COWBOY COUNTRY

A Collection of Recipes

Published by
San Antonio Livestock Exposition, Inc.
San Antonio, Texas 78220
1982

Proceeds from the sale of our Cookbook will go to the Auction Committee to help increase the premiums for our youth.

"Support our youth, buy a cookbook"

Copyright © 1982 by San Antonio Livestock Exposition, Inc.

No part of this book may be reproduced or utilized in any form or by any means, electronic or mechanical, including photocopying and recording, or by any information storage and retrieval system, without permission in writing from the publisher.

International Standard Book Number: ISBN 0-9609848-0-1

First Edition 1982, 10,000 copies

Printed in the United States of America
Taylor Publishing Co.
Fine Books Division
Dallas, Texas 75235

"A Big Texas" thanks to Pat Halpin for our cover pictures of the windmill, yucca, and cactus. He is a Life Member, Director, Trail Boss, and very active on several committees. Pat indeed is a true friend of our San Antonio Stock Show and Rodeo.

COWBOY COUNTRY

Western Cookbook Committee

Chairman

Patricia Blaylock Garza

Co-Chairmen

Rhonda Wolfe   Jesse Garza

Eddie Bender	Larry Simpson
Kathy Bender	Eileen Stewart
Katy DuBose	Mary West Traylor
Anne Oates	Mary Nan West
David Oates	Jim Wolfe
Mr. "Q"	Margaret Wolfe
Bettie Rutledge	Rita Wolma
Shirley Simpson	Ron Wolma

ACKNOWLEDGEMENT

We deeply appreciate all who so generously shared with us their recipes to make this worthwhile project a success. We regret that because of the limited space allotted, we were not able to use every recipe that was submitted.

My sincere thanks to the members of the Western Cookbook Committee for their unselfish support and time that they contributed for this worthy cause.

And last but not least to the Operating Committee that had enough confidence to let us produce this book for you to enjoy for many years to come.

Patricia

FOREWORD

In "forty-nine" a fine group of men said,
"There will be a Stock Show, so let's begin!"

Three decades later, plus a few years more,
Half-a-million people passed through our doors.

The world's greatest stock show (this we all know),
As the San Antonio Livestock Show & Rodeo.

And sitting in the saddle to lead the brigade
Is someone we thank for his generous aid;

HAROLD M. FREEMAN (Mr. Harry to us)
Heads the show with just a little fuss.

He's as Texas, as the Texas skies above
A wonderful gentleman, we all know and love.

It takes a lot of people to make a show
Some are well-known and some you may not know.

Dedicated officers and committee people too,
And fine employees; there are quite a few.

So let's give credit where credit is due;
Give a cowboy cheer for the whole great crew.

With this thought in mind and our best wishes too,
we dedicate this "Cowboy Country" to all of you.

ALLEY B. DANIELS

RECIPE FOR KINDNESS

1 cup of good thoughts
1 cup of kind deeds
1 cup of consideration for others
2 cups of sacrifice
2 cups of well beaten faults
3 cups of forgiveness
4 cups of prayer — faith

Mix thoroughly, add tears of joy, sorrow and sympathy. Flavor with love and kindly service. Fold in four cups of prayer and faith. Blend well. Fold into daily life. Bake well with the warmth of human kindess and serve with a smile anytime. It will satisfy the hunger of starved souls.

AUTHOR UNKNOWN

SAN ANTONIO LIVESTOCK EXPOSITION, INC.

Officers
HAROLD M. FREEMAN
   Life Chairman of the Board

TOM BELL
   Vice Chairman of the Board

NAT PRASSEL
   President

GEORGE HARRIS
   Vice President

GEORGE HAYES
   Vice President

MARY NAN WEST
   Vice President and Secretary

RALPH WINTON
   Treasurer

Executive Commitee

JOSEPH S. MORRIS
ARD E. RICHARDSON
FRANK SEPULVEDA

* * * * * * * * * *

ROBERT B. TATE
   General Livestock Superintendent

MILROY POWELL
   General Horse Show Superintendent

"OUR COWHANDS"

We gratefully acknowledge the generous contributions of the following.

Alamo Cafe
Ancira Winton Chevrolet
Averitt Brokerage/Gary Putnam
Barkley's
Ken Batchelor Cadillac
Eddie and Kathy Bender
Brands Western Ware — Broadway
Brands Western Ware — Walzem
Jewel "Judy" Bryant
John Chavana
Fred Collier
The Cowboy
Crane "Budweiser" Distributing
Crystal Baking Company
D & D Farm and Ranch Supermarket
Al Daniels
Doc Holiday's
Katy DuBose
Frontier Enterprises
Patricia and Jesse Garza
Pat Halpin
Golden Corral — Lou Melchor
International/Mexico Day Committee
Janet Photography
KBUC — Harold Banks
Bobby Kiolbassa
Senator Glenn Kothmann
Cecil Lankford
Leisure Foods
Magic Time Machine
Mueller-Wilson
Anne and David Oates
Pitluk Group
Quarterdeck

Graham "Mr. Q" Quesenberry
Royal Street Crossing
Bettie Rutledge
Sheplers
James Smith
St. Anthony Club
Tom Stolhandske
Tower of the Americas
Union Stockyards
Mary Nan West
West Coast Produce
Wild Wild West
Rita and Ron Wolma
Rhonda and Jim Wolfe
Shirley and Larry Simpson
1776, Inc.

and a "BIG" thanks to all those who attended the Margarita Party who gave so generously and made this "Party" a huge success. We would also like to thank everyone who contributed after we went to press.

COMMITTEES

TABLE OF CONTENTS

Ambassadors

The Ambassadors Committee is a joint effort by the Stock Show and the Chamber of Commerce to develop interest throughout South Texas and attendance at all San Antonio Stock Show and Rodeo events.

STEVE SCHULTZ
CHAIRMAN

CHEESE BALL

2 8-ounce packages cream cheese
2 cups cheddar cheese, shredded
1 tablespoon onion, chopped
1 tablespoon pimiento, chopped
1 tablespoon bell pepper, chopped
1 tablespoon Worcestershire
1 teaspoon lemon juice
¼ teaspoon garlic powder
¼ teaspoon cayenne pepper
Dash of salt

Combine cream cheese and Cheddar cheese thoroughly. Then add remaining ingredients and mix well. Chill, then roll in almonds or parsley.

MARTHA HOFFMANN

SALMON BALL

1 pound can of salmon
1 8-ounce package cream cheese, softened
1 tablespoon lemon juice
1 tablespoon onion, grated
1 tablespoon horse radish
1 tablespoon liquid smoke
¼ teaspoon salt
½ cup of pecans, grated

Drain salmon, mix together, chill overnight. Shape on wax paper, roll in pecans and chill again 1 hour. Before serving put in freezer.

RHONDA WOLFE
WESTERN COOKBOOK
CO-CHAIRMAN

JOE BOY'S HOT SAUSAGE DIP

Fry until done (in large, heavy pot):
2 pounds lean ground beef
2 pounds lean ground pork sausage, hot
1 large onion, chopped
Drain well, then stir in, until blended:
2 pounds Velveeta cheese
2 cans Rotel tomatoes and green chili

Serve warm. Good on tortilla chips, flour tortillas, and rye bread.

THURMAN KENNEDY
GENERAL LIVESTOCK

DESERT CHEESE CENTERPIECE ✓

2 cups cream-style cottage cheese
1 3-ounce package cream cheese
½ cup blue cheese
1 cup whipping cream
Crackers and or fruit

Beat together cottage cheese, cream cheese, and blue cheese until smooth. Gradually beat in whipping cream. Line colander with cheese cloth. Pour in cheese mixture. Tie cheese cloth at top. Let drain overnight in refrigerator. Untie cloth, turn into serving plate. Remove cheese cloth. Decorate top of cheese with lemon leaves or mint leaves. Surround cheese with crackers and or fruit. Brush apples and pears with lemon juice to keep color.

LIBBY JONES
AUCTION SALES

POPEYE DIP

2 boxes frozen chopped spinach
  (thaw, drain, and squeeze off all water)
1 cup fresh parsley, chopped
4 tablespoons green onions and tops, chopped
1 teaspoon salt
2 teaspoons freshly ground black pepper
⅛ teaspoon thyme
½ cup grated Parmesan cheese
Juice of ½ lemon
Garlic powder to taste
TABASCO sauce to taste
Mayonnaise to blend together; about 1 cup

Combine all ingredients using mayonnaise to attain spreading consistency. Make 24 hours ahead to maximize flavor. Serve with assorted crudites and crackers.
Serves 8-10

ROBERT AND SHIRLEY WAGNER
GENERAL LIVESTOCK

THE DIP

5-6 avocados, mashed with salt and lemon
1 large jar Picante sauce
1 14-ounce container sour cream
1 cup Cheddar cheese, grated 1 cup Monterrey Jack
Jalapeño cheese, grated
1 firm tomato, chopped

Layer in the above order in large glass flat pan. Refrigerate. Serve with large corn chips. UM-M-M-GOOD!

FRANCES JOHNSON

SPINACH DIP I

1 package frozen spinach
½ cup onion, chopped
½ cup parsley, chopped
1 tablespoon garlic salt
1½ cups mayonnaise
½ cup sour cream

Cook spinach according to directions. Drain off all water, add other ingredients. Chill 5 hours. Serve with fresh vegetables. Better made the day before.

LIBBY JONES
AUCTION SALES

SPINACH DIP II

1 package chopped frozen spinach
1 cup mayonnaise
1 cup sour cream
1 package vegetable soup mix
1 can water chestnuts, sliced and drained
3 green onions, sliced

Combine mayonnaise, sour cream, soup mix, onions, and water chestnuts. Add spinach. Mix together. Chill. Serve with wheat or rye crackers or hollow out round of pumpernickel bread and stuff with dip.

JOELLA SMITH
INTERNATIONAL/MEXICO DAY

BROCCOLI DIP I

Chopped jalapeño, optional
2 rolls garlic cheese
2 rolls jalapeno cheese
1 can mushroom soup, undiluted
2 packages chopped broccoli,
   cooked and well drained
1 onion, chopped

Brown onion in butter or margarine and the jalapeño's if added. Add the mushroom soup, garlic cheese, jalapeño cheese and cooked broccoli. Serve warm in crock pot or chafing dish, with chips.

PATRICIA GARZA
AMBASSADORS

BROCCOLI DIP II

1 12-ounce package frozen chopped broccoli
½ teaspoon salt
¼ cup water
1 small onion, finely chopped
3 tablespoons margarine
1 can cream of mushroom soup
1 6 -ounce roll garlic cheese
½ teaspoon salt
⅛ teaspoon black pepper
⅛ teaspoon Worcestershire
1 ounce can mushrooms stems and pieces
¾ cup almonds, slivered

Cook broccoli, salt and water. Drain and set aside. Sauté chopped onions in margarine. Add soup, cheese and seasonings and simmer until cheese melts. Add drained broccoli and cook 1 minute longer. Stir to blend. Add drained mushrooms and almonds. (Serve hot — excellent)

SHIRLEY SCHREIBER
AUCTION SALES, BUYER

SOUTH OF THE BORDER DIP

1 large can Rosarita's refried beans, cold,
Your own homemade guacamole spiced up with a little
    Picante sauce
Grated Cheddar cheese
Diced tomatoes and green onions
Diced jalapeño peppers

Spread refried beans to cover a serving dish — then top with the guacamole, garnish with the tomatoes and jalapeños — sprinkle grated cheese over the top and serve with tortilla chips.

SANDRA SESCILA
AUCTION SALES, BUYER

SIX-LAYER DIP

3 large avocados, chopped
⅛ teaspoon garlic powder
⅛ teaspoon garlic salt
1 tablespoon lemon juice
2 tablespoons mayonnaise
1 8-ounce carton sour cream
2 8-ounce jars Picante sauce
¾ cup ripe olives
3 cups tomatoes, chopped
1½ cups Cheddar cheese, shredded

Mix avocados, garlic powder, garlic salt, lemon juice, and mayonnaise. Spread in baking dish. Cover with sour cream. Drain Picante sauce and spoon over sour cream. Layer olives, tomatoes and cheese.

ANNELLA EGBERT
AUCTION SALES

HOT BEEF STROGANOFF DIP

1 cup mushrooms, chopped
½ cup onions, chopped
2 cloves garlic, minced
⅓ cup butter
1 cup sour cream
1 pound beef, coarsely chopped
1 can cream of chicken soup
2 tablespoons cornstarch
½ cup burgundy wine
Salt and pepper to taste

Sauté mushrooms, onion, garlic in butter for 3 minutes. Add paprika, salt, and pepper to taste. Add beef and cook until meat looses its pinkness (about 5 minutes). Add undiluted soup; combine cornstarch with wine, add to mixture, cook until thick.

Cool at this point. This can be frozen or placed in refrigerator. When ready to serve, heat and fold in sour cream. Do not let it come to a boil after adding sour cream. Correct seasonings, garnish with parsley. Serve with flavored wafers or melba toast.
Yields: 5 cups.

MONICA GOSE
LIFE MEMBER

CHILI BEAN DIP

½ to ¾ pound ground meat
½ onion, chopped
2 heaping teaspoons, chili mix
½ to ¾ cup water
1 can refried beans
Picante sauce to taste
⅓ hunk Cheddar cheese

Sauté together, hamburger and chopped onion. Add remaining ingredients and cook to dip consistency.

MARTHA HOFFMANN

HUNGRY MAN DIP

1 pound hamburger meat
1 pound American Cheese, Velveeta may be used
2 teaspoons Worcestershire
½ teaspoon chili powder
1 can of Rotel Tomatoes
   (do not drain)

Brown hamburger, pour off fat, add remaining ingredients, allow cheese to melt slowly. Serve in fondue pot with Tortilla chips.

KAYE BOWIE AND
JOHN H. SAVAGE III
AUCTION SALES

CHILI CON QUESO DE WOLFE

2 Pounds Velveeta cheese
   and
1 Can of Rotel tomatoes and green chilies

Melt cheese, add the tomatoes and green chilies mixing well. (Note: It is best to put the tomatoes and green chilies in a blender for 2 to 3 seconds.) Serve with your favorite chips.

RHONDA WOLFE
COOKBOOK COMMITTEE

MEXICAN DIP

1 can refried beans
1 can jalepeño refried beans
1 small can black olives, chopped
3 scallion onions, chopped
3 small tomatoes, chopped
1 small container sour cream
3-4 avocados, mashed
Cheddar cheese, grated

Mix 2 cans of beans. Put in long pyrex dish. Mix together: olives, chopped tomatoes and chopped onions (use green stems also). Spread on top of beans. Mash avocados and spread on top of above mixture. Spread carton of sour cream next and top with lots of Cheddar cheese.
You can dip it with chips or put it in a tortilla rolled up.

MRS. MARCUS ROBBINS
AUCTION SALES

SPINACH BALLS

2 packages frozen spinach, cooked and drained
1 package stove top stuffing, cornbread mix
½ cup butter, melted
3 eggs, beaten
1 large onion, grated
½ cup Parmesan cheese
1 teaspoon pepper
1 teaspoon thyme
1 tablespoon garlic, optional

Mix all ingredients, shape into 1-inch balls and place on cookie sheet. Bake 25 minutes in a 350 degree oven. Makes about 40 balls. Can be frozen and reheated at 350 degrees or use microwave. An excellent hors d'oeuvres.

REBA ROBERSON
AUCTION SALES

PICADILLO DIP

3 pounds ground beef
3 onions, chopped
3 cloves garlic, chopped
1 1-pound can tomatoes
¾ cup toasted almonds, chopped
1 can water chestnuts, chopped
1 cup white raisins
4 ounces mushroom stems and pieces
1 package 3-Alarm Chili Mix
2 medium potatoes, chopped (raw)
Salt and pepper to taste
1 package masa mix

Combine first 3 ingredients and brown in olive oil. Add remaining, except for package of masa mix, and simmer for about 2 hours. Add masa. Freezes well.

BEVERLY ADAMS GRAY
SOUVENIR PROGRAM

CHICKEN LIVER PATÉ

2 tablespoons butter
1 pound chicken livers
1 tablespoon instant minced onions
2 3-ounce packages cream cheese
1 teaspoon salt
¼ teaspoon nutmeg
⅓ sherry

Melt butter and sauté chicken livers and onions until they are tender. About 10 to 12 minutes. Stir frequently while sauteing. Cut both cream cheese blocks into four cubes. Blend at medium speed — livers, cream cheese, sherry, salt and nutmeg — until smooth. Refrigerate several hours before serving.

BEBE JONES
AUCTION SALES

23

CURRY PATÉ

2 3-ounce packages cream cheese, softened
1 cup sharp Cheddar cheese, shredded
2 tablespoons dry sherry wine
½ teaspoon curry powder
¼ teaspoon salt
1 8-ounce jar mango chutney, finely chopped, (optional)
⅓ cup green onions with tops, finely sliced

Beat together thoroughly cream cheese, Cheddar cheese, sherry, curry powder and salt. Roll into a log or place in a serving bowl. Chill until firm. At serving time, spread with chutney and sprinkle with green unions.

PATRICIA GARZA
INTERNATIONAL/MEXICO DAY

HOT CRAB DIP

2 8-ounce packages cream cheese
2 large cans crab meat, rinsed and drained or
   same amount of frozen crab meat
2 cloves garlic, crushed
½ cup mayonnaise
2 tablespoons yellow mustard
¼ cup white wine
2 tablespoons powdered sugar
Salt and white pepper to taste

Combine all ingredients in a double boiler. Cool and refrigerate 24 hours before serving. Reheat thoroughly and serve in chaffing dish with melba toast rounds. Have plenty of room around the serving area of this dip as guests do not stop until dip is gone!

BEBE JONES
AUCTION SALES

CRAB PATÉ

1 can cream of mushroom soup, undiluted
1 envelope unflavored gelatin
3 tablespoons cold water
¾ cup mayonnaise
1 8-ounce package cream cheese, softened
1 6½-ounce can crabmeat, drained and flaked
1 small onion, grated
1 cup celery, finely chopped
Parsley sprigs

Heat soup in a medium saucepan over low heat; remove from heat. Dissolve gelatin in cold water; add to soup, stirring well. Add next 5 ingredients, and mix well. Spoon into an oiled 4-cup mold; chill until firm. Unmold and garnish with parsley. Serve with assorted crackers. Yield: About 4 cups.

ROBYN MERCHANT
AUCTION AND PROGRAM

MARINATED CARROTS

2 bags carrots, 1 pound each

Cook in salted water, or in 1 can of beef consomme, until tender. Drain, set aside to cool.

Add 1 large bell pepper, diced.

Combine:
2 cans of tomato soup, (do not dilute)
½ cup cooking oil
1 cup sugar
¾ cup vinegar
1 teaspoon prepared mustard
1 teaspoon Worcestershire
½ teaspoon celery seed
Salt and pepper to taste

Mix well. Pour over vegetables. Refrigerate. Serve cold. This will keep for several weeks.

ELIZABETH JACOBS
INTERNATIONAL/MEXICO DAY

CUCUMBER FINGER SANDWICH

1 12-ounce can Spam, chopped　　½ onion
1 8-ounce carton sour cream　　1 cucumber
3 stalks celery　　　　　　　　Salt and pepper

Chop Spam in food processor, add celery and onions. Chop until mixed well. Add salt and pepper to taste. Add sour cream, spread on bread, and top with sliced cucumber.

SANDI HARPER
AUCTION SALES

CHEESE BALLS

1 pound Owens Hot Sausage, uncooked
1 pound sharp Cheddar cheese, grated
¼ cup onions, finely chopped

Mix well with hands and form small bite size balls. Bake in 300 degree oven 25 minutes or until done. Can be frozen.

VERNA SKLOSS

BACON-ONION SPREAD

1 large package cream cheese, softened
1 jar Hormel Real Bacon Bits
2 green onions, chopped
Salt and pepper to taste
Milk

Cream all ingredients in food processor using plastic blade. Use enough milk to make a spreadable consistency. Serve with crisp crackers. Keeps a week if you have leftovers.

J. R. HARTMAN/JENNIFER HARTMAN
CALF SCRAMBLE

FRIED CHEESE
(SAGANAKI)

Kafeletyri or Kasseri cheese sliced length wise ¼ inch thick wedges. (1 pound for 4 people)

2 egg yolks mixed with 2 tablespoons water
Flour
Olive Oil
2 lemons cut in quarters

Dip cheese slices into egg yolk mixture, then into flour coating each side. Use 10 inch skillet, heat ¼ inch olive oil. When oil begins to smoke, add cheese, fry both sides. Remove from skillet, squeeze lemon juice on each slice — Serve hot — 2 slices per person.

NORMAN HITZFELDER
BACHELOR AT LARGE — BUYER

FRIED CHEESE

Cheese Curds
1 cup flour
1 teaspoon salt
1 cup whole milk
1 teaspoon baking powder

Mix with mixer until all blended. Add cheese curds to batter. When well-coated remove and deep-fry until golden brown. (Preheat fryer and maintain at 375°F) Always use peanut oil in deep fryer.

Cheddar cheese cubes may be substituted for cheese curds if these are not available.

MARY FLOWERS
AUCTION SALES

MUSHROOM BALLS 🌿

1 cup biscuit mix
1 cup fresh mushrooms, chopped
1 tablespoon green onions, sliced
1 tablespoon pimiento, chopped
½ teaspoon salt
½ teaspoon celery seed
1 beaten egg yolk
¼ cup dairy sour cream
1 egg white
Cooking oil for deep fat frying

Combine biscuit mix, mushrooms, onion, pimiento, salt and celery seed. Mix together egg yolk and sour cream; stir into dry ingredients just until moistened. Beat egg white to stiff peaks (tip stands straight). Gently fold beaten egg white into mushroom mixture.

Heat oil to 375 degrees and drop batter by tablespoonfuls into hot oil. Fry approximately 2 minutes or until golden brown turning once. Drain on rack and serve hot. Makes 12

JESSE GARZA
WESTERN COOKBOOK
CO-CHAIRMAN

SAUSAGE NIBBLES

3 cups biscuit mix
1 pound hot sausage
Cayenne pepper to taste

Mix all ingredients. Form into bite-size balls. Bake about 20 minutes in 350 degree oven. Keeps for days in a tightly closed container.

OSIE ASHFORD

CHEESE CRACKERS

1 10-ounce package sharp cheese, grated
1 tablespoon onion, grated
2 sticks butter
2 cups flour
2 cups Rice Krispies
1 teaspoon cayenne pepper
Salt to taste

Mix all ingredients and roll into small balls. Place on cookie sheet and press balls with fork. Bake at 350 degrees for 20 minutes.

ROSEMARY VAN HEUVERSWYN
AUCTION SALES

PINEAPPLE-CHEESE BALL

2 8-ounce packages cream cheese, softened
1 8½-ounce can crushed pineapple, drained
2 cups pecans or walnuts, chopped
¼ cup green pepper, finely chopped
2 tablespoons onions, finely chopped
1 tablespoon seasoned salt

In medium bowl, with fork, beat cream cheese until smooth. Gradually stir in crushed pineapple, 1 cup nuts, the green pepper, onion and salt. Shape into a ball. Roll in remaining nuts. Wrap in plastic wrap or foil. Refrigerate until well chilled. Overnight. Makes about 40 appetizer servings.

LIBBY JONES
AUCTION SALES

MUSHROOMS ROYALE

1 pound medium mushrooms, about 3 dozen
3 tablespoons butter or margarine
¼ cup green pepper, finely chopped
¼ cup onion, finely chopped
1½ cups soft bread crumbs
½ teaspoon salt
½ teaspoon thyme
¼ teaspoon turmeric
¼ teaspoon pepper
1 tablespoon butter or margarine

Heat oven to 350 degrees. Wash, trim and dry mushrooms thoroughly. Remove stems; Finely chop enough stems to measure ¾ cup.

Melt 3 tablespoons butter in skillet. Cook and stir chopped mushroom stems, green pepper and onion in butter about 5 minutes or until tender. Remove from heat; stir in remaining ingredients except mushroom caps and 1 tablespoon butter.

Melt 1 tablespoon butter in shallow baking dish. Fill mushroom caps with stuffing mixture; place mushrooms filled side up in baking dish. Bake 15 minutes.

Set oven control at broil and/or 550 degrees. Broil mushrooms 3 to 4 inches from heat 2 minutes.

About 3 dozen appetizers.

ROBYN MERCHANT
AUCTION SALES

MARINATED MUSHROOMS

2 pounds of fresh mushrooms, sliced
¼ cup lemon juice
½ cup cider vinegar
¼ cup water
2 tablespoons onions, chopped
2 tablespoons garlic, minced
1 tablespoon parsley, chopped
½ teaspoon salt
½ teaspoon sugar
⅛ teaspoon oregano
⅛ teaspoon pepper

Clean and slice mushrooms into large pot. Add lemon juice and enough water to cover. Bring to a boil and remove from heat. Drain and place in bowl. Mix remaining ingredients and pour over mushrooms. Marinate overnight before serving.

BOBBY HUGHES
ENTERTAINMENT
CHAIRMAN

MUSHROOMS w/MEAT STUFFING

6 dozen mushrooms

Clean mushrooms by using a small paring knife and taking the centers out of the mushrooms. (Also clean as much of the black substance as you can out.) Take 2 pounds of margarine and over low heat fry mushrooms until they are cooked and turning dark. Drain.

Stuffing:
Sauté in 1 tablespoon butter or salad oil:
1½ pounds ground beef
½ medium onion, chopped
1 clove garlic, finely minced
Drain off excess fat and cool mixture.

Add:
1 cup bread crumbs
1 tablespoon parsley, chopped
½ pound Mozzarella cheese, grated
1 teaspoon pepper
2 eggs, slightly beaten
½ cup milk (if mixture seems dry add more milk)

Mix thoroughly.
Stuff mushrooms and serve hot.

VIVION COLLIER
SOUVENIR PROGRAM

NEW YEAR'S BLACK EYED PEA DIP

Mix the following in a blender:
4 cups black eyed peas, cooked and drained
1 to 5 jalapeño peppers, depends on how hot
**   you wish the dip to be**
1 tablespoon jalapeño juice
1½ medium onion, chopped
1 4-ounce can chopped green chilies
1 clove garlic, minced
In a double-boiler, melt together:
½ pound Old English sharp cheese
½ pound butter

Combine the blended ingredients into the melted cheese and butter. Serve hot with chips or on flour tortillas. Can make ahead of time. This dip freezes well.

BEBE JONES
AUCTION SALES

TEXAS CAVIAR

2 1-pound cans black-eye peas, drained
½ cup olive oil
¼ cup wine vinegar
1 clove garlic
¼ cup thin sliced onion
½ teaspoon salt
Freshly ground black pepper

Put all ingredients in a covered jar. Let stand in refrigerator 2-3 days. Serve small portions on pieces of lettuce leaf or large corn chips.

OSIE ASHFORD

NACHOS DE CAMARON
(SHRIMP NACHOS)

5 pieces shrimp (medium size, cut in half, length wise, cooked)
8 ounces good White Cheese or imported Mexican Chihuahua, grated
1 cup Ernesto's Special Sauce
10 nacho chips
10 slices jalapeño

Ernesto's Special Sauce:
Chop one teaspoon very fine fresh garlic, and sauté in one tablespoon of butter for one minute. Add finely chopped tomatoes (½ cup), one tablespoon of chopped onions, and two finely chopped serrano peppers, add salt to taste. My special sauce makes 1 cup.

Preparation:
Put one piece of shrimp on each chip. Mix the cheese with the sauce and put over each shrimp. Add the jalapeño and put in the oven three minutes.
1 order (or 10) nachos

ENJOY IT!
ERNESTO'S RESTAURANT

SALMON PARTY BALL

1 cup canned salmon, drained
1 8-ounce package cream cheese, softened
1 tablespoon lemon juice
2 teaspoons onion, grated
1 teaspoon prepared horseradish
¼ teaspoon salt
3 drops liquid smoke, optional
½ cup pecans, finely chopped
3 tablespoons snipped parsley

Drain and flake salmon. Combine salmon, cream cheese, lemon juice, onion, horseradish, salt, pepper, and liquid smoke. Mix thoroughly. Chill several hours. Combine pecans and parsley. Shape salmon mixture into ball, roll in nuts and parsley. Chill well. Serve with assorted crackers.

SHIRLEY SCHREIBER
AUCTION SALES

SALMON PUFFS

1 can salmon, approximately 14 ounces
1 egg
½ cup sifted flour
1 heaping teaspoon baking powder

Drain salmon (or you can use tuna) liquid into measuring cup. Put the fish into a mixing bowl and flake, then add egg. Mix well with fork. Add the flour and mix again. It will be very thick. You can add pepper and garlic now if you like. Use ¼ cup of liquid and add the heaping teaspoon of baking powder to it. Beat with a fork until it foams up. It should reach the ¾ cup mark. Pour this into the mixture and mix well. It will now be thin, and that's the secret. Using 2 teaspoons, scoop the mixture out with one spoon and with the other push the mixture into hot oil. They are done in just seconds so keep an eye on 'em. Serve warm with any sauce.

DOROTHY FERGUSON/MONTY FERGUSON
ENTERTAINMENT

APPETIZER MEAT BALLS

1½ pounds ground mixed veal, beef, pork
1 cup seasoned bread crumbs
½ cup chili sauce
1 egg
¼ cup onion, minced
2 tablespoons parsley, chopped
1-1½ teaspoons salt
½ teaspoon TABASCO sauce
½ teaspoon garlic powder
3 tablespoons butter or margarine

Combine meat, bread crumbs, chili sauce, egg, onion, parsley, salt, TABASCO, and garlic powder in large bowl. Shape meat into balls 1 inch in diameter. Or use meatball maker. Pan fry a few meat balls at a time in butter, put into chafing dish. Serve with food picks. Yields 8 dozen.

SHIRLEY KING
GO WESTERN

PIZZA COCKTAIL DIP OR SPREAD

1 8-ounce package cream cheese
1 bottle cocktail sauce
Onion powder
Frozen snow crab, washed and rung out

Season with salt, pepper and onion powder. Decorate with ripe olives or green pepper and chopped parsley. Spread cream cheese on clear glass plate. Sprinkle with lots of onion powder. Then spread bottle of cocktail sauce over cream cheese. Then sprinkle crab and season again and decorate with either olives and parsley. Serve with crackers or chips.

SHIRLEY SCHREIBER
AUCTION SALES — BUYER

PIZZA SNACKS

½ pound Italian sausage
1 tablespoon crushed oregano
1 clove garlic, minced
1 package refrigerated biscuits
1 can tomato paste
1 cup sharp Cheddar cheese, shredded

Brown sausage; drain. Add oregano and garlic. On greased baking sheet flatten biscuits to 4″ circles with floured custard cup; leaving rim. Fill with tomato paste and sausage. Sprinkle with cheese. Bake about 10 minutes at 425 degrees. Trim with olive slices.

MRS. AL SODERSTROM
GO WESTERN

PARESA

6 pounds lean hamburger meat
3 pounds American Cheese, grated
4 or 5 onions, chopped
Juice of 4 to 6 lemons
Salt and pepper generous amounts

Mix together and put in covered dish in refrigerator. Serve with crackers.

MARY ELLEN PENWELL
AUCTION SALES

SPICED PECANS

¾ cup white sugar
1 cup nuts
¼ cup water
2 teaspoons cinnamon

Boil cinnamon, sugar and water in skillet. When well boiled, add nuts and stir until dried. Remove to wax paper and separate. Allow to dry.

MARGO AND AL DANIELS

JALAPEÑO CHEESE STICKS

½ cup butter
1 cup sharp Cheddar cheese, shredded
1 tablespoon water
1 teaspoon Worcestershire
1½ cups flour
10-12 jalapeño peppers, remove seeds and chop in food
  processor
¼ teaspoon salt

Soften butter — add cheese, water and Worcestershire. Stir until well blended; add flour, peppers and salt, mixing well. (Mixture should resemble soft cookie dough.) Turn dough out onto a floured board, roll to ⅛" thickness. Cut into 2½ x ½ strips and place on lightly greased cookie sheet and bake in a 400 degree oven 12-15 minutes or until firm.

SANDI HARPER
AUCTION SALES

SUGARED PECANS

¾ cup white sugar
1 cup whole pecans
¼ cup water

Boil sugar and water in skillet. When well boiled, add nuts and stir until dried. For sugared nuts, stop here. Remove to wax paper and separate. For caramelized nuts keep stirring until moist again. Then remove to wax paper and break apart while still warm.

MARGO AND AL DANIELS

ROASTED PECANS

Preheat oven to 300°
1 cup pecan halves
2 tablespoons butter

Place the pecans and butter in 9 x 13 pan and place in oven, turning pecans about every 5 minutes for 30 minutes.

Turn oven off and mix together:

2 teaspoons soy sauce
½ teaspoon salt
6 dashes of TABASCO sauce

Pour over pecans and place back in oven for about 10 minutes. Turn a couple of times to be sure the pecans don't burn. Remove from oven and drain on paper towel and add more salt if you wish. Store in a tight container. If pecans get soft place in warm oven a few minutes and watch them.

ROSIE GRANGER

SUGAR PECANS

1 pound pecans, shelled
1 cup sugar
1 teaspoon cinnamon
¼ cup water
¾ teaspoon salt
1 teaspoon vanilla

Place pecans in 375 degree oven for 10 minutes, stirring once to keep from burning. Take from oven and cool. In saucepan, mix sugar, cinnamon, salt and water. Bring to a boil until it forms a soft ball in cold water. Add vanilla and beat until creamy, add the pecans and mix until pecans are coated. Pour on buttered plate and break apart when cool.

MARY ELLEN PENWELL
AUCTION AND PROGRAM
COMMITTEE

Entertainment

The Entertainment Committee is a sub-committee of the Special Days. We work together with Special Days to provide the very best entertainment possible during each night of the Stock Show and Rodeo in the Entertainment Center. Professional talent is provided each evening and is the major responsibility of the Entertainment Committee.

BOBBY HUGHES
CHAIRMAN

ROYAL STREET CROSSING

Winner of our Margarita
Tasting Contest

MARGARITA RECIPE

1¼ ounce tequila
¾ ounce triple sec
¼ ounce lime juice
2 ounces sweet and sour

Shake and strain into a cocktail glass rimmed with salt.

Salud, Amor, y pesetas, y bastante tiempo para gastarlas, pero sobre todo — el Amor!!

(Health, love, and riches and time to enjoy them, but above all "Love")

ROYAL STREET CROSSING
Winner — Margarita Contest

BORDER BUTTERMILK

1 can pink lemonade
1 can tequila
Ice

Pour can of frozen pink lemonade into blender; add tequila. Blend. Add ice and blend until frozen. Serves 4.

JOELLA P. SMITH
INTERNATIONAL/MEXICO DAY

May you be in heaven an hour before the devil knows you are dead.

JOHN WAYNE

TEXAS MINT JULEPS 🍃

12 cups bourbon
2 tablespoons sugar
3 cups water
Fresh mint leaves
Finely crushed ice
Fresh mint sprigs

Place bourbon in freezer 24 hours prior to preparing mint julep (the bourbon won't freeze, but it will acquire a syrup like consistency).

For each serving, place ¼ teaspoon sugar in a julep cup add 2 tablespoons water and 7 fresh mint leaves. Stir gently until sugar is dissolved.

Add ½ cup bourbon to each cup, stirring gently. Add enough finely crushed ice to fill cup, stir gently. Place in freezer and freeze at least 3 hours.

Before serving break the ice with a spoon, then garnish each julep with fresh mint sprigs. Yield 24 servings.

BETTIE RUTLEDGE
LIFE MEMBER

COWBOY'S COURAGE

1 shot of Tequila
1 mug of Brew

Grab shot glass between thumb and forefinger. Grab the bar with the other hand. Raise shot glass to mouth and throw head back as far as you can. Holding onto bar as tightly as possible, swallow, and immediately chug-a-lug the brew. Bueno Suerte!

JODI HEAD
Publishing Rep.

CITRUS PUNCH

12 cups sugar
3 pints water
6 packages lime Jello brand gelatin
12 cups hot water
3 cans frozen orange juice
3 cans frozen lemon juice
3 quarts pineapple juice
1 medium size bottle almond extract
3 quarts ginger ale

Boil sugar and 3 pints water for a few minutes until thoroughly mixed. Dissolve Jello in 12 cups hot water — add to first mixture. When ready to serve, add all juices and extract. Put amount needed in punch bowl and add ginger ale to fizz and spice it. For color you may float fruit slices in punch bowl. Served 150

BETTY SMITH
AUCTION SALES

COWBOY MARGARITA

1 jigger (1½ oz.) Everclear   1 ounce fresh lime
½ ounce triple sec   Pinch of salt

Run lime around rim of glass; spin rim in salt. Shake well and strain into glass over crushed ice.

EARL M. HERRING
JUNIOR STEER RIDING

PINK LOVER

1 shot Galiano
1 shot vodka or gin
1 shot créme of almond
1 shot half and half

Mix all ingredients in a shaker, pour into a pretty glass and fill with pineapple juice.

ALBERT AND DIANA MORALES

MARGARITA

Coarse Salt
¾ cup (6 ounce) tequila
¾ cup (6 ounce) triple sec
¾ cup (6 ounce) fresh lime juice
¾ cup coarsley crushed ice (approximately)

Invert glass rims in coarse salt — set aside. In blender, combine tequila, triple sec, lime juice, and crushed ice. Whirl until frothy and well blended. Serve in salt rimmed glass.

TOMMY SMITH
INTERNATIONAL / MEXICO DAY

ARTILLERY PUNCH

1 4-ounce can gunpowder green tea
2 quarts cold water
Juice of 9 oranges
Juice of 9 lemons
1 1-pound package light brown sugar
½ cup firmly packed light brown sugar
2 10-ounce jars maraschino cherries, drained
2 50.7-ounce bottles rhine or catawba wine
1 quart light rum
1 quart rye whisky
1 quart gin
1 25.4 ounce bottle brandy
½ cup benedictine
Champagne or club soda, chilled

Combine tea and water; let stand overnight. Stir fruit juices into tea; strain.

Combine tea and remaining ingredients except champagne in a 3 gallon crock or glass container. Cover lightly, and let stock ferment 2 to 6 weeks.

Strain stock; discard cherries and pour liquid into bottles. Chill as needed. At serving time, dilute each gallon of chilled stock with 1 quart champagne and pour over ice. Yield: about 2½ gallons stock.

COL PAUL BIEDIGER
MAJ RUDY SPANN
WESTERN PARADE

TUMBLEWEED
(After dinner drink)

6 scoops rich, vanilla ice cream
½ ounce brandy
¾ ounce Kahlua
¾ ounce crème de cacao

Blend until smooth. Makes two 6 ounce drinks.

(Can make the drink with Cognac and Amaretto instead of Brandy and Kahlua.)

BEBE JONES
AUCTION SALES

HOT BUTTERED RUM

1 pound butter, softened
1 pound light brown sugar
1 pound powdered sugar
2 teaspoons ground cinnamon
2 teaspoons ground nutmeg
1 quart vanilla ice cream, softened
Light rum
Whipped cream
Cinnamon sticks

Combine butter, sugar, and spices; beat until light and fluffy. Add ice cream, stirring until well blended. Spoon mixture into a 2 quart freezer container; freeze.

To serve, thaw slightly. Place 3 tablespoons butter mixture and 1 jigger rum into a large mug; fill with boiling water. Stir well. (Any unused butter mixture can be refrozen.) Top with whipped cream, and serve with cinnamon stick.
Yield: 25 cups

A FRIEND

PIÑA COLADA

½ cup cream of coconut
1 cup unsweetened pineapple juice, chilled
⅔ cup light rum
2 cups crushed ice

Combine cream of coconut, pineapple juice, rum and ice in a blender and blend at high speed for ½ minute. Pour into chilled glasses and serve with a pineapple spear. 8 servings or 1 quart.

ANNE OATES
WESTERN COOKBOOK

KAHLUA

4 cups water
4 cups sugar
1 fifth vodka
2 vanilla beans
1 2-ounce jar instant coffee

Combine sugar and water; boil 5 minutes. Cool. Dissolve coffee in ¼ cup water. Stir until smooth and add to cool sugar. Halve vanilla beans and place in 1 gallon jar. Add coffee mixture and then whole bottle of vodka. Let stand for 4 weeks. Strain into empty bottle(s).
Happy Drinking!!

ROSE MARIE EICKENROHT
GO WESTERN

KAHLUA

5 cups water
3 cups sugar
3 ounces vanilla extract
11 teaspoons instant coffee
1 5th vodka plus a small
   wine glass

Boil first 4 ingredients 5 minutes, let cool, add vodka. Pour into decorative bottles. Great gift idea.

MARY MENDOZA
SACRAMENTO, CA

AGGRAVATION

1½ ounces kahlua
1½ ounces scotch
Milk

Combine ice cubes, kahlua, scotch and milk in 12 ounce tumbler, stir (pinch of nutmeg optional).

GEORGE B. WOODS
AUCTION SALES

DAIQUIRI PUNCH

1 bottle (4/5 quart) white rum, chilled
1¼ cups (12 ounces) daiquiri mix, chilled
2 quarts carbonated lemon-lime beverage, chilled

In large punch bowl, combine rum and daiquiri mix. Stir in carbonated lemon-lime beverage. Serve immediately.

25 servings (about ½ cup each).

ROBYN MERCHANT
AUCTION SALES

WASSAIL

4 cups pineapple juice
1½ cups apricot nectar
4 cups apple cider
1 cup orange juice
2 sticks cinnamon
2 teaspoons whole cloves
1 teaspoon ground nutmeg
Bourbon to taste

Combine juices in a large saucepan. Tie spices in a cheesecloth bag; add to juice. Simmer mixture over medium heat 30 minutes; remove spice bag. Add bourbon, if desired. Serve hot.

KATY DU BOSE
ADMINISTRATOR COORDINATOR

TEQUILA SOUR

1 tray ice cubes or crushed ice
1 can frozen limeade
1 can water
1 can tequila

Put all ingredients into blender and serve in cocktail glasses. Serves 3 to 4 people.

MARY ELLEN PENWELL
AUCTION SALES

SPRING COOLER

Fill tumbler with ice cubes, about 10-12 ounce, add 1½ ounces of dark rum, fill glass with fresh orange juice, stir, add twist of lime or lemon.

GEORGE B. WOODS
AUCTION SALES

HOW BLOODY MARY
CAME TO BE.

The Bloody Mary was first discovered during the great tomato glut of '54. Faced with a shortage of grapes, vintners put tomatoes in their stomping vats, hoping to create the first tomato wine. A Russian named Barolovsky was quite enamored with a tomato stomper named Mary. While chasing her around the vat, he slipped on a tomato skin and spilled a bottle of vodka which he had hidden in his pocket. And also sustained a minor cut. The vintner thought that he had, indeed, created the first tomato wine. But Barolovsky knew better. And named the drink Bloody Mary, because Mary was some tomato.

BLOODY MARY DRINK

1 No. 5 can tomato juice
¾ cup beef consommé
½ teaspoon TABASCO sauce
½ teaspoon lemon juice
2½ teaspoons Worcestershire
1 teaspoon celery salt
1 teaspoon salt
½ teaspoon pepper

Combine all ingredients and mix well. Store covered under refrigeration. Mix will keep several days. Makes 1½ quarts.

To Prepare Drink:
Fill glass with ice and pour in 1 or more ounces of vodka. Add Bloody Mary mix, stir slightly to blend. Garnish with a lime wedge and/or celery stick.

SAN ANTONIO INTERNATIONAL AIRPORT

MESQUITE BEAN JUICE DRINK
PEMA AND PAPAGO INDIANS

Pick the yellow soft bean of the mesquite bush in July.
Clean and place in large pot with water to cover.
Boil until beans are tender. Cool in pot.
With wooden pounder, pound mesquite beans until pulpy.
Drain through colander, saving liquid for the juice.
This is an ancient and refreshing Indian drink.

BETTIE RUTLEDGE
WESTERN COOKBOOK

FROZEN STRAWBERRY OR PEACH DAIQUIRIS

**16 ounces frozen strawberries or peaches partially
   thawed
1 6-ounce can frozen daiquiri mix or limeade
6 ounces light rum
1 to 2 cups crushed ice (fill blender container)**

Combine all ingredients in blender and blend well. A pretty,
delicious summer drink. Serves 4-6.

JOHN A. BITTER, III
CHAIRMAN
AUCTION SALES

ALMOND LIQUEUR
(On the Trail)

3 cups sugar
2¼ cups water
3 lemons, finely grated rind
1 quart vodka
3 tablespoons almond extract
2 tablespoons vanilla extract

Combine first three ingredients in a Dutch oven, bring to a boil. Reduce heat and simmer 5 minutes stirring occasionally — cool completely. Stir in remaining ingredients, store in airtight containers. Yield 2: quarts.

DAVID OATES
WESTERN COOKBOOK

CRANBERRY PUNCH

2 cans unsweetened pineapple juice
2 bottles cranberry juice
4½ cups water
Dash red food coloring for color

Mix these ingredients in a large coffee percolator. Place the following in the basket:

1 cup brown sugar
2 sticks cinnamon, broken
4½ teaspoon cloves

Let perk, through one complete cycle. Serve hot. Makes 24 cups.
RUBY BOUCHILLON

CHRISTMAS HOOCH
(Hot spiced Drink)

Mix together:
1 can dry lemonade mix
1 can apple drink
1 can presweetened ice tea mix
2 teaspoons powdered cinnamon
1½ teaspoons powdered clove

Store dry in a gallon jar.

Serve steaming hot as follows:
  1 mug boiling water
  1 scoop hooch mix

ORANGE JULIUS

½ of 6-ounce can (⅓ cup)
  frozen orange juice concentrate
½ cup milk
½ cup water
¼ cup sugar
½ teaspoon vanilla
5 or 6 cubes of ice

Combine all ingredients in blender container; cover and blend until smooth, about 30 seconds. Serve immediately. Makes about 3 cups.

SUMMERTIME TEA

1½ cups sugar
6 small tea bags
1 quart boiling water
1 6-ounce can frozen lemonade concentrate,
   thawed and undiluted
1 6-ounce can frozen orange juice concentrate, thawed
   and undiluted
2 quarts cold water.

Add sugar and tea bags to boiling water, stir well. Cover and steep 5 minutes. Remove tea bags, squeezing gently. Stir in all of the remaining ingredients, serve tea over ice. Yield: 3½ quarts.

BETTIE RUTLEDGE
LIFE MEMBER

ORANGE SPICED TEA

1 package lemonade mix, sweetened
1 4-ounce jar Tang
1½ cups sugar
1 teaspoon cinnamon
½ cup instant tea
1 teaspoon cloves

Mix thoroughly. Store in jar with tight lid. To serve, put 2 or 3 teaspoons in a cup, add hot water and stir.

MARY ELLEN PENWELL
AUCTION SALES

SPICED TEA

¾ cups of sugar
½ cup of instant tea
½ cup sweetened lemon flavored instant tea
1 cup of Tang
2 teaspoons of cinnamon
1 teaspoon of cloves

Blend all together. Use 2 teaspoons of above mixture to one cup of boiling water.

KITTY ALONSO
INTERNATIONAL/MEXICO DAY

LEMONBERRY PITCHER PUNCH

4 scoops lemonade mix
4 cups water
½ cup cranberry juice cocktail
1½ cups carbonated lemon-lime beverage, chilled
Ice cubes

Combine drink mix and water in a large pitcher; stir until mix is dissolved. Add cranberry juice cocktail and lemon-lime beverage. Add ice cubes. Pour into tall glasses. Makes 1½ quarts. For large party, double or triple the recipe.

MARY ELLEN PENWELL
AUCTION SALES

Go Western

The Go Western Committee was formed in 1978 with the purpose of publicizing the San Antonio Stock and Rodeo, and with the idea that being as everyone is a "cowboy" or "cowgirl" during stock show time, that all should wear western wear for all occasions.

With this in mind the committee presents the Go Western Gala which ushers in the rodeo season each year.

The "Gala" is held in the Joe and Harry Freeman Coliseum in late January just preceding the rodeo, and it is the night to enjoy fabulous entertainment, gourmet foods, see the latest in western wear, dance, and be with friends.

The Go Western Gala has grown to be the largest party that is associated with the rodeo. The tickets are a sell out each year and everyone looks forward to this particular event.

GEORGE HAYS
CHAIRMAN

POTATO SOUP
(KARTOFFELSUPPE)

Beef soup bone
3 quarts water
Coarsley ground black pepper and salt to taste
2 medium onions, chopped
½ cup celery, chopped (optional)
6 to 8 potatoes, peeled and boiled

Bring soup bone to boil in water. Add rest of ingredients except potatoes and simmer for 2 hours. Remove bone. Mash potatoes thoroughly, add to broth and reheat. Parsley may be added. Serves 6 to 8.

MRS. EVELYN TATUM
SPECIAL DAYS
FREDERICKSBURG, TX

PANADA
(Soup)

2 potatoes
1 tablespoon celery (optional)
2 slices white bread
Cream or milk, small amount
Butter, small amount

Peel and cube potatoes, add diced celery, cover well with water and cook until soft.

Toss bread cubes in buttered skillet until light brown, add bread to boiled potatoes and boil one minute, blend in blender and return to stove, add cream or milk and butter, heat and serve.

MICKEY HUBER
CALF SCRAMBLE

TAMU VEGETABLE SOUP

1 soup bone
Pot about ¾ full water
Salt
Cook about 15-30 minutes — skim off scum,
Add:
1 can whole tomatoes
2 cans tomato sauce
Cook while preparing these following vegetables:
2 carrots — sliced very thin
1 onion — chopped fine
1-2 stalks of celery
Add more salt — cook until tender
Add:
Corn
Handful of macaroni
Cook again until tender

*VALERIE OATES McDONALD
AND FRIENDS*

This "concoction" was created by my daughter and her friends during their first year at Texas A&M University.

*ANN OATES, SECRETARY
COMMITTEE OFFICE*

AVOCADO SOUP

3 fully ripe avocados
1 cup chicken broth
1 cup light cream
1 teaspoon salt
¼ teaspoon onion salt
White pepper to taste
1 teaspoon lemon juice
Lemon slices as garnish

Mash the avocados. Blend with the chicken broth in blender until smooth. Combine with cream and seasonings. Pour into glass container, cover and refrigerate for 3 hours or overnight. Stir in lemon juice, garnish with lemon slices and serve chilled.

CAROLYN PILLOT
AUCTION SALES

BROCCOLI SOUP

2 10-ounce packages frozen broccoli, chopped,
    cook according to directions
2 chicken bouillon cubes
½ teaspoon oregano
1½ cups milk
½ of liquid from broccoli
2 10-ounce cans cream of chicken soup
Salt and pepper to taste

Cook broccoli with bouillon cubes and add milk and liquid from broccoli. Add cream of chicken soup and seasonings. Put in blender and mix. Heat and serve.

SHIRLEY SCHREIBER
AUCTION SALES

TEXAS SOUP

Pinto beans, cooked
3 slices bacon
2 medium onions, finely chopped
2 cloves garlic, minced
1 16-ounce can of tomatoes, cut up
1½ cup brown rice, cooked
2 teaspoons salt
½ teaspoon paprika
¼ teaspoon pepper

In dutch oven, cook bacon until almost crisp. Add onion and garlic. Cook and stir until tender, but not brown. Stir in cooked beans, tomatoes, rice, salt, paprika, and pepper. Add 2 cups liquid from beans and 2 cups water (as necessary). Bring mixture to boil, cover and simmer 1 hour, stirring occasionally.

JAY M./MARY LEE TAYLOR
CALF SCRAMBLE

TORTILLA SOUP

12 corn tortillas, cut in julienne strips
¼ cup oil
3 green peppers, quartered
2 tomatoes, peeled, seeded and chopped
1 onion, minced
1 garlic clove, minced
¼ cup oil
8 cups chicken broth
3 cups sharp Cheddar cheese, grated

Fry tortillas in oil until golden. Drain. Sauté green peppers in the remaining oil until browned. Drain and tear into pieces. Sauté tomatoes, onion, and garlic in ¼ cup oil until soft. Add chicken broth and bring to a boil. Divide the tortilla strips, peppers, and cheese among 6 soup bowls and pour the boiling soup over them. Serves 6.

DEBBIE KANE
GO WESTERN

GAZPACHO

2 large tomatoes, peeled
1 large cucumber, pared and halved
1 medium onion, peeled and halved
1 medium green pepper, quartered and seeded
1 jar pimiento, drained
2 12-ounce cans tomato juice
⅓ cup olive oil
⅓ cup red wine vinegar
¼ teaspoon TABASCO
1½ teaspoons salt
⅛ teaspoon coarsely ground black pepper
2 cloves garlic, split
½ cup packaged croutons
¼ cup chopped chives

In electric blender, combine one tomato, half the cucumber, half the onion, a green pepper quarter, the pimiento, and ½ cup tomato juice. Blend, covered and at high speed, 30 seconds, to puree the vegetables.

In a large bowl, mix the pureed vegetables with remaining tomato juice, ¼ cup olive oil, the vinegar, TABASCO, salt and black pepper.

Refrigerate mixture, covered, until it is well chilled — about 2 hours. At the same time, refrigerate six serving bowls.

Meanwhile, rub inside of small skillet with the garlic, reserve garlic. Add rest of oil; heat. Sauté the croutons in oil until they are browned. Set aside until serving time.

Chop separately remaining tomato, cucumber, onion and green pepper. Place each of these, and the croutons, in separate bowls. Serve as accompaniments.

Just before serving time, crush reserved garlic. Add to chilled soup, mixing well. Sprinkle with chopped chives. Serve the gazpacho in chilled bowls.
Serves 6

ROBIN GLASSCOCK
AUCTION SALES

"MEXICAN" CHICKEN SOUP

6 chicken breasts
2 carrots, grated
3 stalks celery, chopped
1 large onion, chopped
3 green onion tops, chopped
1 can garbanzos
½ cup raw rice
⅛ cup fresh cilantro, chopped
1 serrano chili pepper, sliced
1 avocado, chopped

In large kettle boil chicken breasts in 6 quarts of water. Reserve chicken broth adding to it 2 tablespoons chicken bouillon granules, to flavor. Shred or chop chicken from bones and return to broth. Add all the remaining except chopped avocado. Add more water if necessary. Serve in soup bowls and decorate with chopped avocado and chopped fresh tomato.

BEVERLY ADAMS GRAY
CHAIRMAN
QUEENS CONTEST,
SAN ANTONIO, TX

CHEESE SOUP

¼ cup butter
½ cup onion, diced
½ cup carrots, diced
½ cup celery, diced
¼ cup flour
1½ tablespoons cornstarch
1 quart chicken broth
1 quart milk
⅛ teaspoon baking soda
1 cup Cheddar, grated
1 cup Velveeta, grated
½ cup American cheese

Melt butter in pot, add onion, carrots, and celery. Sauté over low heat until soft. Add flour and cornstarch and cook until bubbly. Add chicken broth and milk and make a smooth sauce. Add baking soda and cheeses. Season with salt and pepper. Add parsley a few minutes before serving. Serves 8.

STEVE SCHULTZ
CHAIRMAN
AMBASSADORS

VEGETABLE-CHEESE SOUP

2 cups potatoes, diced
1½ cups onion, chopped
1 cup carrots, sliced
1 cup celery, chopped
2 cups water
¼ cup butter
6 teaspoons instant chicken bouillon or
6 chicken bouillon cubes
2 cups milk
½ cup flour
3 cups Cheddar cheese, shredded
1 teaspoon dry mustard
⅛ teaspoon cayenne pepper
½ cup beer (optional)

In a large pot, combine potatoes, onion, carrots, celery, water, butter and bouillon. Bring to a boil, reduce heat, cover and simmer for 30 minutes or until vegetables are tender. In a small bowl, blend milk and flour until smooth. Gradually stir into vegetable mixture. Add cheese, mustard and pepper. Cook, stirring constantly, until cheese melts. If desired, stir in beer, heat through and serve.

MARY FLOWERS
AUCTION SALES

CREAM OF WILD RICE SOUP

1 6-ounce package Long Grain and Wild Rice Mix
1½ tablespoons butter
1 cup onion, chopped
1½ tablespoons flour
1 teaspoon salt
¼ teaspoon mace
Few twists freshly ground black pepper
3 13¾-ounce cans chicken broth
1 pint half and half or light cream
½ cup dry white wine
Sour cream or chopped parsley for garnish

Cook rice mix as package directs. Melt butter in Dutch oven; add onion and sauté, stirring until tender, about 8 minutes. Stir in flour, salt, mace and pepper. Add cooked rice, chicken broth, half and half and wine. Heat, stirring until mixture just comes to the boiling point. Remove from heat. Ladle about 1½ cups soup into blender; cover and blend until smooth. Pour this into a large bowl. Repeat until all of soup is blended. Return soup to Dutch oven and heat, stirring occasionally until heated through. Serve garnished with a small spoonful of sour cream or a sprinkle of chopped parsley. Makes 2½ quarts.

May be made day before and refrigerated. Reheat gently, stirring. Thin with a little milk, if desired.

BEBE JONES
AUCTION SALES

MUSHROOM SOUP

1 pound fresh mushrooms, ¾ pound chopped and
   remainder cut in thin slices for garnish
8 tablespoons butter, softened
2 cups green onions,
   chopped (include tops, about 4 inches)
2 tablespoons flour
5 cups chicken broth
1½ cups heavy cream
Salt and pepper

Combine butter and onions. Transfer to kettle and simmer,
covered, for 15 to 20 minutes. Add flour and make a roux.
Add broth little at a time, stirring until it thickens slightly.
Add mushrooms and simmer partially covered about 10
minutes. Puree the soup, preferably in a food mill, but a
blender may be used. Return the mixture to the kettle and
stir in cream ½ cup at a time until desired consistency is
reached. Taste for seasoning. To serve place sliced
mushrooms in tureen or individual bowls and pour hot soup
over them. Serves 6.

ELIZABETH JACOBS
INTERNATIONAL/MEXICO DAY

ROSIE'S CHILI

2 pounds coarse ground meat
1 cup celery, diced
1 large onion, chopped
1 large bell pepper, chopped
1 pod garlic, chopped
1 large jalapeño chopped
4 strips bacon, fried crisp
½ teaspoon salt
½ teaspoon black pepper (or) mix ¼ teaspoon
   black pepper and ¼ teaspoon cayenne pepper
2 tablespoons chili powder
¼ teaspoon cumin
¼ teaspoon oregano
2 cans kidney beans
1 1-pound can quartered tomatoes
1 can tomato paste

Brown meat in 1 tablespoon shortening. Put meat aside. Fry bacon, remove from pan and sauté onions, celery, and green bell pepper in bacon grease. Put all ingredients (except spices) into a 6 quart pot. Bring to a boil and simmer for 2½ hours. Add the spices at this time and continue to cook at low heat to your taste.

ROSEMARY VAN HEUVERSWYN
AUCTION SALES

SUMP'IN ELSE CHILI ℔

1½ pounds lean ground meat
1 can pinto beans
6 strips bacon, fried crisp
2 cans beer
1 cup green onions, chopped
3 tablespoons chili powder
½ garlic clove, minced
½ teaspoon cominos
1 can whole tomatoes

Brown ground meat in skillet with bacon. Mash garlic, cominos, and whole tomatoes together in that order. Place all together in pot and cook at 350 degrees for 1 hour. Salt and pepper to taste.

SHIRLEY AND LARRY SIMPSON
WESTERN COOKBOOK

CHILI

3 pounds chili meat (Venison is good also)
1 medium onion, chopped
4 cloves garlic, minced
4 tablespoons bacon drippings
6 to 8 teaspoons beef bouillon, (or cubes)
6 to 8 tablespoons chili powder
2 tablespoons flour
1 teaspoon cumin seed
1 teaspoon oregano
Salt and pepper to taste
2 bay leaves

Brown meat, onions and garlic in bacon drippings. Add beef bouillon and 6 to 8 cups water. Simmer 30 minutes. Mix next five ingredients with enough water to blend. Add to meat along with the bay leaves. Simmer at least one hour and correct seasonings to taste.

DOTTIE BIEDIGER
AUCTION SALES

HOSS CHILI

Soak 4 dark red dried peppers in boiling water about 5 minutes or until soft. Remove seeds and chop fine. Set aside. Render out about 1 pound beef suet and discard any remaining pieces or residue. Cube 4 pounds sirloin. Get suet grease hot until almost smoking, throw in comino seed, and then add meat *immediately* — brown well. Add chopped peppers along with 4 cloves garlic and salt. Cover meat with water and cook about 1½ hours, or until meat is very tender. Add chili powder to taste. To thicken, add 2-3 tablespoons corn masa with water until smooth.

ROBYN GLASSCOCK
AUCTION SALES

MENUDO

Water
10 pounds fresh tripe
2 cans Hominy
8 pigs feet
2 to 3 teaspoons salt and pepper and chili powder
2 serrano chili peppers
3 teaspoon flour
Cominos to taste
3 to 4 pods fresh garlic
1 teaspoon oregano

Cut tripe into small cubes place in pot with water add salt, pepper to taste. Grind cominos, fresh garlic, serrano peppers and oregano in a morter and pedestal or mocahete. Boil pigs feet separately with salt and pepper to taste, when tender add only the pigs feet one by one to tripe and discard the water. Brown a small amount of flour and chili pepper in a separate skillet add a little water to make paste and then add to menudo. Add the homony and simmer for 2 to 3 hours. Serves 15 to 20.

MAYO ZUNIGA
Horseshoer
Charlotte, Texas

CHICKEN GUMBO

2 tablespoons oil
½ cup onions, chopped
½ cup green peppers, chopped
4 cups chicken broth
1½ cups canned tomatoes
1 bay leaf
⅛ teaspoon powdered thyme
1½ cups fresh or frozen okra, sliced
¾ teaspoon salt
¼ teaspoon black pepper
½ cup cooked rice
1 cup cooked chicken, diced

Heat the oil in a saucepan; sauté the onions 10 minutes. Add the green peppers, broth, tomatoes, bay leaf and thyme. Bring to a boil, add the okra, salt and pepper, and cook over low heat 15 minutes. Stir in the rice and chicken. Heat and serve. Serves 6.

MARY FLOWERS
AUCTION SALES

D & J'S OKRA GUMBO

Shortening or oil
Okra, small carton or so
Tomatoes, about 1 can
Rotel Tomatoes and Green Chilies is good too
Onions, enough so you do not cry
Salt and pepper to taste

Sauté the okra and onions in the shortening or oil for just a little while. Add the tomatoes and just a little water together with the salt and pepper, cover and let cook until the okra is tender.

DAVID OATES AND
JESSE GARZA
WESTERN COOKBOOK

SEAFOOD GUMBO

1 cup salad oil
1 cup all-purpose flour
2 large onions, chopped
2 stalks celery, chopped
1 large green pepper, chopped
6 cloves garlic, minced
1 gallon warm water
4 cups okra, sliced
3 tomatoes, peeled and chopped
2 tablespoons salt
Red and black pepper to taste
2 pints oysters, undrained
1 pound fresh or frozen crab meat
2 pounds fresh or frozen shrimp, peeled and deveined
½ cup parsley, chopped
½ cup green onion, chopped w/tops
Hot cooked rice

Combine oil and flour in an iron pot over medium heat; cook, stirring constantly, until the flour is copper color (about 15 minutes). Add green pepper, garlic, onion and celery, stirring constantly, until vegetables are tender. Do not let browned flour burn! Gradually add one gallon warm water in small amounts, blending well after each addition. Add tomatoes and okra and bring mixture to boil. Reduce heat and simmer, stirring occasionally, for about 1½ hours. Add salt, pepper and seafood. Bring gumbo to a boil and simmer 10 minutes. Add green onion tops and parsley and simmer 5 minutes. Serve the gumbo over hot rice.

MERLE GIBSON
SOUVENIR PROGRAM

CREOLE GUMBO

2 medium stalks celery, chopped
1 small onion, chopped
½ cup green pepper, chopped
2 tablespoons cooking oil
1 clove garlic, minced
1½ teaspoons salt
1 tablespoon Worcestershire
1 can (2 cups) tomatoes, undrained
1 6-ounce can tomato paste
1 10-ounce (1½ cups) frozen okra, package
   partially thawed and cut into ½" pieces
1 cup shrimp
1 cup (about 6 ounce) crab meat, flaked
1 tablespoon parsley, chopped

In large saucepan, cook celery, onion and green pepper in oil until tender. Stir in garlic, salt, Worcestershire, tomatoes and tomato paste. Cover and simmer 30 to 35 minutes. Add remaining ingredients; continue simmering, covered 15 to 20 minutes or until okra is tender. Serve over rice. 6 to 8 servings.

Note: 1 4½-ounce can shrimp, drained, or 7-ounce package frozen shrimp, partially thawed, may be used.
   A 1-pound can of sliced okra, drained, may be used for frozen okra.

ROBYN MERCHANT
AUCTION SALES

UNCLE BUSH'S MISSISSIPPI GUMBO

1 piece bacon
1 teaspoon bacon fat
1 bay leaf
1 teaspoon Worcestershire
2 cups cooked shrimp
16 okra pods — canned or fresh, cut
1 large onion, chopped
1 small green pepper, chopped
1 bunch celery, chopped
½ cup canned tomatoes
1 tablespoon filé powder
1 can crabmeat
1 clove garlic
2 tablespoons flour
3 cups chicken stock or consommé
½ teaspoon thyme
Salt and pepper to taste

Cut bacon in small pieces and put in kettle with fat. Fry 2 minutes. Add cut okra, chopped onion and chopped green pepper. Cook 5 minutes over low heat. Add garlic and flour and stir. Add consommé, celery (chopped), tomatoes, thyme, bay leaf, Worcestershire, salt and pepper to taste. Simmer 1 hour covered. Add shrimp and crab. Cook 2 minutes. Add filé powder just before serving.

You can boil some chicken breasts, shred and add to gumbo in place of crab or in addition to.

JESSE F. GARZA
INTERNATIONAL/MEXICO DAY

7 TO 12 BEEF STEW

Shortening
4 medium onions, chopped
7 pounds chuck, cut up for stew meat
1 cup flour, shake cup to pack down
3 quarts water
¼ cup, plus 1 tablespoon beef bouillon
2 teaspoons ground cumin
1 tablespoon chervil
1 teaspoon basil
1 tablespoon, plus 1 teaspoon paprika
3 teaspoons black pepper
1 teaspoon mustard
1 quart carrots, cut in 1 inch pieces
4 cups celery, coarse chopped w/some leaves
6 medium potatoes, cut in large cubes
4 medium onions, cut in eighths

In large roasting pan:
Melt enough shortening to brown the meat. Brown bones from roast in the oven while stew meat is browning. When meat is brown and all juice and water have cooked out, stir in flour. Stir until flour is browned. Add onions (chopped), and water. Stir until well mixed and add browned bones. Add beef bouillon and all spices, plus mustard. Stir until well mixed. Cover and simmer on low heat approximately 1 hour or until meat is tender. Add celery, and onions cut in eighths. Stir, cover and simmer approximately 30 minutes. Add carrots and simmer covered until carrots are almost tender. Then add potatoes, and simmer until potatoes are done. This will feed 24 hungry people.

MR. "Q"

BEERY BEEF STEW

¼ cup flour
1 teaspoon salt
½ teaspoon pepper
2 pounds stew meat, cubed
½ cup olive oil
2 pounds onions, peeled and sliced
1 clove garlic, crushed
1 tablespoon soy sauce
1 giant size or 2 regular cans of beer.
1 tablespoon Worcestershire
1 tablespoon steak sauce
1 teaspoon dried thyme
½ teaspoon bay leaf — crumbled
2 pounds potatoes, pared and quartered
4 medium carrots, chunked
Boiling water
Parsley

Coat the cubed meat in the flour, which has been mixed with the salt and pepper; set aside. In a large pot, heat ¼ cup of olive oil and sauté the onion and garlic until tender, about 5 minutes. Remove onions from pot, add the remaining oil. Heat and add the floured meat, browning it on all sides. Return the onion-garlic mixture along with three sauces and herbs. Mix well, bring mixture to boil. Reduce heat; cover and simmer for 1 hour and 30 minutes. Add the pared, quartered potatoes to the stew with just enough boiling water to make enough juice for them to cook in. After about 15 minutes add the carrots. In another 20 minutes or so, when the potatoes are tender, you are ready to serve. Sprinkle some parsley on top just before carrying the pot to the table.

4 to 6 servings.

OSIE ASHFORD

CHICKEN BRUNSWICK STEW 𝒲

2 3-pound chickens
Water to cover
2 tablespoons salt

Wash whole chickens, place in large pot, cover with water and salt and bring to boil. Reduce heat and let simmer.

Add the following:
6 large ears corn cut from cob
   or 1 No. 2 can whole corn
5 medium onions, chopped
1 pound okra, sliced
2 large green peppers, chopped
5 large ripe tomatoes, peeled and chopped
   or 1 No. 2½ can
½ pound salt pork, lean
2 pounds lima beans
1 teaspoon TABASCO sauce or 1 pod red pepper
½ teaspoon black pepper
2 bay leaves.

Continue to boil until meat separates from bone. Reduce heat very low until stew barely simmers. Stir frequently so that stew does not stick to bottom of boiler. Taste and add more seasoning if desired.

In 2 or 3 hours the stew will be a perfectly blended mixture of chicken meat and vegetables, of thick mushy consistency. Remove bones and serve piping hot. Serves about 10.

WESTERN COOKBOOK

LAMB STEW

2-3 pounds breast of lamb
1 large onion, chopped
1-2 cloves garlic, crushed
1 can stewed tomatoes
Carrots, potatoes, and
  celery, diced
Salt and pepper to taste

Brown meat in oil. Add onion and garlic. When onion and garlic are tender add stewed tomatoes. Cook 40 minutes or until amost tender. Add vegetables, salt, and pepper and cook until tender. Add small amount of flour for thickening.

JERRY AND LINDA ANOOSHIAN
AUCTION SALES-BUYER

NAVAJO MUTTON OR LAMB STEW

Any kind of mutton or lamb cut can be used. For economy this recipe uses neck bones.

2 pounds mutton or lamb neck bones
6 cups water
3 medium potatoes, peeled and cut into small pieces
1 onion, cut into small pieces
1 stalk celery, without leaves, cut into small pieces
3 roasted green chilies, peeled, seeded, and chopped.

Put all the ingredients in a heavy pot and bring to a boil. Then simmer for 1½ hours until done. Add salt to taste after cooking.

Carrots, peas, squash, tomatoes and corn can also be used in this stew.

BETTIE RUTLEDGE
AUCTION SALES

COWBOY GOULASH
(from an old genuine cowboy)

2 tablespoons fat
1 pound hamburger
1 teaspoon each salt and pepper
1 teaspoon paprika
1 medium onion, chopped
1 green chili, chopped
1 jalapeño, chopped
8 ounces noodles, medium width
12 ounces canned tomatoes

In a large cast-iron skillet brown meat in the fat. Add the onion and cook until glossy. Add seasoning, chili, and jalapeño. Stir thoroughly. Break up the tomatoes and add to mixture. Shake the noodles on top. Cover and cook on low heat for 20 minutes. Stir thoroughly and serve.

BETTIE RUTLEDGE
WESTERN COOKBOOK

HACIENDA STEW

1 pound hamburger meat
¾ cup onions, chopped
1 cup celery, cut
1 No. 2 can tomatoes
½ teaspoon pepper
1½ teaspoons salt
1 cup diced American cheese
2 cups wide noodles

Cook meat in 2 tablespoons oil with onions for 5 minutes. Add celery, salt and pepper and cook 5 minutes. Then add tomatoes, uncooked noodles, and cheese. Cover and cook until noodles are tender, reduce heat.

MRS. ARIEL HABY

OVEN BEEF STEW

2½ pounds stew meat, 1 inch cubes
1 cup celery, coarsely chopped
4 medium carrots, sliced
3 medium potatoes, cubed
3 medium onions, chopped
1 10-ounce package frozen peas or green beans
3 or 4 tablespoons quick cooking tapioca
2 beef bouillon cubes
2 tablespoons salt
1 tablespoon sugar
Fresh ground black pepper
⅛ teaspoon ground thyme
⅛ teaspoon rosemary leaves
⅛ teaspoon ground marjoram
¼ cup red wine

Combine all ingredients in a 5 quart casserole. Cook covered at 250 degrees for 5 hours. After 3½ hours, stir well, continue cooking. Yield about 15 servings. Serve over rice.

Hints: Use chicken or beef bouillon as cooking liquid instead of water.
Add fresh mushrooms, sautéed in butter or lemon butter.
Add a few drops of bottled brown bouquet sauce.

LEA BEASLEY
JUNIOR STEER RIDING

COUNTRY STEW

2 pounds boneless beef,
  1½ inch cubes
Flour
2 tablespoons fat
4 cups boiling water
1 teaspoon lemon juice
1 teaspoon Worcestershire

2 small bay leaves
2 teaspoons salt
½ teaspoon pepper
1 clove of garlic, minced
6 carrots, quartered
8 small onions, whole
3 potatoes, quartered

Dredge beef with flour. Brown well on all sides in hot fat. Add remaining ingredients, except carrots, onions, and potatoes, simmer for 2 hours, stirring frequently. Add vegetables, cook 30 minutes longer or until vegetables are tender. Thicken stew with flour.

BETTIE RUTLEDGE
AUCTION SALES

RANCH-HAND POTATO AND CABBAGE SOUP

¼ cup onion, chopped
2 tablespoons oil
3 cups water
1 teaspoon salt
2 cups potatoes, diced
2 cups cabbage, chopped
1 large can evaporated milk

Cook onion slowly in oil until yellow. Add water, salt, potatoes, and cabbage. Cook until tender (20 minutes). Add milk and reheat. Serve with chopped parsley, a dash of paprika or toasted bread cubes. Makes 6 portions.

ELIZABETH JACOBS
INTERNATIONAL/MEXICO DAY

General Livestock

Some fifty dedicated businessmen and Ranchers ban together each year. forming the General Livestock Committee.

This committee is directly responsible for the continuous upgrade of quality Stock, Farm and Ranch equipment, and the promotion of our Rural Youth in General Agri-business.

TOM BELL
CHAIRMAN

SHOE PEG CORN SALAD

1 cup onion, chopped
1 cup bell pepper, chopped
1 cup celery, chopped
1 can shoe peg corn
1 can French cut string beans
1 cup frozen green peas,
   mushrooms or cauliflower flowerets
Combine the above.

Bring to a boil:
⅔ cup sugar
⅔ cup vinegar
½ cup oil
1 teaspoon salt

Pour over vegies and stir until cool.
Optional: Chopped pimientos

CALISTA MARSHALL
AUCTION SALES

MACARONI SALAD

¾ cup mayonnaise
1 teaspoon salt
¼ teaspoon dried basil leaves
1 8-ounce package elbow macaroni, cooked, drained
1 cup cucumber, diced
1 cup celery, diced
¼ cup green pepper, diced
¼ cup radishes, sliced
2 tablespoons green onion, sliced thinly
2 medium tomatoes, diced
Salad greens

Stir together first 3 ingredients. Add remaining ingredients; toss. Cover; chill. Serve on salad greens. Makes 8 cups.

MRS. RUBY PIRCHER
AUCTION SALES — BUYER

AVOCADO SALAD

1 3-ounce package lime Jello brand gelatin
1 cup boiling water
¼ small onion, grated
2 3-ounce packages cream cheese
½ cup pimiento, chopped
2 medium avocados, chopped or mashed
¼ green pepper, chopped
1 cup celery, chopped
½ cup mayonnaise

Dissolve gelatin in boiling water. Let cool. Add onion, cream cheese, pimiento and avocados. Add remaining ingredients and mix well. Refrigerate until set. Serve on lettuce leaves. Yield: 8 servings.

ROBERT AND SHIRLEY WAGNER
GENERAL LIVESTOCK

OLIVE SALAD

4 10-ounce jars salad olives
4 cloves garlic, crushed
1 bell pepper, chopped fine
1 stalk celery, chopped fine
Oregano
Crushed Italian red pepper
Bristole olive oil

Drain olives. Rinse thoroughly — at least 4 times. Slice and place in large mixing bowl. Add garlic, bell pepper, and celery. Sprinkle about 1 teaspoon oregano and crushed Italian red pepper (½ teaspoon). Blend mixture well. Stir in Bristole olive oil — just enough to hold mixture together and *do not saturate*. Place mixture back into jars and refrigerate at least 24 hours. Flavor is better if refrigerated 45 hours. Servings 20-25.

EILEEN/ELMER CRUMRINE
RURAL YOUTH

COLD SPICED FRUIT

1 to 2 unpeeled oranges, sliced and seeded
1 20-ounce can pineapple chunks
1 16-ounce can sliced peaches
1 16-ounce can apricot halves
1 29-ounce can pear halves
1 cup sugar
½ cup white vinegar
3 sticks cinnamon
5 whole cloves
1 3-ounce package cherry flavored gelatin

Cut orange slices in half; place in a sauce pan and cover with water. Simmer until rind is tender; drain and set aside. Drain canned fruits well, reserving all of the pineapple juice and half of the peach and apricot juice. Combine reserved juice, sugar, vinegar, cinnamon, cloves and gelatin; simmer 30 minutes. Combine fruits, including orange slices in a 9 cup container; pour hot juice mixture over fruit. Refrigerate at least 24 hours. Yield about 15 servings.

Hint: As the fruit dwindles and there is juice left, add a little fruit of your choice to the container, either fresh or canned. This keeps a long time in the refrigerator and is delicious until it is all gone.

MRS. E. R. LITTLETON
(RAY'S PUMP SERVICE)
AUCTION SALES

GUACAMOLE RING

2 envelopes unflavored gelatin
1 cup water
2 tablespoons lemon juice — I like 3 tablespoons
1 teaspoon salt
½ teaspoon garlic powder
½ teaspoon hot sauce — I like 1 teaspoon
4 medium avocados, smashed
½ cup onion, finely chopped

In small saucepan sprinkle gelatin over cold water. Let stand 1 minute. Stir over low heat until gelatin is dissolved (5 minutes). Stir in lemon juice, salt, garlic powder, and hot pepper sauce.

In a large bowl, combine gelatin mixture and avocados. Beat well. Add onion. Pour into 5 cup ringmold pan. Chill until firm. Serve as appetizer, salad, or spread for crackers.

HINTS:
Oil pan before pouring blended mixture into it. For salad: add chopped peeled ripe tomatoes — 1 cup — along with the onions — or — when you turn chilled ring on lettuce leaves on serving plate — fill center of ring with chilled cherry tomatoes.

EILEEN CRUMRINE/ELMER CRUMRINE
RURAL YOUTH

COKE SALAD

1 large box cherry Jello brand gelatin
2 cups Coca-Cola — ice cold
1 8-ounce package cream cheese, dissolved in
2 cups hot water
½ cup celery, finely chopped
½ cup nuts, chopped
Maraschino cherries

Mix Jello with 1 cup hot water, add cheese cut in pieces, adding the 2 cups of water. Let set until congealed and add additional ingredients.

MRS. FRANCES A. CARTER

BING CHERRY SALAD

1 can bing cherries, pitted
2 boxes black cherry Jello brand gelatin
1 can crushed pineapple
1 cup pecans
1 small Coca-Cola

Bring juice of cherries and pineapple to boil; add Jello, stir until dissolved. Add Coke, chopped nuts, pineapple, cherries and mix lightly. Place mixture in decorative mold and let set. Serve on lettuce with mayonnaise or sour cream topping.

ANNE OATES
WESTERN COOKBOOK

CRANBERRY JELLO SALAD

2 cups water
1 large package cherry Jello brand gelatin
1 cup orange juice
1 cup raw cranberries
½ cup finely chopped pecans
2 small apples
1 cup sugar

Heat water to boil and pour over Jello. Stir; cool. Stir in orange juice; chill until syrupy. Run cranberries through food chopper. The berries do better if frozen. Peel apples, chop fine; add sugar and nuts. Mix well; add to cranberries. Fold into slightly thickened Jello. Pour into 1½ quart mold and chill.

ROBYN MERCHANT
AUCTION SALES

HORSERADISH SALAD

1 3-ounce lime Jello brand gelatin
1 3-ounce lemon Jello brand gelatin
2 cups boiling water
1 cup drained crushed pineapple
1 cup mayonnaise
1 can condensed milk
1 cup chopped pecans
2 heaping tablespoons horseradish
3 tablespoons lemon juice
¼ teaspoon salt
1 small carton cottage cheese

Mix Jello with water. Chill until partially set. Blend in remaining ingredients. Use an 8 inch square pan or mold. Makes 10 servings.

ROBERT AND SHIRLEY WAGNER
GENERAL LIVESTOCK

TRAVELING CONGEALED SALAD

1 can cherry pie filling
1 5-ounce can crushed pineapple
1 large cherry gelatin
½ teaspoon plain gelatin

Blend above and bring to boil. Cool. Add ½ cup chopped nuts and ⅔ cup chopped celery. Mold and chill. Can be served one to eight days after making as it keeps nicely. This is an ideal dish to carry to covered dish affairs. Easy to make and can be made ahead of time.

RUTH RENEAU
READY-TO-COOK POULTRY

PINEAPPLE CHEESE SALAD

1 3-ounce package lemon Jello brand gelatin ⎞ Stir
1 cup boiling water ⎠

1 cup crushed pineapple, drained
2 tablespoons lemon juice
Pineapple syrup and enough cold water to make another
    cup
1 teaspoon pineapple flavoring
1 cup Cheddar cheese, shredded
1 cup whipped cream or
    Cool Whip brand topping

Dissolve Jello in boiling water, add lemon juice, and flavoring. Chill until partly conjealed. Fold in crushed pineapple, cheese, and whipped cream. Refrigerate.

MRS. FRANCES A. CARTER

COOL GREEN GELATIN SALAD

1 package lemon gelatin
1 package lime gelatin
1 cup boiling water
1 14-ounce can sweetened condensed milk
1 pint large curd cottage cheese
1 cup mayonnaise
1 13 or 15 ounce can crushed pinneapple,
   in heavy syrup

Empty lemon and lime gelatin into large mixing bowl. Pour in boiling water and stir until gelatin is dissolved. Pour in sweetened condensed milk, cottage cheese, mayonnaise and pineapple. Stir until smooth and pour into rectangular baking dish. Refrigerate until firm. Cut into squares and serve on lettuce leaf.

ROBYN MERCHANT
SOUVENIR PROGRAM

LIME JELLO SALAD

1 package lime Jello brand gelatin
2 packages cream cheese
1 cup celery, chopped
¾ cup crushed pineapple
1 cup pecans, chopped
1 cup whipping cream

Mix Jello in 1 cup hot water. Add Jello mixture to cream cheese and whip. Gradually add cream and whip until fluffy. Fold in pineapple celery and pecans. Chill, serve on lettuce leaf.

PATRICIA ANN GARZA
WESTERN COOKBOOK

ORANGE-COTTAGE CHEESE SALAD

1 2-pound carton cottage cheese
1 small container of Cool Whip brand topping
2 small or 1 large package orange Jello brand gelatin
1 small can mandarin oranges

Mix cottage cheese and Cool Whip together — just fold gently. Add mandarin oranges cut into bite-size pieces. Sprinkle orange Jello over all, gently fold. Chill. May be served as salad on lettuce leaf or as a side dish. DELICIOUS!!

ELIZABETH JACOBS
INTERNATIONAL/MEXICO DAY

CHALUPA BAR
For a quick party try a Chalupa Bar.
Chalupa shells
Refried Beans
Onions, Chopped
Cheddar cheese, grated
Lettuce, chopped
Guacamole
Pico de Gallo
Salsa*
Place in decorative containers and have everyone help themselves

*SALSA
  1 serrano chili, finely chopped
  1 tomato, chopped
  1 teaspoon onion
  Makes about ½ cup. If you like it hotter add more pepper.

CONGEALED APRICOT PINEAPPLE SALAD

Serves 20
1 tall can crushed pineapple, drained
½ cup sugar
1 cup water
6 ounce package apricot Jello brand gelatin
2 cups cold water

Note: Use pineapple juice and add enough cold water to make the above 2 cups.

1 8-ounce package cream cheese
1 cup chopped pecans or less
1 cup grated carrots
1 large Cool Whip brand topping

Combine sugar and 1 cup water and heat, then add Jello (dissolve good). Put in softened cream cheese (left at room temperature) and add 2 cups of water and pineapple juice, pineapple, carrots and pecans. Put in refrigerator until starting to congeal then fold in Cool Whip and put in 9 x 12 pyrex cake pan.

MICKEY HUBER
CALF SCRAMBLE

JELLO-COTTAGE CHEESE SALAD

1 large can crushed pineapple
2 cans mandarin oranges, drained
1 large carton cottage cheese
2 small packages apricot Jello brand gelatin, no water
1 medium carton Cool Whip brand topping

Mix all ingredients and chill.

REBA ROBERSON
AUCTION SALES

STRAWBERRY NUT SALAD

2 packages strawberry gelatin
1 cup boiling water
1 20-ounce packages frozen sliced strawberries thawed
1 1-pound 4 ounce can crushed pineapple
3 medium ripe bananas, mashed
1 cup walnuts, coarsely chopped
1 12" x 8" x 2" baking dish
1 pint sour cream
1 head lettuce

In a large kettle or saucepan, combine gelatin and boiling water, stirring until gelatin is dissolved. Fold in all at once, strawberries (with juice), drained pineapple, bananas, and walnuts. Turn half of the strawberry mixture into the baking dish as first layer. Refrigerate until firm (about 1½ hours). Evenly spread top with sour cream. Gently spoon on rest of strawberry mix. Refrigerate. Just before serving, cut dish of salad into 12 squares. Serve on lettuce leaves. 12 servings.

ROBYN MERCHANT
AUCTION SALES

RASPBERRY SALAD

2 3-ounce packages raspberry gelatin
1½ envelopes of Knox unflavored gelatin or 1½
   tablespoons
2 cups hot water
2 cans whole berry cranberries
1 large carton sour cream

Mix the unflavored gelatin into the cold water. Bring just to a boil, mix in two packages of raspberry gelatin. Add the cranberries and stir in sour cream. Mix well and pour into 9" by 12" pan. Sets quickly. 20-24 squares.

LEE NOONAN
RURAL YOUTH

APFELSALAT (APPLE SALAD)

6 apples, peeled and diced
2 egg yolks, beaten
½ teaspoon lemon juice
½ teaspoon salt
½ teaspoon white pepper
1 teaspoon mustard
1 tablespoon vinegar
1 tablespoon sugar
1 cup cream

Mix all ingredients except apples and cream. Bring to boil over low heat, stirring constantly. Remove from heat, add cream, and beat until it is cool. Pour mixture over apples and mix thoroughly.

MRS. EVELYN TATUM
SPECIAL DAYS
FREDERICKSBURG, TEXAS

FRUIT SALAD

2 red sweet apples, cut
2 green tart apples, cut
3 oranges, cut
5 bananas, sliced
1 small can pineapple rings, cut
2 cups coconut, shredded
1 small jar maraschino cherries
1 cup nuts, chopped
1 small carton whipping cream
4 tablespoons sugar

Cut all fruits in bite size pieces and place in bowl. Pour whipping cream on fruit and add some of the cherry juice. Let stand in refrigerator for at least 1 hour before serving. Serves approximately 8.

CHERI HUGHES/BOBBY HUGHES
ENTERTAINMENT
CHAIRMAN

CHERRY-PINEAPPLE SALAD

1 large can crushed pineapple, drained
1 can condensed milk
1 can cherry pie filling
1 large container whipped topping
1 cup pecans

Mix together one at a time by hand. Chill. Serves a lot.

SHERI/TERRY LOPER
ENTERTAINMENT

FRUIT SALAD

1 20-ounce can chunk pineapple, packed in own juice
1 3⅝ regular size instant vanilla pudding
1 11-ounce can mandarin oranges
1 can cherry pie filling
Sliced bananas

Mix pineapple (do not drain) with pudding mix. Add cherry pie filling, mandarin oranges (drained), and add sliced bananas. (I use at least 3). Ready to serve. May be made ahead and then fold in bananas shortly before serving. Good with all types of meat. Serves 8.

MRS. DALTON F. NEILL
GENERAL LIVESTOCK

FIVE CUP SALAD

1 cup chunk pineapple
1 cup small marshmallows
1 cup coconut
1 cup mandarin oranges
1 cup sour cream

Mix and chill in refrigerator for at least 3 hours and serve.

HARRY BOGGESS

AMBROSIA DELIGHT

1 apple (peeled or unpeeled as you prefer)
1 orange
2 bananas
1 small can crushed (or chunk size) pineapple
1 cup coconut
1 small jar green cherries
1 small jar red cherries
1 cup pecans
1 cup small marshmallows (all white or mixed colors)

Cut apple, orange and bananas up in small pieces.
Add coconut, pineapple, and both cherries (save enough cherries to decorate top of salad).
Add pecans but save enough whole pecans to decorate top of salad.
Add marshmallows but save enough to decorate top of salad.
Mix all of above ingredients well.

Dressing:
1 egg, well beaten
3 to 4 tablespoons vinegar (depending on desire for tartness)
1½ cups sugar (1 cup may be used to lessen sweetness)

Mix well — place over very low heat and stir *constantly* until dressing thickens.
Remove from fire and let cool. Add to salad and mix well.
Place cherries, marshmallows, and pecans over top of salad and sprinkle lightly with coconut.
Refrigerate for about 30 minutes before serving — keep any remainder refrigerated until consumed.

This recipe can be enlarged depending on the number of people being served — the above amount will serve 6 people adequately.

PEGGY AUSTIN
FOR WYNN D. MILLER

ENCORE SALAD

1 can small whole green beans
2-3 carrots, cut in rounds
Radishes, according to preference
1 bell pepper, cut in rings
1 can water chestnuts
1 small jar stuffed olives
1 can whole mushrooms
1 can pimientos, chopped
1 head cauliflower
⅓ cup oil
⅓ cup vinegar

Mix all ingredients. This will keep in the refrigerator several days.

JAMIE BROWN
JUNIOR STEER RIDING

PEA SALAD

Stir together: ½ cup mayonnaise, 1 teaspoon sugar, ½ teaspoon nutmeg, 1½ teaspoons prepared mustard. Set aside.

6 slices bacon, cooked and crumbled
6 ounce Swiss cheese, sliced matchstick size
1½ cup frozen peas, run hot water over and allow to drain
2 quarts salad greens, salt and pepper to taste.
1 small red onion, cut in strips
2 stalks celery, sliced

Mix together all salad ingredients and toss lightly with salad dressing mixture.

MARY FLOWERS
AUCTION SALES

THREE-BEAN SALAD

1 pound can French cut green beans
1 pound can yellow wax beans
1 pound can red kidney beans
½ cup green pepper, minced
½ cup onion, minced
½ cup salad oil
⅔ cup white or wine vinegar
¾ cup sugar
1 teaspoon salt
½ teaspoon pepper

Drain all three cans of beans. Combine drained beans, green pepper, and onion. In another bowl combine salad oil, vinegar, sugar, salt, and pepper. Add liquid to bean mixture and stir until beans are coated. Refrigerate for 24 hours. Before serving, drain liquid from beans and put them in lettuce-lined bowl. Yields 4 to 6 servings.

MRS. RUBY PIRCHER
AUCTION SALES — BUYER

PORK AND BEAN SALAD

1 large can pork and beans
1 bell pepper, sliced in ¼ inch squares
1 tomato, sliced in ¼ inch squares
1 bundle green onion or shallots
2 tablespoons of mayonnaise

Mix all ingredients together and chill before serving.

WALLACE L. BOLDT
AUCTION SALES

TACO SALAD BOWL

1 pound ground chuck
½ clove garlic, crushed
1 4-ounce can green chilies, finely chopped
1 pound canned tomatoes, drained
1 teaspoon salt
⅛ teaspoon pepper
2 quarts bite-size pieces crisp salad greens
4 ounces to 1 cup Cheddar cheese, grated
1 6-ounce package corn chips, regular size
1 cup green onions, chopped
10 tomatoes, coarsely chopped

In skillet sauté meat and garlic until meat is brown — 10 minutes. Drain excess fat. Add green chilies, tomatoes, salt and pepper; mix well. Cook over low heat, uncovered 30 minutes. Just before serving, in large chilled salad bowl, arrange lettuce, cheese, corn chips and green onions with cooked meat mixture; *toss lightly* until well combined. Garnish with chopped tomatoes. Serve immediately.

SANDI HARPER
AUCTION SALES

BEST-EVER FRESH CAULIFLOWER SALAD

1½ cups raw flowerets, or small head
6 green olives, cut in halves or fourths
1 cup carrots, grated
1 cup green peas, cooked and drained
½ cup Cheddar cheese, cubed
⅔ cup mayonnaise
Salt and pepper

Cut cauliflower into flowerets. Cut olives into 2 or 4 pieces. Mix all ingredients together. Salt and pepper to taste. Should be made the night before and allowed to season. Keeps for several days.

Tuna, ham, or chicken (cubed) may be added for variety.

RON SNOWDEN
JUNIOR STEER RIDING

D — SALAD

1 medium head lettuce
1 bunch green onions, chopped
1 head cauliflower, broken
1 package frozen English peas
1 16-ounce jar mayonnaise
Bacon bits

Starting with shredded lettuce, place each ingredient into a bowl in layers. Spread with mayonnaise and sprinkle with bacon bits. Cover and allow to stand in refrigerator for 24 hours before serving.

JAMIE BROWN
JUNIOR STEER RIDING

STUFFED AVOCADO

1 large ripe avocado
Lemon juice
Lettuce leaves
FILLING:
2 cups cooked chicken, cubed
½ cup orange sections, halved
½ cup green grapes, cut in half
¼ cup walnuts, chopped
¼ cup onion, chopped
DRESSING:
5 tablespoons olive oil
2 tablespoons fresh lemon juice
2 tablespoons fresh parsley, chopped
1 tablespoon fresh basil, chopped or
1 teaspoon dried basil
Salt and pepper to taste

Combine filling ingredients and chill for an hour. At the same time, mix dressing ingredients in a jar with a cover. Chill. At serving time cut avocado in half, lengthwise, remove pit, and brush with lemon juice to prevent discoloring. Mix filling and dressing (shake dressing well first) and heap on each avocado half. Arrange on a bed of crisp lettuce leaves.

ROSE MARIE EICKENROHT
GO WESTERN

BEAN SALAD

Drain and place in bowl:
1 No. 2 can cut green beans
1 No. 2 can wax beans
1 can red kidney beans
Add:
1 large green pepper, sliced thin
1 large sweet onion, sliced thin
Blend together:
1 cup vinegar
1 cup sugar
¼ cup salad oil

Add to vegetables, toss lightly and chill in refrigerator for 12 to 24 hours.

ELIZABETH JACOBS
INTERNATIONAL/MEXICO DAY

BEAN SPROUTS SALAD

2 cups well washed and drained fresh bean sprouts
4 tablespoons of vinegar
Salt
Dash of Worcestershire
½ teaspoon minced fresh ginger

Mix all ingredients. Serve cold. Serves 4.

RHONDA WOLFE
WESTERN COOKBOOK

CUCUMBER SALAD

1 small package lemon or lime Jello brand gelatin
1 cup hot water
1 small can crushed pineapple with juice
Salt
1 cucumber, peeled and chopped, remove large seed
3 tablespoons mayonnaise
½ cup chopped pecans

Dissolve Jello in hot water; when cool, add mayonnaise stirring until dissolved. If it does not dissolve readily it may be mixed with hand beater. Add pineapple and juice, cucumber and pecans. When partially set fold in ½ cup whipped cream or use ½ of 9 ounce tub of Cool Whip and allow several hours to congeal.

VIVION COLLIER
SOUVENIR PROGRAM

MARINATED CARROT SALAD

5 cups cooked carrots, sliced
1 small green pepper, sliced
1 medium onion, chopped
1 can tomato soup
¼ cup salad oil
½ cup vinegar
¾ cup sugar
1 tablespoon Worcestershire
1 teaspoon salt
1 teaspoon pepper

Combine soup, oil, vinegar, sugar, Worchestershire, salt, and pepper. Add carrots, green peppers, and onions. Mix well and let stand overnight.

MRS. ARIEL HABY

MARINATED VEGETABLE SALAD
(For a snack, salad or vegetable)

1 cup salad oil, light oil
1½ cups white vinegar
4 tablespoons sugar
1½ teaspoons salt
½ teaspoon basil
½ teaspoon oregano leaves
½ teaspoon garlic salt
1 large cauliflower, sliced
1 can pitted ripe olives (6 ounces), sliced
1 medium green pepper, chopped
4 raw carrots, sliced
4 ribs celery, sliced
OPTIONAL:
1 large onion, chopped
½ pound fresh mushroom caps

Combine first 7 ingredients. Stir in vegetables. Refrigerate in large container, tossing often. Can be made day before serving.

SHIRLEY SCHREIBER
AUCTION SALES

VEGETABLE SALAD

2 cups celery, chopped
½ cup purple onion, chopped
2 cups green peppers, chopped
4-ounce jar pimiento, chopped
2 1-pound cans French green beans, drained
1 package frozen green peas
2 teaspoons salt and pepper

Dressing:
1 cup sugar   ¾ cup cider vinegar
½ cup salad oil   2 teaspoons water

Add to vegetables and mix well. Refrigerate overnight. Drain before serving.

JOHN J. WILLIAMS
JUNIOR STEER RIDING

106

MEXICAN POTATO SALAD

4 medium potatoes
½ cup oil
⅓ cup vinegar
2 teaspoons chili powder
1 teaspoon seasoned salt
¼ teaspoon salt
½ teaspoon hot pepper sauce
8-ounce can whole kernel corn, drained
½ cup celery, sliced
½ cup carrots, shredded
½ cup red or green pepper, chopped
½ cup sliced ripe olives, pitted
¼ cup red onion, chopped
Tomato wedges

In 2-quart saucepan cook potatoes in boiling water until tender; about 35 to 40 minutes. Drain while still slightly warm; peel and cube. In small bowl, combine oil, vinegar, chili powder, salt and pepper sauce; add to warm potatoes, tossing gently to coat cover. Chill 1 hour. Gently fold in remaining ingredients. If desired, garnish with tomato wedges and additional olives. Serve chilled. 8 to 10 servings.

MARY ELLEN PENWELL
SOUVENIR PROGRAM

COLE SLAW

1 head cabbage, grated
1 medium bell pepper, chopped
1 large can tomatoes
1½ cups sugar
1 tablespoon salt
Black and red pepper to taste

Mash, bruise, and squeeze with hands the above ingredients. After thoroughly mixed, cover with white vinegar (almost one cup). Cover bowl, let set out at room temperature for at least 24 hours. Place in covered container in refrigerator ... will keep 2 months. Great with BBQ.

WANDA J. ECRETTE
RURAL YOUTH

CABBAGE SLAW

1 large head cabbage, sliced
1 large onion (use purple for color), sliced
1 cup sugar, (less 2 tablespoons)
1 tablespoon mustard seed
1 tablespoon celery seed
2 tablespoons salt or more according to taste
¾ cup salad oil
¼ cup white vinegar

Combine the first 3 ingredients and set aside. Boil the 2 tablespoons sugar and the other ingredients. Pour over cabbage mixture. Keep in air-tight container for 24 hours before serving. Will keep up to three weeks in refrigerator.

THOMAS REAVIS
INTERNATIONAL/MEXICO DAYS

OVERNIGHT CABBAGE SLAW

½ medium cabbage, sliced
1 small sweet onion
½ medium green pepper
2 carrots
⅔ cup vinegar
⅓ cup vegetable oil
½ cup sugar
1 teaspoon salt
¼ teaspoon pepper

Shred sliced cabbage, onions, pepper, and carrots: Mix together. Add vinegar, oil, sugar, salt, and pepper together. Mix well. Pour mixture over vegetables, stir well. Cover and refrigerate at least 8 hours before serving. At serving time stir and drain. Makes 6 (1 cup) servings.

M. D. SMITH

WILTED SPINACH SALAD

Cut roots and tough stems from one pound spinach. Wash thoroughly in cold water. Drain, shake out water and blot dry. Tear leaves into bite size pieces. Mince 6 green onions. Mix with spinach. Mash 1 clove garlic and cover with 1 tablespoon salad oil. Let stand 30 minutes. Discard garlic. Sauté 3 slices bacon. Reserve bacon drippings. Beat together:

1 egg
1 tablespoon sugar
1 tablespoon tarragon vinegar
1 tablespoon wine vinegar

Pour slowly into warm bacon fat, stirring constantly until mixture has thickened slightly. Pour over spinach mixture and toss well. Crumble bacon strips and sprinkle over salad.

CAROLYN PILLOT
AUCTION SALES

SHRIMP AND RICE SALAD

2 cups cooked cooled rice
2 cups cooked cleaned shrimp
½ green pepper, chopped
2 green onions, chopped
1 cup raw cauliflower, chopped
10 stuffed olives, sliced
Juice of half a lemon
Salt and pepper to taste
½ cup mayonnaise

Combine rice, shrimp, green pepper, green onions, cauliflower, olives, lemon juice, salt and pepper. Mix well and then add mayonnaise. Chill well.

SHIRLEY SCHREIBER
AUCTION SALES — BUYER

SHRIMP MOLD

1 10¾-ounce can tomato soup
1 can water
1 8-ounce package cream cheese
1 cup mayonnaise
2 envelopes Knox gelatin, dissolved in ¼ cup cold water
¼ cup green onions, chopped fine
½ cup celery, chopped fine
3 cans broken shrimp or
　2 cans shrimp and 1 can crab
Black pepper and TABASCO sauce to taste

Rinse shrimp before using, then chop. Bring soup and water to boil. Add cream cheese that has been cut in small pieces. Add mayonnaise and dissolved gelatin. Add remaining ingredients. Pour into greased 9 inch mold. Serve on lettuce with assorted crackers.

ROBERT AND SHIRLEY WAGNER
GENERAL LIVESTOCK

HOT CHICKEN SALAD

2 cups chicken, cooked and diced
1 cup celery, chopped
½ cup pecans, chopped
1 tablespoon onion, grated
½ cup mayonnaise
1 can mushroom soup

Mix and put in a baking dish. Bake for 30 minutes at 350 degrees. Sprinkle potato chip pieces over the top.

MRS. JACK SELLERS
WESTERN PARADE

GODDESS CASHEW CHICKEN SALAD

4 cups chicken, cooked and cubed
1 cup celery, sliced
½ cup green pepper, chopped
¼ cup green onion, chopped
2 tablespoons pimiento, chopped
½ teaspoon salt
½ cup Green Goddess salad dressing
⅓ cup cream, whipped
¾ cup cashews
6 small tomatoes
6 hard cooked eggs, if desired

In large bowl, combine chicken, celery, green peppers, onion, pimientos and salt, toss lightly. In small bowl gently fold dressing into whipped cream. Combine chicken, vegetable mixture, and dressing, tossing lightly. Chill, just before serving, fold in cashews.

To serve, spoon salad in and around tomatoes on individual lettuce-lined plates. Garnish with egg wedges. Refrigerate leftovers. 6 servings.

MARY ELLEN PENWELL
AUCTION SALES

SEPTEMBER LUNCHEON SPECIAL CHICKEN SALAD

2 cups chicken, chopped and cooked
1 cup celery, chopped
1 6-ounce package long grain and wild rice mix
    cooked and chilled
2 tablespoons green onion, finely chopped

Dressing:
½ cup mayonnaise
½ cup plain yogurt
2 tablespoons lemon juice
½ teaspoon honey

LEE NOONAN
RURAL YOUTH

PICO DE GALLO

Garlic
2-3 fresh tomatoes, chopped
½ onion, chopped
Cilantro, chopped
1 or 2 chilies to taste, Serrano or Jalepeño, chopped
2 avocados, chopped
2 limes
Salt and pepper

Mash garlic in press and rub around in mixing bowl. Combine tomatoes, onion, cilantro, and peppers, mix well. Cut avocado and mix lightly with other ingredients. Squeeze lime juice over mixture, salt and pepper to taste. Store in air-tight container. Will keep for several days in refrigerator.

GEORGE B. WOODS
AUCTION SALES

RO'S EASY SALAD

1 15-ounce can midget baby corn whole, drained
2 15-ounce cans artichokes in brine, drained
1 can hearts of palm, drained and quartered
2 to 4 tablespoons stuffed olives, sliced

Put all of the above in bowl and pour over any Italian salad dressing and toss lightly. Chill for 2 to 3 hours in your refrigerator and serve on lettuce leaves.

ROSEMARY VAN HEUVERSWYN
AUCTION SALES

Western Cookbook

This year a proposal to publish a cookbook for the San Antonio Livestock Show and Rodeo was presented and approved by the Operating Committee. Proceeds from the sales of our cookbook will go to the Auction Committee to help increase the premiums for our youth.

With the support and help from the many that submitted recipes we were able to publish this book for your pleasure. We sincerely hope you have many hours of joy reading it and most of all "happy eating."

PATRICIA ANN GARZA
CHAIRMAN

"HARRY SCHNEIDER'S" FAMOUS BAR-B-Q SAUCE

1 large onion, chopped fine
¼ cup cooking oil
¼ cup vinegar
¼ cup brown sugar
2 cups catsup
1 cup water or beer
2 teaspoons prepared mustard
2 teaspoons Worcestershire
1 teaspoon salt
½ teaspoon pepper

Cook the chopped onion in the oil over low heat until the onions are tender, do not brown. Then add the rest of the ingredients, stir well and simmer over low heat for 30 minutes. Put the sauce on the meat only after the meat is nearly done, or about 30 minutes before serving. This sauce is good on almost any kind of meat. Makes about 1 quart of sauce.

HARRY SCHNEIDER
AUCTION SALES

RED BAR-B-QUE SAUCE

¼ cup salad oil
1 cup onion, finely chopped
1 clove garlic, minced
1 cup water
¾ cup catsup
⅓ cup lemon juice
3 tablespoons sugar
2 tablespoons Worcestershire
1 tablespoon prepared mustard
1 teaspoons salt
Dash of hot pepper sauce

Cook onion and garlic in salad oil until just tender. Add remaining ingredients; simmer uncovered 15 minutes. Sauce can be stored in refrigerator. Excellent on grilled pork.

A. J. KALLUS
CALF SCRAMBLE
HALLETTSVILLE, TX

RUM SAUCE

1 stick oleo or butter
1 cup sugar
½ cup Karo syrup
¼ teaspoon salt
1 cup evaporated milk
½ cup rum

Combine oleo, sugar, Karo and salt, cook over low heat stirring constantly for four minutes. Mixture will be a little thick. Remove from heat and gradually stir in milk. When mixture is completely cooked, add rum and beat vigorously. If mixture separates while in refrigerator, beat again before using. May be served hot or cold. Great over hot apple pie and ice cream.

CARRIE AND RICKY

RÉMOULADE

2 cloves garlic, chopped fine or pressed in garlic press
1 cup mayonnaise
¼ cup chili sauce
¼ cup catsup
1 teaspoon mustard
½ cup oil
1 teaspoon Worcestershire
1 teaspoon black pepper
Dash of TABASCO sauce, optional
Dash of paprika, optional
1 onion, grated
2 tablespoons water

Combine all ingredients in blender or small mixing bowl; mix until well blended.

Refrigerate several hours before serving. This sauce may be used as a salad dressing or seafood sauce.

ELMO J. BOUCHILLON
GREENVILLE, MISSISSIPPI

SECRET BARBECUE SAUCE

2 teaspoons salt
1 teaspoon black pepper
2 teaspoons mustard
2 teaspoons chili powder
1 tablespoon TABASCO sauce
2 tablespoons Worcestershire
½ cup brown sugar
½ cup white sugar
1 cup vinegar
2 cups water
¼ cup bacon drippings
3 cloves garlic, finely chopped

Mix all ingredients together. Bring to boil, then simmer slowly for 30 minutes. This sauce has much more flavor if made the day before. Refrigerate overnight, and heat to luke warm the next day, before sopping on meat.

JACK HUMMEL
SUPT. CALF SCRAMBLE

MEAT "SOP"

This is a great basting "sop" for barbeque:
Cover bottom of pan with salt. Squeeze juice of 3 lemons into pan. Also use lemon rinds. Pepper to taste, sprinkle with garlic salt. Add 2 chopped onions, 1 pint water, 1 pint vinegar, 1 stick oleo. Bring to a boil and simmer 15 to 30 minutes.

SAUCE FOR CHARCOAL BROILED STEAK

1 pod garlic, finely chopped
1 cup lemon juice, fresh
2 cups Wesson Oil
1 tablespoon oregano

Finely chop garlic, and put in quart jar. Add other ingredients. Shake real well (has more flavor if made day before). Use as much sauce needed to marinate steaks for about an hour before cooking, leaving as much garlic as possible in jar. This will keep indefinitely in refrigerator, and as the sauce gets low in jar, you can keep adding to it. In adding to it, if lemons are not handy, substitute vinegar, add a little garlic powder, oregano, and Wesson Oil. Always shake well before marinating meat.

GLEN O. HUMMEL, JR.
CHAIRMAN, CALF SCRAMBLE

LEMON MARINADE FOR POULTRY

¾ cup wine vinegar
3 teaspoons lemon juice
1 medium onion, minced
1 clove garlic, crushed
¼ cup parsley, chopped
1 bay leaf
⅛ teaspoon thyme
⅛ teaspoon tarragon
2 teaspoons salt
½ teaspoon pepper

Mix all together and brush over chicken. Repeat about every 15 minutes while chicken is cooking.

RHONDA WOLFE
WESTERN COOKBOOK

BARBEQUE SAUCE FOR STEAKS AND CHICKEN

1 cup vinegar
Juice of 4 lemons
1 of the lemons' peel, diced
⅓ cup Worcestershire
3 bay leaves
½ cup of oleo
1 garlic clove, minced

Mix together and bring to boil.
Sprinkle meat with lemon pepper and spread barbeque sauce over meat while cooking.
Sprinkle chicken with paprika before cooking.

A. H. CADWALLADER III
AUCTION SALES

COCKTAIL SAUCE

½ cup catsup
½ cup chili sauce
1 teaspoon Worcestershire
3 drops TABASCO sauce
2 tablespoons white horseradish
2 tablespoons onion, chopped

Mix all of the above ingredients and chill. Terrific with boiled shrimp or oysters on half-shell.

RICKY BLAYLOCK

DIPPING SAUCE

1 32-ounce bottle catsup
Juice from 2 large lemons
1 14-ounce bottle horseradish

Mix well and season with salt and TABASCO sauce to taste.

SHIRLEY AND LARRY SIMPSON
JUNIOR STEER RIDING

TARTAR SAUCE

1 cup mayonnaise
⅓ cup sweet pickle relish
⅓ cup onion, chopped
Salt to taste

Combine all of the above ingredients and chill. Great with fried shrimp, oysters or fish.

JESSE F. GARZA
WESTERN COOKBOOK

BRANDY HARD SAUCE

¼ cup butter, softened
2 cups powdered sugar
2 to 3 tablespoons brandy

Beat butter in small bowl until fluffy. Beat in powdered sugar and enough brandy for desired consistency. Serve at room temperature. Makes 1 cup.

RON WOLMA
WESTERN COOKBOOK

MUSHROOM SAUCE

3 tablespoons butter or margarine
1 cup fresh mushrooms, sliced
3 tablespoons flour
Dash cayenne
1 can condensed chicken broth, undiluted
¼ cup half and half

Melt butter in saucepan, add mushrooms; sauté stirring occasionally, about 5 minutes. Remove from heat; stir in flour and cayenne until smooth. Add chicken broth and half and half. Cook over medium heat stirring constantly, until boiling. Reduce heat; simmer 3 minutes. Makes 8 servings.

KATHY BENDER
AUCTION SALES

BARBEQUE SAUCE

¼ cup butter
¼ cup vinegar
¼ cup catsup
¼ cup lemon juice
¼ cup Worcestershire
1 onion, chopped
1 clove garlic, minced
½ teaspoon salt
¼ teaspoon pepper
3 shakes TABASCO sauce
Few grains red pepper

Melt butter in sauce pan. Add lemon juice, vinegar, catsup, Worcestershire sauce, and spices. Bring to a boil and pour over meat to be barbequed.

ADRIANNE DALTON

PICANTE

2 large cans Rotel Tomatoes, crushed
1 small can Rotel Tomatoes with Green Chilies
1 large onion, chopped coarse
1 small bell pepper, chopped coarse
Jalapeño peppers, about four, chopped coarse
2 medium cloves garlic, chopped super fine
   (can substitute garlic powder)
¼ cup vinegar
½ cup water
2 tablespoons sugar
Salt and pepper to taste

Mix ingredients in large cooking pot. Bring to a boil and then simmer about one hour.

Optional: Add additional jalapeño pepper to taste if desire hotter sauce.

Yield: About 2 quarts.

JEFF HABERSTROH
BRANDS-BROADWAY

TASTY ITALIAN SAUCE

s, Toppin's and Coverin's

1½ to 2 pounds of Italian sausage
2 medium to large onions, white or yellow
2 green peppers, red pepper can also be used
Mushrooms, canned or fresh
1 cup of wine, optional
2 or 3 16-ounce cans of tomato sauce,
   depending on how thick you want it
1 tablespoon Worcestershire
3 tablespoons brown sugar
2 teaspoons garlic powder
1 teaspoon each ginger, clove, and cinnamon
2 tablespoons Italian seasoning (approximately)
2 shakes or so of pepper
Salt to taste, if you must

Get your skillet out and put the sausage, onions, pepper, and mushrooms in and brown until sausage is done. While that is simmering away, combine the rest of the ingredients in a sauce pan, stir well, and bring to a slow boil. Drain the skillet of goodies *well.* Add to sauce and turn down temperature so it will simmer without sticking for at least 1 hour. Stir occasionally.

From here you're on your own. I cook my sauce for at least 2 hours, and I've found it tastes even better the second day. It can be frozen if you wish to make larger amounts. This sauce can be used for many things, such as spaghetti sauce, lasagna, etc. Pour over any macaroni or even noodles and of course pizza! Mmm-good!

BONNIE PASCUZZI
ALAMO TRAIL RIDE

SHA'S CAESAR DRESSING

2 eggs
2 teaspoons lemon juice
3 cloves garlic
2 teaspoons salt

1 teaspoon black pepper
2 teaspoons Worcestershire
½ cup Parmesan cheese
1½ cups salad oil

Blend all ingredients in blender or food processor.

Serve cold over tossed salad or any particular vegetable.

SHA HAYS
GO WESTERN

PRALINE SAUCE TOPPING

1½ cups light brown sugar
⅔ cup white Karo syrup
4 tablespoons real butter (no substitute)
1 small can evaporated milk
Pecan halves

Mix and boil first three ingredients. Cool to lukewarm. Add evaporated milk. Stir well. Toast 1 or 2 cups of whole pecan halves a few minutes with very little salt and butter. Add sauce before serving over vanilla ice cream.

Good warm or cold.

JUNIOR STEER RIDING

HONEY DRESSING

⅓ cup undiluted concentrate for lemonade
   or limeade, thawed
⅓ cup honey
⅓ cup salad oil
1 teaspoon celery seed

Beat until smooth with rotary beater. Double recipe will use up a 6 ounce can lemonade.

MRS. HARRIS/FRED HARRIS
READ TO COOK POULTRY

THOUSAND ISLAND DRESSING ℐ

1 cup mayonnaise
¼ cup chili sauce
2 hard boiled eggs, chopped
2 tablespoon green pepper, chopped
2 tablespoon celery, chopped
1 tablespoon onion, chopped fine
1 teaspoon paprika
½ teaspoon salt

Combine all ingredients and store in a tightly sealed container and place in refrigerator. Approximately 2 cups.

SPICY FRENCH DRESSING

1 cup vegetable oil
1 cup mayonnaise
1 10¾-ounce can tomato soup
½ cup firmly packed brown sugar
⅓ cup vinegar
1 teaspoon dry mustard
1 teaspoon garlic salt
½ teaspoon onion salt
½ teaspoon celery salt
¼ teaspoon paprika
¼ teaspoon Worcestershire
Dash of hot sauce

Combine all ingredients in container of electric blender. Process on low speed until thoroughly blended. Chill at least 2 hours.

Yield about 4 cups.

BETTIE RUTLEDGE
AUCTION SALES

BATTER FOR ONION RINGS

1 can of beer
1½ cups of flour
Salt and pepper (lots)

Mix well, let set for 3 hours without stirring. Dip onion rings and fry as usual. Also excellent for shrimp.

MARY ELLEN PENWELL
AUCTION SALES

ONION RING BATTER

1 cup beer, not cold
1 cup flour

Mix ingredients and let stand for 2 to 3 hours. Dip rings and fry to golden color with medium heat in shortening or oil (use enough to cover). Also good for egg plant, green tomatoes, squash, okra, etc.

MILROY POWELL
GENERAL HORSE SHOW
CHAIRMAN

POSSUM FRITTERS

Frying Batter:
1¾ cup flour
3 teaspoons baking powder
½ teaspoon salt
1 egg, slightly beaten
1 cup milk
1 tablespoon cooking oil

Mix dry ingredients — combine egg, milk and oil. Pour into flour mixture and stir until smooth.

Clean squash (okra, egg plant, etc.). Cut into small cube pieces and mix into batter. Drop by spoonfulls into hot oil and deep fry.

JUANITA BROWN
JUNIOR STEER RIDING

BASIC WHITE SAUCE*

2 tablespoon butter
2 tablespoon flour
¼ teaspoon salt
¼ teaspoon pepper
1 cup milk

Melt butter, blend in flour add salt and pepper and whip lightly while stirring in the milk. Stir constantly with wire whip until thick and smooth.
*To make the Basic White Sauce thinner, decrease flour by 1 tablespoon.
To make the Basic White Sauce thicker, increase flour by 1 tablespoon.

VARIATIONS:
Add Cheddar cheese to make cheese sauce.
Add curry powder to make curry sauce for vegetables.

Calf Scramble

Fun and action are the name of the game in the annual San Antonio Stock Show and Rodeo Calf Scramble. Of the many exciting rodeo highlights, none is more fun, especially for the spectators.

Twenty youngsters (boys and girls), ages 12-15 are pitted against 10 calves in the arena. The aim of each youngster is to halter a calf and get it over the finish line. Sound easy? Not so!!! The calves have to be caught barehanded, haltered, and then dragged, pushed, led or coaxed across the finish line.

In each performance, every calf is a winner for some youngster. The top four places pay $400, and the next six pay pro-rated amounts according to the amount of money donated. One of the reasons behind offering this event, besides just plain fun, is to promote participation in educational activities. That's why the winners must use the certificates to buy livestock for FFA or 4-H projects or to save for a college scholarship.

GLEN HUMMEL, JR.
CHAIRMAN

CREPES RELLENO

Crepes:
1 cup milk
2 eggs
⅓ cup cornmeal
⅔ cup flour
Dash of salt
Filling:
⅓ cup onion, chopped
1 tablespoon vegetable oil
1 pound ground beef
1 8-ounce jar taco sauce
¼ cup sunflower nuts
¼ teaspoon ground cumin
⅛ teaspoon garlic powder
Topping:
Guacamole
Dairy sour cream
Shredded sharp Cheddar
  cheese

For crepes: combine all ingredients; mixing until smooth. For each crepe, fill ¼ cup dry measure half full. Pour into hot lightly greased crepe pan or 6 to 7 inch skillet; immediately tilt pan to cover bottom evenly with thin layer of batter. Cook 45-60 seconds or until top looks dry. Turn, cook about 20 seconds. Stack crepes between sheets of wax paper.

For filling: sauté onion in oil, add meat, browning lightly; drain. Stir in taco sauce, sunflower seeds (nuts), cumin, garlic powder; simmer about 5 minutes. Heat over to 325 degrees. Fill each of 12 crepes with ¼ cup meat mixture, roll up. Place seam side down in 13x9 inch baking dish, cover with aluminum foil. Bake at 325 degrees for 10-12 minutes or until heated enough through. Serve with guacamole, sour cream, and shredded cheese. Makes 12.

COL. MAXIMO VIRGIL
INTERNATIONAL/MEXICO DAY

EGG SOUFFLE

10 slices white bread, crust removed
Butter both sides, cut into fourths
Grate together:
  ½ pound sharp cheese
  ¾ pound Longhorn cheese
Alternate layers of bread and cheese in casserole, starting
  with bread and ending with cheese.

Beat 8 eggs with 3 cups milk, 2 teaspoons mustard, 2 teaspoons salt and pepper. Pour over bread and cheese.
Refrigerate over night or freeze. Sprinkle chopped jalapeno
on top if desired and also sausage. Bake 1 hour at 375
degrees. Set casserole in tray of water.

NOBLE J. — TOPSY TAYLOR
CALF SCRAMBLE

MEXICAN OMELET

4 eggs beaten
2 tablespoons green chilies, chopped
2 tablespoons green olives, chopped
2 teaspoons butter or margarine
¼ cup Cheddar cheese, shredded

Combine eggs, chilies, and olives; blend well. Melt butter in
a 10 inch omelet pan or heavy skillet until just hot enough to
sizzle a drop of water. Pour egg mixture into pan. As mixture starts to cook, gently lift edges of omelet and tilt pan to
allow uncooked portion to flow underneath. When egg mixture is set and no longer flows freely, sprinkle cheese over
half of omelet. Fold omelet in half and slide onto plate.
Yields 2 servings.

COL. MAXIMO VIRGIL
INTERNATIONAL/MEXICO DAY

MEXICAN QUICHE (NO CRUST)

½ cup butter, melted
10 eggs
Salt
½ cup flour
1 teaspoon baking powder
1 pound Monterey Jack cheese, grated
1 8 ounce can chopped green chilies, drained
1 pint cottage cheese

Lightly butter 9×13 inch pan. Beat eggs slightly. Add flour, baking powder, and salt. Blend. Add butter, chilies, cottage cheese, and grated cheese. Pour into pan. Bake at 400 degrees for 15 minutes and then at 350 degrees for 35 to 40 minutes until golden. Serves 8-10.

SHIRLEY SCHREIBER
AUCTION SALES

HAM AND MUSHROOM QUICHE

1 pie shell
⅔ cup green onions, chopped
½ tablespoon butter or margarine
⅔ cup fresh mushrooms, chopped
¾ cup ham, cubed
½ cup milk
4 eggs
1⅔ cup Monterrey Jack cheese, grated

Bake pie shell 5 to 7 minutes. Sauté onion in butter, add mushrooms and continue to sauté for 2 to 3 minutes. Beat the eggs and milk until well blended. Add the onions, mushrooms, ham, and cheese and mix lightly. Pour into pie shell and bake at 350 degrees for 30 minutes or until mixture is set.

PATRICIA AND JESSE GARZA
WESTERN COOKBOOK

QUICK QUICHE LORRAINE

1 9 inch pie shell
6 eggs, beaten
8 slices bacon, crisp-cooked, drained and crumbled
1 cup Swiss cheese, shredded
1¼ cups half-and-half, light cream or milk
½ teaspoon salt
⅛ teaspoon nutmeg
⅛ teaspoon pepper

Brush inside of the pie shell with a small amount of the beaten eggs. Prick bottom and sides with fork. If using a pie plate, bake shell in preheated 450 degree (F) oven 5 minutes or until light golden brown. If using a metal pie pan, bake shell at 425 degree oven. Set pie shell aside. Reduce oven temperature to 375 degree for pie plate, 350 degree for metal pie pan. Stir together bacon and cheese. Put into pie shell. To the beaten eggs, add remaining ingredients. Beat until well blended. Pour over bacon/cheese mixture. Bake in preheated oven 35 to 40 minutes or until knife inserted near center comes out clean. Let stand 5 to 10 minutes before serving.

PATTI POCHER
JUNIOR STEER RIDING

JALAPEÑO CHEESE

6 jalapeños chopped and seeded

In bottom of pan place 20 ounces grated sharp Cheddar cheese, then jalapeños. Beat 8 eggs and pur on top of jalapeños.
Bake at 275 degrees for 45 minutes. Can be taken from pan and frozen.

ANNELLA EGBERT
AUCTION SALES

ASPARAGUS AND CHICKEN QUICHE

Unbaked 10 inch deep pie shell
1½ cups chicken, chopped
1 10-ounce package frozen asparagus, cooked
4 slices cooked bacon
½ cup Swiss cheese, grated
4 eggs
1 tablespoon flour
½ teaspoon salt
2 cups light cream
2 tablespoons Parmesan cheese
Dash of paprika

Arrange asparagus in bottom of pie shell, spoke fashion. Top with chicken, crumbled bacon and Swiss cheese. Beat eggs, flour, salt and cream together and pour over asparagus. Sprinkle with Parmesan cheese and paprika. Bake at 375 degrees for 45-50 minutes until set. Let stand 10 minutes before serving. Makes 8 servings.

BEBE JONES
AUCTION SALES

JALAPEÑO PIE

1 unbaked pie crust
1 7-ounce can jalapeños, washed and cut
8 ounces grated Cheddar cheese
4 eggs, beaten well
Pinch of salt in egg batter

Lay jalapeños in bottom of pie shell, next the 8 ounces of grated Cheddar cheese. Then pour the egg mixture over this. Bake at 350 degrees for 20-25 minutes until set. Serves 4-6.

NANCY CHILDRESS

SPINACH QUICHE

½ small onion, finely chopped
1 cup sharp Cheddar cheese, grated
1 cup plain yogurt
1 tablespoon flour
2 eggs
1 teaspoon salt
¼ teaspoon pepper
dash nutmeg
1 can chopped spinach
1 9-inch pie crust

Preheat oven to 450 degrees. Bake crust 10 minutes or lightly brown. Cool, sprinkle ½ cheese and onion over crust. Beat eggs well, add yogurt, flour, seasonings, remaining cheese and onion. Stir in spinach and pour into crust. Bake on lowest rack 15 minutes. Reduce heat to 350 degrees and bake 30 minutes more. Serves 6.

MRS. AL SADERSTROM
GO WESTERN

CHILAQUILLA

2 onions, chopped
2 cloves of garlic, minced
3 1-pound cans whole tomatoes
2 cans green chilies
2 pounds Monterrey Jack cheese
16 corn tortillas

Chop 2 onions, 2 cloves of garlic and sauté in 3 tablespoons of butter. Add 3 1-pound cans of whole tomatoes and 2 cans of green chilies, seeded, chopped and drained. Simmer 30 minutes. Quarter tortillas and drop in sauce to soften. Grate the cheese and make two layers of tortillas, sauce, and cheese in a 2½ quart dish.

Bake for 30 minutes at 350 degrees. Serves 8-10.

CAROLYN PILLOT
AUCTION SALES

JALAPEÑO PIE

Use 13 x 9 inch pan
Grated Longhorn cheese — enough to cover bottom of
pan
Diced jalapēnos — enough to cover bottom pan lightly
1 dozen eggs, whip-up, pour over cheese and jalapeños

Bake at 350 degrees for 30 minutes, cut into squares and
serve. Makes 8 servings.

ROBERT AND SHIRLEY WAGNER
GENERAL LIVESTOCK

PIMIENTO CHEESE

Melt 2 pounds Velveeta in double boiler. Add cut up pimientos (1 small jar 4 ounces). Add 1 jar of cut up pimiento stuffed olives 5 ounce size. Add ¼ to ½ cup of sweet pickle
relish. Remove from burner and slowly add 1 pint of Miracle
Whip Salad Dressing. Store in plastic container with good
tight lid. Will last indefinitely. Optional — Add a third cup of
chopped and seeded jalapeño.

MRS. NAT PRASSEL

PIMIENTO CHEESE

1 pound grated Longhorn cheese
1 small jar chopped pimiento
1 teaspoon grated onion
Chopped jalapeño, optional

Mix together with mayonnaise until creamy. Can be used on
sandwiches, crackers, for stuffed celery, or to stuff
jalapeños, sliced lengthwise and seeded.

MARY ELLEN PENWELL
SOUVENIR PROGRAM

SNAPPY CHEESE BAKE

1 quart milk
6 eggs
1½ cups biscuit mix
2 small cans whole green chilies
1 pound mellow Cheddar cheese, shredded

Butter oblong baking dish (2 quart). Drain and rinse green chilies. Split chilies and lay flat on bottom of pan. Cover with shredded cheese. Combine biscuit mix, eggs and milk. Beat until smooth. Pour over cheese and chilies. Bake at 350 degrees for 50 to 60 minutes or until set.
Recipe may be halved. Delicious with brisket!

CHARLOTTE COOK

JALAPEÑO PEPPER PIE

¾ jalapeños peppers
1 pound Cheddar cheese
6 eggs

Butter quiche pan. Slice peppers into pan. Grate cheese over peppers. Beat eggs and pour over the cheese. Bake at 350 degrees for 30 minutes. Can be served cool or hot.

STEVEN SCHULTZ
AMBASSADORS

HUEVOS RANCHEROS

1 8-ounce jar Picante sauce
1 large tomato, chopped
8 eggs
4 corn tortillas, warmed
Butter
*Ranchero sauce:

Heat Picante sauce and chopped tomato in a sauce pan. Set aside and keep warm. Fry eggs sunny side up. Place 2 fried eggs on a warm tortilla and top with ranchero sauce. Serve immediately. Serves 4.

*Ranchero sauce may be used on top of poached, scrambled eggs, as a filling for omelets or as a sauce for steaks.

BEBE JONES
AUCTION SALES

VALLEY PEPPER CASSEROLE

3 4-ounce cans roasted green chilies, remove seeds and
   split open
Lay flat in casserole
Layer sliced Monterrey Jack cheese,
Layer of Cheddar cheese
Continue layering for 7 layers
2 small cans evaporated milk
4 eggs
3 tablespoons flour

Shake or mix well the last three ingredients and pour over
top of 7 layers. Bake 30-40 minutes at 350 degrees. Before
serving, warm can of tomato sauce and pour over top.

BILL DUGAT, JR.
CALF SCRAMBLE

SUNDAY BRUNCH STRATA

2 cups ham, diced
2 cups American cheese, diced
12 slices bread, cubed and crust removed
½ cup onion, chopped
½ cup green pepper, chopped
12 eggs
4 cups warm milk
1 teaspoon salt
2 tablespoons bacon grease

Combine bread, onion, green pepper, ham, and cheese.
Pour into 13 x 9 buttered casserole. Beat eggs and add
milk, salt, and bacon grease. Pour over bread mixture.
Refrigerate overnight. Bake in 325 oven for approximately
1¼ hours or until set. Serves 8 to 10.

ANNE FLEENOR

DEVILED EGGS

12 eggs
¾ cup of mayonnaise
1 tablespoon white vinegar
1 teaspoon dry mustard
1½ teaspoons Worcestershire

¾ teaspoon salt
⅛ teaspoon pepper
⅛ teaspoon paprika
Parsley sprigs

Hard-cook eggs, remove shells and let eggs cool completely. Halve eggs lengthwise. Take out yolks, being careful not to break whites. Press yolks through sieve into medium bowl. Add remaining ingredients, *except* parsley; mix with fork until smooth and fluffy. Lightly mound yolk mixture in egg whites. Garnish each with parsley sprig. Makes 12 servings.

JIMMY WOLFE
ENTERTAINMENT

EGGS A LA COWGIRL
DATES BACK TO GALVESTON IN 1909

Take shallow baking dish, put 2 large tablespoons butter, in a little bit of milk, then a layer grated cheese, break a number of eggs (your choice of number) very carefully in the dish, keeping them separate. Season with salt and pepper to taste. Sprinkle more cheese on top. Put in oven and as soon as cheese is brown, serve.

BETTIE RUTLEDGE
WESTERN COOKBOOK

BOWL OF CEREAL

Get bowl milk
Pour cereal in bowl
Pour milk on cereal
Get a spoon
Eat it!!

ALLYSON WOLFE, AGE 4

Special Days

It is with great pride that we recognize the San Antonio Stock Show as truly an area show. Each year we set aside a special day for each area to honor the cooperative communities that make our show a success. It is our way of saying "thanks" to these area groups for their continuing support to the Livestock Exposition. With the addition of the Harry Freeman Entertainment Center, we now have the facilities and room to provide space for the special days groups to gather, perform, entertain, and have a home away from home for their own communities.

GEORGE P. HARRIS
CHAIRMAN

HOME MADE SAUERKRAUT

Shred fresh cabbage. Put in quart jars with some green dill in the bottom, press down tight in the jar, leave little space below the neck of the jar.

Add 1 teaspoon salt (canning salt)
1 teaspoon sugar

Add boiling water almost up to the neck of the jar. Pour hot water on slowly. Seal good and store in a dark place. Ready to eat in 6 to 8 weeks.

CHILI SAUCE

18 large ripe tomatoes
3 green peppers, chopped fine
6 onions, chopped fine
2 cups vinegar
1 cup sugar
3 tablespoons salt
1 teaspoon cloves
1 teaspoon allspice
1 teaspoon cinnamon

Boil all of the above ingredients for one hour. Bottle and seal. Makes eight pints.

HOME MADE SAUSAGE

1 pound canning salt to 40 pounds of meat
15 tablespoons home ground black pepper
1 teaspoon saltpetre
1 box mustard seed
1 cup brown sugar
1 tablespoon or more garlic, minced

You can use 100% pork or up to ½ ground beef. Mix dry ingredients. Sprinkle over meat and add garlic. Mix well. Stuff into casings and smoke. Can be made into patties and frozen.

HOMEMADE WINE

2 cups grapes
1 cup sugar

Place grapes and sugar in quart jar and fill with cold water, leaving a little space at top and seal loosely; put in a dark place. Let stand for six weeks. Drain the juice from the grapes and strain through a cloth; fill into clean dry jars or bottles. Do not seal completely. Ready to drink in 30 days. This recipe is for one quart. Recipe may be increased to fit your needs.

HOMEMADE MAPLE SYRUP

1 cup water
2 cups sugar
½ teaspoon maple flavoring

Boil one cup water and stir in sugar until dissolved. Add maple flavoring. To make a thicker syrup ½ to ¾ cup of white Karo Syrup may be added and ½ teaspoon more of maple flavoring.

MARY ELLEN PENWELL
AUCTION AND PROGRAM COMMITTEE

CANNING GREEN BEANS

Green Beans
Water
Salt

Wash and snap beans. Place beans in blancher and bring water to boil. When water boils, immediately take out of water and place in hot sterilized jars. If you are using pint jars put a ½ teaspoon salt on top of the beans; for a quart use a teaspoon. Add the water to the beans that they were blanched in. Put the cap and ring on the jars and place in a pressure cooker. Let the pressure rise to 10 pounds and pressure for 7 minutes. Remove from burner and let pressure go down. Remove jars and tighten caps.

MR. AND MRS. ELMO J. BOUCHILLON
GREENVILLE, MISSISSIPPI

CANNED TOMATOES

Select firm ripe tomatoes; scald and peel. Cut into pieces and cook seven minutes. Add 1 teaspoon salt to a quart of tomatoes and pack into sterilized jars.

WESTERN COOKBOOK

TOMATO SAUCE

12 cups tomatoes, ground
3 onions, chopped very fine
⅛ teaspoon cayenne pepper
¼ cup salt
¼ cup sugar
1 teaspoon black pepper
¼ cup vinegar

Combine all of the above ingredients. Boil until done about 15 minutes. Pour into sterilized jars and seal while hot. Great for chili, soup or stews.

WESTERN COOKBOOK

YELLOW CORN HOMINY

Place 2 quarts of dry field corn in a large enameled pan or pot. 8 quarts water and 2 ounces of lye. Boil vigorously for 30 minutes, then allow to stand for 20 minutes. Rinse off lye with real hot water four times. Follow with cold water to cool for handling.

Work hominy with hands until dark tips of kernels are removed (about 7 minutes). Separate the tips from corn by floating them off. Add water to cover hominy about 1 inch and boil 5 minutes, change water, repeat 5 times. Then cook until kernels are soft (30 to 50 minutes) and drain. This will make 6 quarts of hominy.

Pack hominy into jars to 1 inch of top. Add 1 teaspoon of salt to each quart jar. Fill to ½ inch of top of jar with water in which the corn was cooked (the last time) or boiling water, put on lid, screw band on tight.

Quarts — 70 minutes — 10 lbs. pressure
Pints — 60 minutes — 10 lbs. pressure

Remove from cooler, let stand for 6 hours at room temperature before storing in dark place.

PAUL D. SHIRES

SPECIAL SWEET MUSTARD

Mix together:
1 cup sugar
1 tablespoon flour.

2 eggs
1 small jar mustard
½ cup vinegar
2 teaspoons butter

Beat eggs well and slowly add mustard. Add ½ cup vinegar and butter until melted. Add dry ingredients (sugar and flour). Cook slowly until thick, stirring constantly. Keeps for weeks. Excellent with ham, pork or cold cuts.

SHIRLEY SCHREIBER
AUCTION SALES

ZUCCHINI RELISH

4 quarts zucchini slice lengthwise into eighths and then slice into quarter inch pieces
4 medium green peppers, seeded and chopped
4 medium onions, peeled and chopped fine
Place in earthenware, enamelware or stainless steel container
Cover with brine using 6 tablespoons coarse salt to 1 quart water
Soak at least 12 hours Drain well
In enamelware or stainless steel container mix
1 quart cider vinegar
4 cups sugar

In cloth bag place 2 tablespoons whole mixed pickling spices and ½ teaspoon each celery seed and mustard seed. Bring just to a boil. Add vegetables and bring just to a boil again. Remove spices and place relish in sterile jars. Seal and process 15 minutes in boiling water bath. Approximately 5 quarts.

EILEEN STEWART
WESTERN COOKBOOK

COUNTRY APPLESAUCE

2 pounds tart cooking apples
½ to ⅔ cup of sugar, depending on tartness of apples

Wash, core, and pare apples; cut into quarters. In medium saucepan, bring ½ cup water to boiling, add apples and bring to second boil. Reduce heat, simmer, covered 20 to 25 minutes; stir occasionally. Add water, if needed. Stir in sugar until well combined. Serve warm or cold makes about 3 cups.

JIMMY WOLFE
ENTERTAINMENT

ZUCCHINI PICKLES

10 pounds zucchini sliced ¼ inch thick.
Soak in brine of:
   1 quart water to 6 tablespoons pickling salt for 12
   hours or more.
Drain from brine and add boiling water to cover.
Quickly drain and pack pickles in sterile jars.
Bring the following just to a boil and pour over pickles.
½ gallon vinegar
6 ½ cups sugar
1 ounce whole pickling spices
6 sticks cinnamon
½ tsp. whole cloves
2 tablespoons lime water

Seal and process 15 minutes in boiling water.

To make lime water use 1½ teaspoons calcium oxide and 2 cups soft water. Stir well, allow to settle and use the clear water only. Approximately 6 quarts.

EILEEN STEWART
WESTERN COOKBOOK

JALAPEÑO JELLY

6½ cups sugar
1½ cups vinegar
1 cup bell peppers, ground
¼ cup jalapeño pepper, seeded and ground

Combine ingredients. Bring to a full rolling boil. Stir ingredients all the time while cooking. Remove from heat and immediately add:
1 6-ounce bottle Certa
Now add a little green coloring. (Just to make it pretty)

MRS. RUBY PIRCHER
AUCTION SALES — BUYER

SQUASH RELISH

Cut up the following in food processor:
20 cups squash (1 squash= approximately 1 cup)
½ to 1 cup hot peppers
8 medium onions
3 bell peppers
2 red sweet pimiento
½ cup salt

Mix vegetables and pour salt over. Let set overnight — rinse and chop in food processor. Prepare syrup.

SYRUP:
5 cups vinegar (90 grain)
5 cups sugar
2 teaspoons tumeric
2 teaspoons black pepper
1 teaspoon celery seed
½ teaspoon nutmeg

Bring to boil — drop vegetables in hot syrup and boil 5 minutes. Place into jars — hot bath process 10 minutes.

JAN HERRINGTON
AUCTION SALES

PEAR BUTTER

Wash pears. Do not peel. Slice. Add small amount of water to start cooking. Cook until very soft. Press through colander. To each cup pulp, add ½ cup sugar. (Spice may be added, ½ teaspoon cinnamon to 3 cups pulp.) Cook until thick, stirring frequently to prevent scorching. Pour into sterilized jars and seal while hot.

MRS. R. W. PIRCHER
AUCTION SALES — BUYER

RIPE CANTALOUPE PRESERVES

2 pounds firm ripe cantaloupe
4 cups sugar
1 juice of lemon

Peel cantaloupe and cut in thin slices 1½ inches long. Mix sugar and cantaloupe and let stand over night at room temperature 12 hours in a cloth covered pot. Then add lemon juce, cook until clear. Pour into half-pint jars to within ½ inch of top. Put on cap, screw band firmly tight. Process 5 minutes in boiling water bath. Yield: 4 half-pints. (Hint: store in a cool, dry dark place and 70 degrees or lower.)

PAUL D. SHIRES

WELCH'S GRAPE JELLY

2 cups Welch's grape juice
3 cups sugar
½ bottle Certo fruit pectin

Bring to a boil for 1 to 1½ minutes at full boil; remove from heat and add ½ bottle Certo. Let stand a few minutes and skim with metal spoon. Pour into hot jars and seal with wax.

MARY ELLEN PENWELL
AUCTION SALES

MOCK STRAWBERRY PRESERVES

8 cups figs, peeled and
   sliced
6 cups white sugar
2 large or 4 small boxes strawberry gelatin
1 box Sure-Jell

Mix sugar and gelatin with figs. Slow boil for 20 minutes. Then add jelling agent and boil 2 minutes longer. Then put into prepared jars and seal.

MARY ELLEN PENWELL
AUCTION AND PROGRAM COMMITTEE

STRAWBERRY JAM

4 cups strawberries
7½ cups sugar
1 pouch Certo fruit pectin

Wash and hull berries. Wash and scald jars and lids, keep them hot. Place a handful of the berries in a food processor and process for 2 to 3 seconds. Continue this until you have processed all the berries. Place the fruit in a large pot. I use the bottom to a blancher but make sure it is at least a 6 to 10 quart capacity. Add the sugar and stir. Bring to a full rolling boil and boil hard for 1 minute. Immediately stir in the Certo fruit pectin. Skim off the top with a pastry brush and metal spoon. Put into hot jars immediately. Wipe rims, cover jars with hot lids and screw bands on tight. Have the water boiling in canner and put the jars on the rack of the canner and place in the boiling water. Boil for 5 minutes. Remove jars from canner and let cool.

PATRICIA GARZA
WESTERN COOKBOOK

PLUM JAM

2 quarts tart plums, chopped, approximately 4 pounds
6 cups sugar
1½ cups water
¼ cups lemon juice

Combine all ingredients in a kettle, bring to boil slowly, stirring occasionally, until sugar dissolves. Cook rapidly almost to jellying point about 20 minutes. To prevent sticking, stir frequently as mixture thickens. Pour mixture, boiling hot, into hot jars, leaving ¼ inch head space. Adjust caps, process 15 minutes in boiling water bath. Yield: about 4 pints.

MARY ELLEN PENWELL
AUCTION AND PROGRAM COMMITTEE

CACTUS JELLY

6 quart pot
4½ cups sugar
½ cup lemon juice
1½ cups cactus juice
1 6-ounce bottle Certo fruit pectin

In the 6 quart pot combine the sugar, lemon juice and cactus juice and bring to a rolling boil stirring frequently. Add the 1 bottle of Certo and return to a rolling boil and boil hard for 1 full minute stirring constantly. Remove the scum and pour into sterile jars and top with parafin wax.

Note: If a four quart container is used you may reduce the recipe in half.

PICKLED CAULIFLOWER

Cauliflower
Dill seed, or fresh dill
Hot peppers
Garlic
Mustard Seed
Salt
Water
Vinegar

Separate cauliflower into flowerets. Pack into sterile jars. To each quart, add 1 teaspoon dill seed, 3 small hot peppers, 1 pod garlic, 1 teaspoon mustard seed, and 2 tablespoons salt. Bring to a boil 4 cups of water and 1 cup of vinegar. (Judge by amount of jars to be filled). Pour boiling liquid over cauliflower and seal immediately. Do not use for 4 weeks.

MARY ELLEN PENWELL
SOUVENIR PROGRAM

PICKLED JALAPEÑO PEPPERS

Wash the peppers and pack 'em tightly in scalded jars
Then combine (in a sauce pan):
1 cup vinegar
¼ cup water
¼ cup olive oil
1 teaspoon salt
1 teaspoon mixed pickling spice

Bring all this stuff to a boil over a full gas flame. Open the hot jars containing the saucy jalapeno peppers, and cover the peppers with the mess you've mixed and boiled. Leave about ¼ inch space at the top of the jars. Slam the lids back on the jars and process in boiling water bath for 10 minutes — start counting time as soon as the water returns to boiling.

PICKLED SQUASH

8 cups squash, sliced
2 cups onions, cut up
1 cup green pepper, cut up
½ cup regular salt
BRINE MIX:
1 cup white distilled vinegar
1½ cups of sugar
1 teaspoon celery seed
1 teaspoon mustard seed
1 small jar pimiento

MIX DIRECTIONS:
Salt down squash and onion and let it sit one hour. After one hour, drain off liquid. Bring brine to boil and add green pepper, squash, onion and pimiento. Continue until it boils again. Put in jars.

Store for two weeks, then chill before eating

LUCILLE JOHNSON

BEET PICKLES

3 quarts small beets, peeled and cooked
2 cups sugar
1 tablespoon whole allspice
1½ teaspoon salt
2 sticks cinnamon
3½ cups vinegar
1½ cups water

To cook beets, first wash and drain. Leave 2 inches of stems and taproots. Cover with boiling water and cook until tender, about 35 or 45 minutes. Combine all ingredients; simmer for 15 min. Pack beets into hot sterilized jars leaving ½ inch head space. Cut larger beets in half if necessary. Remove cinnamon. Bring liquid to boiling. Pour boiling hot over beets leaving ½ inch headspace. Seal and process in hot water bath for 30 minutes.

Yield: 6 pints.

CHARLYNE WILLIAMS AND JOHN J. WILLIAMS
CO-CHAIRMAN CALF SCRAMBLE

PICKLED OKRA

1 quart okra, do not remove stems
Hot pepper, as you like
1 cup water
2 buttons garlic, minced
3 small dill heads
2 quart apple vinegar
Salt as you wish

Wash okra and pack in jars along with the dill, garlic and hot peppers; heat to boiling the remainder of ingredients and pour over contents in jar. Seal. Let stand 3 weeks before using. Real good if chilled before using.

MARY ELLEN PENWELL
AUCTION AND PROGRAM COMMITTEE

PICKLED OKRA

1 hot pepper, 1 for each jar
1 garlic clove, 1 for each jar
3½ pounds small okra pods
1 teaspoon dill seeds for each jar
1 pint white vinegar
4 cups water
⅓ cup salt

Place hot pepper and garlic in hot sterilized jars. Remove part of stem from each okra pod. Pack okra into jars. Add dillseeds. Combine vinegar, water, and salt in a saucepan; bring to a boil, and simmer about 5 minutes. Pour over okra. Adjust lids; process in boiling-water bath at simmering temperature (180 to 200 degrees) for 10 minutes. Let pickles stand several weeks before opening. Yield: 4 to 5 pints.

ROBERT AND SHIRLEY WAGNER
GENERAL LIVESTOCK

PICKLED EGGS

2 cups white vinegar
2 tablespoons sugar
1 medium onion, sliced and separated into rings
1 teaspoon salt
1 teaspoon pickling spice
12 hard boiled eggs

Combine all ingredients except eggs in saucepan. Simmer over low heat 10 minutes. Arrange eggs in two 1-quart jars. Pour 1 cup vinegar mixture over eggs in each jar. Cover tightly and refrigerate overnight. Eggs may be stored up to 2 weeks in refrigerator.

MARY ELLEN PENWELL
AUCTION SALES

FROZEN CUCUMBERS

2 quarts cucumbers, do not peel, slice very thin
1 onion, large, sliced very thin
2 tablespoons salt
1½ cups sugar
½ cup vinegar
¼ teaspoon pepper

Slice the cucumbers and onion very thin and put in a large glass or crockery bowl. Mix the sugar, salt, vinegar and pepper and pour this mixture over the cucumbers and onion. Let set for about 2 hours. Put in *small* containers and freeze. To serve, thaw slightly. These will stay crisp in the refrigerator for several days. If you like sweet pickles, you will love these.

JENALYN SCHNEIDER
AUCTION SALES

FREEZING SQUASH AND EGGPLANT

Slice and wash. Put in water and boil until it begins to tender. Drain and put into freezer container add a little of the water and let cool. Ready to put into freezer.

MUSTARD/TURNIP GREENS

Wash and pick over greens, place in boiling water and boil for 5 minutes. With a cooking fork remove greens and put in freezer container and cover. Let cool, and place in freezer. Note: no water need be added enough from the greens will be sufficient.

CORN

Cut corn from cob be sure and scrape cob to get all the juice/milk. Cook corn until the juice/milk thickens. Let cool, put into freezer containers and freeze.

PEAS AND BUTTERBEANS

Shell and wash beans. Place in blancher, bring to boil and boil for 10 minutes. Drain beans or peas and spread out to cool. I set mine in front of the air conditioner. Let water cool also. When the beans or peas and water are completely cooled fill your freezer containers with the beans or peas adding the water to slightly cover. Ready for freezing.

MY MAMA

BEEF SAUSAGE

10 pounds lean ground beef
5 teaspoons mustard seed
5 teaspoons crushed peppercorns
3 teaspoons garlic salt
5 teaspoons liquid smoke
5 teaspoons black pepper
10 teaspoons Mortons Quick Cure salt

Mix and knead all ingredients well. Refrigerate 24 hours. Knead well again and refrigerate for another 24 hr. Shape into about 12 rolls about 2 inches by 10 inches Place on a broiler pan to drain. Bake about 10 hours at 150 degrees, uncovered. It makes its own casing. Wipe outside of each baked roll with paper towel. Refrigerate 48 hours before using. Freezes well.

MRS. BILLE F. BUSBY
BOERNE, TEXAS

HOMEMADE BEEF SALAMI

3 pounds lean ground beef
1½ cups water
3 tablespoons Morton's Tender Quick Meat Cure Salt, not regular salt
2 teaspoons liquid smoke
¼ teaspoon garlic powder
4 tablespoons dehydrated minced onion
Small pinch salt

Mix all ingredients (by hand), in order listed. Blend well. Divide into rolls about 2 to 3 inches in diameter. About 8 or 9 inches long. Wrap each roll in saran wrap. Place in meat tray or coldest part of refrigerator for 24 hours.

Remove saran wrap — place rolls on broiler tray (to allow drip) and bake on center rack at 300 degrees for one hour. Reduce heat to 275 degrees and cook another 15 minutes. (Adjust cooking time if larger rolls). Cool on rack, wrap in foil, store in refrigerator. May be frozen also.

BETTY WOMMACK

Life Membership

The San Antonio Livestock Exposition is a non-profit Corporation, incorporated under the laws of the State of Texas for "the encouragement of agriculture by the maintenance of public fairs and exhibitions of stock."

Aside from the prestige of being a Life Member and being among the outstanding ranchers, farmers and businessmen of nine states and 2 foreign countries, the support and benefit our youth receive from the show cannot be measured. It is with your help that makes our show so outstanding.

BOB COOK
CHAIRMAN

PIZZA BREAD

Dough:

1¼ cup warm water
1 package dry active yeast
3 tablespoons oil
¼ cup dry milk

1 tablespoon sugar
1 teaspoon salt
3¾ cup flour

Pour water in bowl, dissolve yeast in water. Stir in remaining ingredients and beat 3 minutes at medium speed with dough beaters. Add remaining flour and knead until smooth. Divide into 3 parts and roll each into a 12" square.

Filling:

3 cups salami, chopped
1½ cups pepperoni, chopped
3 cups grated Monterrey Jack cheese
¼ cup green olives, chopped
½ cup black olives, chopped

Sprinkle garlic salt, oregano and parmesan cheese on each square. Put ⅓ of filling on each square and roll up, jelly roll style. Let rise in warm place until double in size. About 1½-2 hours. Bake in a 375 degree oven for 30 minutes. Can be frozen after baking, thaw and warm. Serves: 25 slices per loaf.

BETTY SMITH
GO WESTERN

LONE STAR BEER BISCUITS

4 cups biscuit mix
1 tablespoon sugar
1 can beer, (Lone Star)

Mix and roll out as other biscuits. Bake 25 to 30 minutes.

MARGIE V. HABY

CRACKLIN' CORN BREAD

Not many of us make crackling any more, so we use chicharrones. Be sure they are fresh by keeping them in the refrigerator. Just before using them, put them in a pan in the hot oven for a few minutes. Let them cool and cut them into crumbs.

1 cup corn meal	2 eggs
½ cup flour	1 cup milk
2 teaspoons baking powder	3 tablespoons shortening
½ teaspoon salt	¾ cup cracklings
1 tablespoon sugar	

Sift together dry ingredients. In another bowl, beat eggs slightly and add milk. Then add this to the dry ingredients and mix well. Have shortening hot in baking pan, pour 2 tablespoons of shortening into batter and mix. Fold cracklings into batter. *Do not beat.* Pour batter into hot greased baking pan (7×11 inch). Bake at 400 degrees for 25 to 30 minutes or until done and golden brown on top. Southern cooking!!!

MARTHA A. (RITA) JIMENEZ
CHIEF OPERATOR SAN ANTONIO LIVESTOCK SHOW
AND LIFE MEMBER

SOUR DOUGH BISCUITS

1 cup warm water
1 package dry yeast, dissolved in hot water
4 teaspoons baking powder
1 teaspoon soda
1 teaspoon salt
1 cup sugar
¾ cup oil
2 cups buttermilk
6 cups flour

Mix above ingredients together. Will keep in refrigerator for 2 weeks. Pull off as much as you need, form into biscuits and bake at 350 degrees until brown.

ED BENDER
AUCTION SALES

SPANISH CORN BREAD

2 cups yellow cornmeal
⅓ cup melted shortening
½ teaspoon salt
1 tablespoon sugar
2 eggs
½ teaspoon soda
¾ cup buttermilk
1 can cream-style corn
2 green jalapeño peppers, canned
1 cup cheese, grated

Mix first 7 ingredients as for regular bread. Add corn and peppers. Pour half of the mixture into a large greased iron skillet. Place half of the cheese over the batter. Spoon remaining batter into skillet; top with remaining cheese. Bake for 25 minutes at 500 degrees.

JIM TOBE ATKINSON
JUNIOR STEER RIDING

MEXICAN CORN BREAD

1 can cream-style corn
1 cup buttermilk
½ cup vegetable oil
2 eggs beaten
1 cup cornbread mix
1 4–ounce can chopped green chilies, drained
1½ cups sharp Cheddar cheese, divided,
   shredded

Combine corn, buttermilk, oil, and eggs; mix well. Stir in cornbread mix. Pour half of batter into a greased 9 inch square pan. Sprinkle with green chilies, and half of cheese. Pour remaining half of batter over top and sprinkle with remaining cheese. Bake at 350 degrees for 45 minutes to 50 minutes. Cut into squares. Yields: 9 servings.

TRAIL RIDE CAMP-SKILLET CORN BREAD

1 teaspoon sugar
1 teaspoon salt
½ teaspoon baking soda
1 teaspoon baking powder
1 cup water-ground cornmeal
1 egg
½ cup buttermilk
1 tablespoon bacon fat or other shortening

For this recipe, mix sugar, salt, soda and baking powder at home. Put enough for 2 or 3 batches in individual plastic bags, put them in a jar and label. Mix dry ingredients in small bowl. Beat egg and buttermilk together in 4 cup measure and stir in dry ingredients. Heat bacon fat in iron skillet and pour in batter. Cover and "bake" over fairly low heat 10 minutes. Turn over onto cover and slide back into skillet. Cover and "bake" 10 minutes longer.

BETTIE RUTLEDGE
WESTERN COOKBOOK

SOUTHERN CORNBREAD

2 cups cornmeal
1 teaspoon soda
1 teaspoon salt
2 eggs, beaten
2 cups buttermilk
¼ cup bacon drippings

Combine cornmeal, soda, and salt; stir in eggs and buttermilk. Heat bacon drippings in an 8-inch iron skillet until very hot; add drippings to batter, mixing well.

Pour batter into hot skillet, and bake at 450 degrees about 25 minutes or until bread is golden brown. Yield: 8 to 10 servings.

ANNE FLEENOR

MEXICAN CORN BREAD II

1 can cream style corn
1 cup corn meal
1 cup buttermilk
½ teaspoon baking soda
1 teaspoon salt
1 large onion, chopped
2 hot peppers, chopped
2 eggs
6 ounces Longhorn cheese, grated

Beat eggs slightly and add corn, corn meal, oil, baking soda and salt. Add buttermilk. Fold in seasoning and cheese. Bake in 400 degree oven in large pan until done — approximately 30 minutes.

BUTCH GRAHAM
AUCTION SALES

CHEESE AND GARLIC FLAVORED CORNBREAD STICKS

½ cup flour
½ cup yellow cornmeal
2 tablespoons sugar
½ 7/10 ounce envelope cheese-garlic salad dressing mix, about 3 ½ teaspoons
1 egg
1 8 ¾ -ounce can cream style corn
2 tablespoons vegetable oil
Few dashes bottled hot pepper sauce

In a mixing bowl, combine flour, cornmeal, sugar, salad dressing mix, and baking powder. Combine beaten egg, corn, vegetable oil, and hot pepper sauce. Add to dry ingredients. Stir just until moistened. Spoon batter into well-greased corn stick pans, filling about two thirds full.

Bake at 425 degrees about 15 to 18 minutes. Makes about 12 corn sticks.

PAT McGUIRE

ANGEL BISCUITS

5 cups flour
¾ cups Crisco
1 teaspoon soda
1 teaspoon salt
3 teaspoons baking powder
3 tablespoons sugar
2 packages dry yeast, dissolved in ½ cup lukewarm water
2 cups buttermilk

Mix all dry ingredients together. Cut in Crisco until mixture is like cornmeal. Add water, yeast and buttermilk. Mix until flour is moistened. Store in covered bowl in refrigerator. Take out any amount you need. Can be cut out or dropped. Bake at 350 degrees until done.

MARY ELLEN PENWELL
AUCTION SALES

DINNER ROLLS

⅔ cup milk
2 teaspoons salt
⅔ cup warm water
2 tablespoons sugar
4 beaten eggs

½ cup sugar
6 tablespoons flour
2 packages dry yeast
6 cups flour

Scald milk; stir in ½ cup sugar, salt and butter. Let cool. Combine water and 2 tablespoons sugar in large bowl; add yeast. Stir until yeast is dissolved. Stir in cooled milk mixture and eggs. Mix well. Add 3 cups flour and mix well, then add remaining flour. Turn onto floured surface and knead only until smooth and elastic. Place in greased bowl and cover with damp cloth. Let rise until doubled. Punch down. Shape into ¾ inch balls. Place 3 balls in each cup of muffin pan. Cover and let rise again.
Bake at 375 degrees until brown. Yields: 3 dozen.

CHERI HUGHES/BOBBY HUGHES
ENTERTAINMENT CHAIRMAN

MONKEY BREAD

1 cup milk
1 cup butter melted
4 tablespoons sugar
1 teaspoon salt
1 package of dry yeast
3½ cups flour

Combine milk, ½ cup butter, sugar and salt in a saucepan; heat until butter is melted. Cool to 105 to 115 F. Stir in yeast until dissolved. Place flour in large bowl. Make a well in the flour and pour in liquid. Stir until blended. Cover and let rise until doubled in bulk, about 1 hour and 20 minutes. Turn dough out on a floured surface. Roll ½ inch thick; cut into 3 inch squares. Dip each square into remaining butter. Layer squares in a 10 inch tube or bundt pan; let rise until doubled; about 30 or 40 minutes. Bake at 375 degrees for 30 or 40 minutes.

MARY ELLEN PENWELL
AUCTION AND PROGRAM COMMITTEE

QUICK YEAST ROLLS

1 cup buttermilk, lukewarm
¼ teaspoon soda
1 package yeast
2 tablespoons sugar
3 tablespoons melted shortening
½ teaspoon salt
2-2½ cups flour

Stir yeast into milk, add soda, sugar, salt and shortening. Add flour to make stiff dough. Let stand for 10 minutes. Work out and roll into rolls.
Bake at 350 degrees for 15 minutes. Makes 18 large rolls.

SANDRA NAGEL
AUCTION SALES

BOLILLOS (MEXICAN ROLLS)

33.8 ounces warm water
4½ pounds flour
¼ pound sugar
1 scant teaspoon salt
1 round teaspoon yeast (granular) (melted in lukewarm water)
⅓ pound shortening

Mix above ingredients in bowl. Let rise 1½ hours. Make into balls. Let rise 45 minutes. Make into bolillos (football shapes). Brush with milk and salt just before baking in oven 450 degrees for 15 to 18 minutes.

JAMES DOCKERY/PEGGY DOCKERY
JUNIOR STEER RIDING CHAIRMAN

NEVER-FAIL REFRIGERATOR ROLLS

½ cup salad oil
½ cup sugar
1 cup water + 1 cup water
2 packages yeast
1¼ teaspoon salt
6 cups flour — unsifted

Mix oil, sugar and 1 cup water. Add 1 cup water with yeast dissolved in it; then stir in flour and salt. Knead until smooth, takes only a few minutes. Let rise, until double in bulk (about 2 hours). Make into rolls, let rise 2 hours before cooking.

Bake in 375 degree oven until lightly browned.

May be placed in refrigerator for several days after making. Let rise 2 hours after making into rolls.

RON SNOWDEN
JUNIOR STEER RIDING

MILROY'S-JALAPEÑO AND CHEESE CORN BREAD

1 cup yellow cornmeal
½ cup flour
2 teaspoons baking powder
1 teaspoon salt
1 teaspoon sugar

Sift dry ingredients together into bowl and add:

1 egg
1 cup milk
3 tablespoons Wesson Oil or melted shortening
1 cup Cheddar cheese, grated
2 tablespoons jalapeños, finely chopped

Grease cast iron skillet, use 8″ or 9″ for thickness desired, Cook in 450 degree oven for 20 minutes.

MILROY POWELL
HORSESHOW

MEXICAN CORN BREAD

1 package cornbread mix
2 eggs
½ cup milk
1 12-ounce can Mexicorn
1 medium onion, grated
1 cup Cheddar cheese, grated
1 hot jalapeño pepper
1 small clove of garlic, minced

Mix cornbread mix, eggs, and milk until eggs blended thoroughly. Then add the remaining ingredients. Mix all together and pour into 2 foil baking pans, or use well greased iron skillet, or other baking dish. Bake 25 to 30 minutes at 400 degrees or until firm.

MRS. ODO J. RIEDEL

CHIFFON PANCAKES

¼ cup butter or ½ stick of oleo
½ cup powdered sugar
1 egg, well beaten
1 cup flour
2 teaspoons baking powder
¼ teaspoon soda
¼ teaspoon salt
⅓ cup sweet milk

Blend butter and sugar real well until fluffy. Add all the remaining ingredients in the order given. Drop 1 heaping tablespoonful in hot electric fry pan or griddle. Serves 4 people.

SYLVIE "DUTCH" KLAEVEMAN

PANCAKES HOME-STYLE

Beat 1 egg until light, add 1 cup buttermilk
Blend 1 cup flour, minus 1 tablespoon, add 1 tablespoon waterground cornmeal (other flour such as wheat, buckwheat, etc. but keep proportions the same)

1½ teaspoon baking powder
1½ teaspoon baking soda — sift dry ingredients together.

Add dry to liquid and beat well, add 2½ tablespoons melted butter or oil and beat until smooth and shiny. Bake on moderate griddle, turn once.

BARBARA VRETIS
INTERNATIONAL/MEXICO DAY

BLUEBERRY STREUSEL MUFFINS

⅓ cup sugar
¼ cup butter or margarine, softened
1 egg
2⅓ cups all-purpose flour
1 tablespoon, plus 1 teaspoon baking powder
½ teaspoon salt
1 cup milk
1 teaspoon vanilla extract
1½ cup fresh or frozen blueberries, (thawed)
½ cup sugar
⅓ cup all purpose flour
½ teaspoon ground cinnamon
¼ cup butter or margarine, softened

Combine ⅓ cup sugar and ¼ cup butter in a small mixing bowl, creaming until light and fluffy. Add egg, beating well. Combine 2⅓ cups flour, baking powder, and salt, add to creamed mixture alternately with milk, stirring well after each addition. Stir in vanilla extract and fold in blueberries. Spoon batter into greased muffin cups, filling ⅔ full. Combine ½ cup sugar, ⅓ cup flour, and cinnamon; cut in ¼ cup butter until mixture resembles crumbs. Sprinkle on top of muffin batter. Bake at 375 degrees for 25 to 30 minutes or until golden brown. Yield: 1½ dozen.

Note: If using frozen blueberries, rinse and drain thawed berries, pat dry with paper towels. This will prevent discoloration of batter.

ROBYN MERCHANT
AUCTION SALES

BRAN MUFFINS

6 cups bran
2 cups boiling water
1 cup melted shortening
4 eggs
3 cups sugar
5 cups flour
5 teaspoons baking powder
2 teaspoons salt
1 quart buttermilk

Mix bran, boiling water and shortening; set aside. Beat eggs with sugar. Mix together flour, baking powder and salt. Mix all together with buttermilk, fold together until well mixed and bake in muffin tins at 400 degrees for 15 to 20 minutes. Dough keeps refrigerated up to 6 weeks.

MARY ELLEN PENWELL
AUCTION AND
SOUVENIR PROGRAM

MINI SAUSAGE MUFFINS

1 pound hot bulk sausage
1 cup all purpose flour
1 cup cornbread mix
2 ounces pimiento, drained and chopped
1 cup french onion dip
½ cup milk
Parmesan cheese

Brown sausage, drain, reserve 2 tablespoons drippings. Combine flour, cornmeal, sausage, pimiento, dip, and milk and reserved drippings. Stir to moisten. Fill greased mini muffin tins ⅔ full. Sprinkle with Parmesan cheese. Bake 25 minutes at 350 degrees.

MONICA GOSE
LIFE MEMBER

ITALIAN EASTER BREAD

1 tablespoon lemon extract
1 package dry yeast
1 tablespoon grated lemon rind
6 tablespoons sugar
6 tablespoons Wesson oil
6 eggs
Dash salt
5 cups sifted flour (approximately)

Beat eggs well. Add sugar, salt, oil, and yeast dissolved in ¼ cup warm water. Add lemon extract and rind. Add 3 cups flour and then gradually add more flour until mixture is not sticky. Knead until smooth — approximately 5 minutes. Cover bowl with towel for 20 minutes. Divide in three parts and form braid, pinching ends. Flour cookie sheet and place dough under towel until it rises double in size — Bake 300 degrees until golden brown. Cool and frost with glaze. Sprinkle with colored confetti sprinkles.

GLAZE:
2 cups powdered sugar
½ teaspoon pure lemon extract
2 tablespoons milk (approximately)

Combine all above ingredients, adding more milk if necessary to spread easily. Use sprinkles while icing is soft or they won't stick.

MAXINE KAY CHAVANA
SOUVENIR PROGRAM

BROWN AND SERVE SALLY LUND ROLLS

1 envelope active dry yeast
¾ cups warm water, 105-115 degrees
¼ cup sugar
2 teaspoons salt
¾ cup warm milk
½ cup margarine, softened and cut in pieces
3 eggs, room temperature, beaten
5-6 cups flour

In large warm bowl, sprinkle yeast into warm water and stir until dissolved. Stir in sugar, salt, butter, milk, and eggs. Stir in 3 cups flour. With wooden spoon, beat until well mixed, about 1 minute. Beat in about 2¼ cups additional flour to make a soft dough that leaves sides of bowl. Cover with cloth and let rise in warm, draft free, place until doubled. About 1 hour. Stir down and divide dough into 24 smooth balls. Place in greased muffin cups. Cover and let rise until doubled. Bake in pre-heated 250 degree oven 25 minutes or until roll springs back when lightly touched. Cool in pans 25 minutes. Remove to racks and cool completely. Seal in plastic bags or containers. Refrigerate up to one week or freeze up to one month.

When rolls are needed: Thaw amount needed. Place rolls on greased baking sheet. Bake in preheated 400 degree oven 10-15 minutes or until thawed.

Makes 24 dinner rolls.

BETTY SMITH
GO WESTERN

CINNAMON FRUIT BISCUIT CRUNCHIES

1 10-ounce can Hungry Jack refrigerated flaky biscuits
½ cup sugar
½ teaspoon cinnamon
¼ cup margarine or butter, melted
10 teaspoons plum, strawberry, peach or other preserves

Heat oven to 375 degrees. Separate biscuit dough into 10 biscuits. Combine sugar and cinnamon. Dip both sides of biscuits in melted margarine, then in sugar mixture. Make deep thumb print in center of each roll: fill with 1 teaspoon preserves.

Bake in ungreased 15 x 10 inch jelly roll or 13 x 9 inch pan at 375 degrees for 15 to 20 minutes or until golden brown. Serve warm or cool.

MRS. NAT PRASSEL

PUMPKIN BREAD 𝓌

1 cup vegetable oil
3 cups sugar
4 eggs
1½ teaspoons nutmeg
1½ teaspoons cinnamon

1½ cups pumpkin
1 cup water
3½ cups self-rising flour
1 cup raisins
1 cup nuts

In a large mixing bowl, beat oil, sugar, and eggs until smooth. Blend in spices, pumpkin and water. In another bowl mix flour, raisins and nuts. Stir flour mixture into creamed mixture thoroughly. Pour batter into 3 greased 1 pound coffee cans to within 1½ inches of top. You may find it best to use four cans. Bake at 350 degrees for 1 hour or until toothpick inserted in center comes out clean. Cool in pan 15 minutes. To serve, slice and spread with cream cheese or plain.

SAUSAGE BREAD

1 pound hot sausage
1 ½ cups brown sugar
1 ½ cups white sugar
2 eggs, beaten
3 cups flour, sifted
1 teaspoon ginger

1 teaspoon baking powder
1 teaspoon pumpkin pie spice
1 teaspoon soda
1 cup strong coffee
1 cup raisins
1 cup chopped walnuts

Combine sausage and sugars. Stir until blended. Add the eggs and mix thoroughly. Sift flour, ginger, baking powder and pumpkin pie spice. Stir soda into strong coffee. Add flour mixture and coffee alternately to meat mixture, beating well. Pour boiling water over raisins and let stand five minutes; drain well and dry raisins. Fold raisins and nuts into meat mixture. Pour in greased pans. Bake 1 hour at 350 degrees.

ANNELLA EGBERT
AUCTION SALES

SALLY LUNN BREAD

1 package dry yeast
1 cup warm water
½ cup butter or margarine
⅓ cup sugar

3 eggs
4 cups flour
½ teaspoon salt
¼ cup non-fat dry milk

Soften yeast in warm water. Cream butter until light and fluffy. Add sugar gradually and beat well. Add slightly beaten eggs. Sift together flour, salt, and dry milk solids, and add to the creamed mixture, alternately with the softened yeast. Beat until smooth. Let rise in warm place until doubled in bulk. Again beat well. Pour into well greased tube pan. Let rise to double in bulk. Bake at 350 degrees for 25 to 40 minutes.

ARLINE HARRIS/FRED HARRIS
READY TO COOK POULTRY

ZUCCHINI BREAD

1 cup salad oil
3 cups sugar
4 eggs
⅔ cup water
3½ cups flour
1½ teaspoons salt
2½ cups zucchini, steamed and mashed
2 teaspoons soda
3 teaspoons cinnamon
3 teaspoons nutmeg
1 cup raisins
1 cup nuts, walnuts or pecans, chopped

Steam and drain zucchini; then mash. Sift flour, salt and spices. Add raisins and nuts; mix well. Beat eggs, then add eggs, oil, water, and sugar into mixture. Mix Well. Bake in 3 greased and floured loaf pans. Bake at 350 degrees for 40 minutes or until done. Best if served cold.

ROBYN MERCHANT
AUCTION SALES

FLOUR TORTILLAS

4 cups flour
2 tablespoons salt
⅛ teaspoon baking powder
⅔ cup shortening
1 cup plus 3 tablespoons hot water

Combine flour, salt, and baking powder; stir well. Cut in shortening with a pastry blender until mixture resembles coarse meal. Gradually stir in water, mixing well. Shape dough into 1½ inch balls. Roll each out on a lightly floured surface into a very thin circle. Circle should be about 6 inches in diameter.

Heat an ungreased electric skillet to 375 degrees, cook tortillas about 2 minutes on each side or until lightly browned. Pat tortillas lightly with spatula while browning the second side if they puff during cooking. Serve hot. Yields: 2 dozen.

ROLLED DUMPLINGS

2 cups flour
⅓ cup shortening
2 teaspoons baking powder
1 teaspoon salt
Milk to make soft dough

Mix and let stand 20 minutes; roll thin about ¼ inch, and cut in small squares. Drop a few at a time into chicken broth (or beef broth); when they rise, remove with slotted spoon and keep warm. Drop in more until all cooked — drop back into stock and serve hot.

For chicken:
Cook hen or pieces (breasts and thighs); when meat falls from bones discard bones and skin — cut remainder into bite size pieces and hold for dumplings. Use about 2 tablespoons of parsley or parsley flakes and 1 finely cut pimiento in the stock to make it pretty.

IN MEMORY OF MARVIN BEAM

JALAPEÑO HUSH PUPPIES

2 cups yellow cornmeal
1 teaspoon baking soda
1 teaspoon salt
2 tablespoons flour
1 tablespoon baking powder
6 tablespoons onion,
chopped
1½ cup buttermilk or milk
1 egg
Chopped jalapeños to taste

Mix all dry ingredients, add chopped onion, jalapeno, milk, and egg, beat together. Drop by spoonfuls into deep fat fryer. They will float when done, drain on paper towel.

Yields: 2 dozen

JIMMIE HUIZAR
AUCTION SALES

HUSH PUPPIES

Hot oil for deep frying
½ cup corn meal
2 tablespoons flour
⅛ teaspoon salt
⅛ teaspoon rubbed sage
¼ teaspoon baking soda
¼ teaspoon baking powder
1 egg
2 tablespoons chopped onion
⅓ cup buttermilk
Dash red pepper

Combine all of the ingredients. Use teaspoon to dip mixture into hot oil. Dip spoon in water each time to make mixture roll out smoothly. Makes approximately 20 Hush Puppies.

JESSE F. GARZA
WESTERN COOKBOOK

HUSH PUPPIES

2 cups corn meal
1 cup flour
1 tablespoon salt
4 teaspoons sugar
2 cups finely chopped onion
4 teaspoons baking powder
2 eggs
2 cups milk, approximately (if prefer buttermilk then add pinch of soda)

Mix dry ingredients with chopped onion; milk added to beaten egg. When paste-like consistency drop from teaspoon into deep hot fat. When done they will float. Drain on absorbent paper and serve hot!

Fit for a king rather than the hounds!

FRANK FLOWERS
AUCTION SALES

NAVAJO FRY BREAD

4 cups white flour
1 tablespoon baking powder
1 teaspoon salt

Mix the above ingredients together. Add 1½ cups warm water to dry ingredients. Knead until dough is soft and elastic and does not stick to bowl. (If necessary add a little more warm water.) Shape dough into ball the size of small peach. Pat back and forth by hand until dough is about ½ or ¼ inch thick and round. Make a small hole in center of round. Melt 1 cup shortening in heavy frying pan. Carefully put the rounds into hot fat one at a time. Brown on both sides. Drain on paper towel and serve hot.

BETTIE RUTLEDGE
AUCTION SALES

FRIED INDIAN SQUAW BREAD

3 cups all-purpose flour, sifted
1 teaspoon salt
3 teaspoons baking powder
1 tablespoon granulated sugar
1 tablespoon melted butter
1½ cups water
Fat for deep frying
Powdered sugar
Squaw bread syrup

Sift first 4 ingredients; add butter and water. Mix thoroughly. Drop by tablespoons into hot fat (375 degrees on a frying thermometer.) Cook for 2 to 4 minutes, or until brown. Drain on paper towels, sprinkle with powdered sugar. Serve hot with squaw bread syrup. Makes 6 servings.

Squaw Bread Syrup
Put 1 cup light brown sugar, 2 cups light corn syrup, 2 tablespoons bacon fat, and 1 teaspoon maple flavoring in saucepan. Heat to boiling.

BETTIE RUTLEDGE
WESTERN COOKBOOK

TRAIL CAMP TOAST OR HOT BREAD

I use my 10 inch square cast-iron skillet on one of the burners for toasting. I grease it lightly with fat or oil, depending on what's available and what we're eating. It will toast 6 slices of bread or make 6 cheese sandwiches if you cut them in half lengthwise and fit the halves in closely. It makes marvelous toasted English muffins, which are very good in camp because they do not become stale like ordinary sliced bread or bought rolls and biscuits. The 10-inch iron skillet makes French toast (again, cut slices in half) or 4 to 6 pancakes at a time, bakes biscuits and retoasts the halves when biscuits are left over. For your choice of hot bread to go with spaghetti for example, heat skillet with a thin wipe of olive oil or butter; toast bread on both sides, sprinkle with garlic salt. Reheat biscuit halves by toasting in buttered skillet. Fry bacon or sausage in skillet, remove and keep warm, drain excess fat and toast breakfast muffins or white bread in skillet. Or brush with reserved bacon fat to reheat Skillet Corn Bread, cut in halves across. Think ahead — never wash this skillet if there's a flavor in it you can use for your next camp meal; naturally, if food is burned or stuck to it, you must clean it.

BETTIE RUTLEDGE
AUCTION SALES

SPOON BREAD

¾ cup white corn meal
2 cups milk
3 eggs, separated
1 teaspoon salt
3 tablespoons butter

Heat milk in double boiler over hot, not boiling water. Stir in cornmeal and cook slowly stirring constantly until thick and smooth. Remove from heat and add butter and salt. Cool thoroughly. Beat egg whites stiff. Beat egg yolks and add to meal mixture. Fold in whites. Pour into buttered casserole and bake 30 minutes at 350 degrees. Serve immediately.

SCOTT ABBEY WEST
AUCTION SALES

OKLAHOMA BISCUITS

1 cup oats, rolled white
1 cup milk
½ teaspoon salt
2 tablespoons lard or shortening
1½ cup flour
3 teaspoons baking powder

Pour milk over oats and let stand 10 minutes. Sift together flour, baking powder and salt. Work in shortening, add oats and milk. Mix quickly. Toss on floured board. Cover entire surface of dough with flour. Pat out and cut as for biscuits. Brush tops with milk and bake in 375 degrees for 15 minutes. Yields 9.

BETTY JACOBS
INTERNATIONAL/MEXICO DAY

BUTTERMILK ROLLS

Heat together:
2 cups buttermilk
½ cup margarine

To above heated mixture add:
½ cup sugar
½ teaspoon soda
1 teaspoon salt

When mixture is lukewarm, add 2 packages yeast and 1 tablespoon sugar prepared according to package directions.
Add: 2 beaten eggs
Add flour to make soft dough. (Approximately 6 cups.) Let rise (cover bowl with damp cloth) about 3 hours. Punch down. Roll out in small batches on floured board. Cut with biscuit cutter, fold over, and let rise on cookie sheet 1 hour. Bake 350 degrees until pale brown.

CAROLYN BRINKMAN
GENERAL LIVESTOCK

ORANGE/WALNUT BREAD

2 large oranges
1 cup water
1 cup granulated sugar
½ cup packed brown sugar
2 tablespoons oleo
3 cups flour
3 teaspoons baking powder
1 teaspoon salt
1 egg
1 cup milk
¼ cup chopped walnuts

1. Pare rind of oranges thin with vegetable parer. Slice rind into paper thin sticks with *no* white. Simmer 30 minutes until tender, drain.
2. Combine granulated and brown sugar and oleo with rind. Heat stirring constantly 5 minutes or until butter melts and sugars dissolve, set aside.
3. Sift flour, baking powder, and salt into medium size bowl.
4. Beat egg, stir in milk and then orange rind mixture. Stir in dry ingredients. Bake in greased loaf pan 9×5×3.
5. Bake in 350 degree oven 1 hour. Cool in pan 5 minutes, then turn out on wire rack and cool completely.

JIM DOCKERY/PEGGY DOCKERY
JUNIOR STEER RIDING CHAIRMAN

BANANA NUT BREAD

Cream 1 cup sugar with ¼ cup shortening

Add:
2 eggs slightly beaten
1 cup crushed bananas
2 cups biscuit mix
½ cup chopped nuts

Mix. Pour batter into non-stick pan and bake at 350 degrees for 30 to 45 minutes. Using toothpick, bake test.

ROSEMARY VAN HEUVERSWYN
AUCTION SALES

AVOCADO BREAD

1 egg, beaten
½ cup ripe avocado, mashed
½ cup buttermilk or sour milk
1 cup pecans, chopped
2 cups flour, sifted

¾ cup sugar
½ teaspoon baking powder
½ teaspoon soda
¼ teaspoon salt

Combine egg, avocado, buttermilk, or sour milk, and pecans. Sift dry ingredients together and add avocado mixture. Mix only until flour is moistened. *Do not overblend.* Bake in greased and floured loaf pan 1½x4½ in preheated 350 degree oven for 1 hour. If glass pan is used, reduce heat by 25 degrees. Test with toothpick for doneness. The loaf should have a green valley down the middle with a light brown crust on either side. Turn the loaf out of the pan as soon as you can, and let it cool right side up on a rack. This bread will be better flavored after it has matured into the second day. Slice very thin and spread with cream cheese. This is delicious with coffee or tea or just by itself!!

MARY NAN WEST
VICE-PRESIDENT/SECRETARY
SAN ANTONIO LIVESTOCK EXPOSITION, INC.

ROCKET SPOON BREAD

2 cups milk or buttermilk
2 teaspoons salt
¼ teaspoon soda
¼ cup sugar
7 cups flour

4 teaspoons baking powder
¾ cup corn oil
2 packages dry yeast
1 cup warm water

Dissolve yeast in warm water. Combine other ingredients, add dissolved yeast. Place dough in covered bowl in the refrigerator, spooning out as much as needed. Bake in greased and floured loaf pan or greased for dinner rolls. Bake at 425 degrees, 25-30 minutes. You can also bake, wrap in foil, and freeze. Just pop in the oven before serving.

DEBBIE KANE
GO WESTERN

(BUCHTA) CZECHOSLOVAKIAN CHRISTMAS BREAD

Warm 2 cakes fresh yeast or 2 packages dry yeast in small amount of warm water. Let rise.

Take:

16 cups flour = #5 bag	**½ pound margarine**
1 pound butter	**1 tablespoon salt**

Mix like pie dough, put grated lemon rind plus

½ teaspoon nutmeg or to taste
1½ cup sugar diluted in warm milk
2 egg yolks beaten
Stir good.

Warm enough milk, about 2 cups, add little at a time to make it workable. Add beaten egg whites. *Let rise* to *twice* the size. Add raisins about 1 cup plus 1 package almonds diced. Make into loaves or braids and let rise good. Beat egg yolks and brush loaves before baking. Bake at 400 degrees 15 minutes. Then bake 350 degrees 45 minutes.

MRS. FRANCES A. CARTER
(RECIPE IN FAMILY FOR GENERATIONS —
MOTHER AND FATHER WERE FROM PRAGUE,
CZECHOSLOVAKIA)

BEER BREAD

2 cups biscuit mix
1 cup beer
1 egg
½ cup sugar

Mix together. Grease and flour loaf pan. Bake at 350-375 degrees, oven heat varies, for about 30-35 minutes.

PAT BIESENBACH

JEFF'S BEER BREAD

Preheat oven to 425-450 degrees, hot oven.
Oil muffin tin, 24 muffins.
Combine and stir together:

3 cups self rising flour
3 tablespoons sugar
1 can or bottle of beer, 12 ounces

Spoon into muffin tins
Bake about 20 minutes or until done.
If any are left over, store in air-tight containers to keep soft.

THURMAN KENNEDY
GENERAL LIVESTOCK

BRAUNES WEIZENBROT (WHOLE WHEAT BREAD)

1 tablespoon margarine
1 tablespoon salt
1 tablespoon sugar
1 cup All Bran
1 quart hot water
2 cakes compressed yeast
1 tablespoon sugar
1 cup warm water, 115 degrees F.
3 cups whole wheat flour
3 cups rye flour
6 cups white flour

Mix first 5 ingredients in large bowl. In small bowl, dissolve yeast and sugar in warm water. Add to bran mixture. Stir in flours. Knead on floured board 10 minutes or until smooth and elastic. Place in greased bowl, cover and set to rise in warm place until double in bulk, about 1½ hours. Punch down. With well greased hands knead lightly for a minute or so, shape into 4 loaves and place in greased 9x5x3 inch pans. Cover and let rise until doubled, about 1 hour. Bake at 350 degrees F. for 50 to 60 minutes or until done.

MRS. EVELYN TATUM
SPECIAL DAYS

Information & Hospitality

The Information and Hospitality Committee was one of the first committee's established by the San Antonio Livestock Exposition to provide information and direction to visitors during the 10-day event. At least two committee people are on duty at the front of the Coliseum to help in any way possible such as lost children, directions to the barns and a multitude of emergencies that happen. It is indeed nice to know that someone is there to help and also extend to each and everyone a hearty
        "Howdy pardner, what can we do for you?"

JACK CONGER
CHAIRMAN

VAL'S INSPIRED LASAGNA

2 pounds of lean ground beef
1 medium size onion, chopped
1 clove of garlic, minced
2 cans of tomato paste
1 can of whole tomatoes
Italian seasoning
Mozzarella cheese
Parmesan cheese
1 16-ounce carton large curd cottage cheese
1 box lasagna noodles
1 egg

Mix the egg and the cottage cheese together and let it set. Brown ground beef and add onion, garlic, and Italian seasoning; season to taste. Salt and pepper to taste. Drain off excess grease. Add 2 cans of tomato paste and whole tomatoes and enough water to make thick sauce. Boil noodles according to directions. Instead of draining them, just run cold water over them until they're cool enough to handle. Grease a large rectangular cake pan and spread a little sauce on the bottom. Layer 3 noodles on the bottom and spread the cottage cheese mixture thinly over the noodles. Do the same to the meat sauce. Sprinkle Parmesan cheese on the meat sauce and do the same with the Mozzarella. Repeat until all the noodles are used. Be sure you end up with the Mozzarella cheese on the top. Place in a preheated oven of 350 degrees and bake until the cheese turns golden brown. Serves approximately 6.

VALERIE McDONALD
LIFE MEMBER

BAKED MACARONI AND CHEESE

8 ounce package macaroni
3 tablespoons butter
2 tablespoons flour
1 teaspoon salt
¼ teaspoon pepper
2 cups milk
¼ to ½ pound Cheddar cheese, grated
1 tablespoon onion, grated
½ teaspoon dry mustard
1 teaspoon Worcestershire
½ cup buttered bread crumbs

Cook macaroni as directed.

To make white sauce:
Melt butter, add flour, salt and pepper. Stir until well blend-ed. Remove from heat. Gradually stir in milk and return to heat. Cook, stirring constantly until thick and smooth. Combine white sauce, cheese, onion, mustard and Worcestershire. Add cooked macaroni. Place in greased casserole. Top with bread crumbs. Bake at 375 degrees for 25 minutes.

ELIZABETH "BETTY" JACOBS
INTERNATIONAL/MEXICO DAY

SPANISH VERMICELLI

1 package Vermicelli
1 package McCormick Chili Mix
1 stick margarine
1 can stewed tomatoes

Brown Vermicelli in margarine. Add Chili Mix and stewed tomatoes. Simmer until all tomato juice is absorbed.

SONNY HILD
AUCTION SALES

CRAZY SPAGHETTI

1 pound ground round
1 large onion, chopped
5 ounce bottle soy sauce
1 medium head cabbage, shredded
1 4-ounce can mushrooms
1 16-ounce can bean sprouts
1 8-ounce can water chestnuts
1 pound package spaghetti

Cook meat with onion until brown and tender. Reduce heat, pour ⅓ of soy sauce over meat, add cabbage, cover and simmer about 5 minutes. Add mushrooms, bean sprouts, water chestnuts and ⅓ of soy sauce, cover and simmer another 5 minutes. Add cooked spaghetti, cover and simmer for just a few minutes and then serve. Serves 8.

REBA ROBERSON
AUCTION SALES

DIRTY RICE

½ stick butter
1 onion, finely chopped
1 bunch green onions, finely chopped
Beef or bouillon base
2 tablespoons soy sauce
2 tablespoons Kitchen Bouquet
3 cups Rice

Chop onion and green onion finely and sauté in butter until soft. Add rice and continue to sauté until rice is brown. Transfer to deep pan, add soy sauce and Kitchen Bouquet and beef base until rice is covered by ½ inch. Cover with aluminum foil and bake at 350 degrees until all moisture is absorbed.

MONICA GOSE
LIFE MEMBER

GRANDMOTHER'S SPAGHETTI

1 large tablespoon bacon grease
2 large onions, chopped coarse 2 pounds ground round
   steak
Salt and pepper to taste
2 cans whole tomatoes, chopped
2 large cans tomato sauce
1 teaspoon cinnamon
½ teaspoon cloves
¼ teaspoon allspice
1 pound spaghetti, cooked and drained
1 pound yellow cheese, grated

In a large skillet, brown meat in bacon grease. Add onions and cook until clear. Add tomatoes and seasoning. Cook down over low heat. Add spaghetti and grated cheese. Serve hot with salad and Italian bread.

SCOTT ABBEY WEST
AUCTION SALES

JALAPEÑO RICE CASSEROLE

3 cups uncooked regular rice
3 cups chicken broth
3 tablespoons butter
3 fresh jalapeños, broiled, peeled, seeded, and chopped
3 8 ounce cartons sour cream
18 ounces Monterrey Jack cheese, shredded

Combine first 3 ingredients in large saucepan, bring to boil. Cover, reduce heat, simmer 25 minutes. Stir in jalapeños. Spoon rice into lightly buttered shallow 3 quart casserole. Sprinkle cheese evenly over sour cream. Bake 350 degrees for 25 minutes.

ANNELLA EGBERT
AUCTION SALES

RICE O'BRIEN

1 cup white rice
2 cups water
3 chicken bouillon cubes
1 teaspoon salt
1¼ cup butter or margarine
½ cup slice green onions
½ cup diced green pepper
3 tablespoons pimiento
½ cup ripe olives

Cook rice in water flavored with bouillon cubes and salt. Heat: ¼cup butter in skillet, add onions and peppers, cook about 5 minutes. Add cooked rice and sauté until vegetables are tender crisp. Fork toss with diced pimiento and sliced pitted ripe olives.

6 servings

GEORGE WILLIAMS
CALF SCRAMBLE

RICE AND RED BEANS

About noon, put ½ package of red beans on the stove in a large boiler. Cover with water. Cover and cook at a slow boil all afternoon, adding water to make a real thick juice. About 1 hour before you plan to eat, put on your Rice, and make by your usual method. Use 1 or 2 cups (one cup will be enough for 5 or 6 people). Then fry quickly in a hot skillet 10 to 12 slices of fat meat or salt meat. Put in with beans. Then saute in the grease 1 onion chopped, 1 garlic section chopped. Add onion, garlic and grease drippings to the beans and salt to taste. Allow to continue cooking until the rice is done. At the table serve with a mound of rice covered by the beans and all its meats and juices.

Have a tossed salad, french bread, coffee and enjoy yourself.

FRANK FLOWERS
AUCTION SALES

RICE AND SOUR CREAM CASSEROLE

1 pound Monterrey Jack cheese
3 cups sour cream, salted
2 cans peeled green chilies, chopped
4 cups cooked rice, salt and pepper to taste
½ cup Cheddar cheese, grated

Mix sour cream and finely chopped chilies; butter a 1½ quart casserole dish well. Season rice with salt and pepper. Layer rice, sour cream mixture and Monterrey Jack cheese in that order. Finish with rice on top; bake at 350 degrees for 30 minutes. During last few minutes of baking, sprinkle with grated Cheddar cheese.

MATT AND MELISSA FATHEREE
ENTERTAINMENT

WILD RICE WITH MUSHROOMS AND ALMONDS

1 cup uncooked wild rice
¼ cup butter or margarine
½ cup slivered almonds
2 tablespoons snipped chives or chopped green onions
1 8 ounce can mushroom stems and pieces, drained
3 cups chicken broth

Wash and drain wild rice. Melt butter in large skillet. Add rice, almonds, chives and mushrooms; cook and stir until almonds are golden brown, about 20 minutes.

Heat oven to 325 degrees. Pour rice mixture into ungreased 1½-quart casserole. Heat chicken broth to boiling; stir into rice mixture. Cover tightly; bake about 1½ hours or until all liquid is absorbed and rice is tender and fluffy.

6 to 8 servings.

ROBYN MERCHANT
AUCTION AND SOUVENIR PROGRAM

Pioneer Staples

LASAGNA I

1 pound ground beef
1 tablespoon salad oil
1 clove garlic, minced
1 tablespoon parsley flakes
1 tablespoon basil
1 teaspoon salt
1 No. 2 can, 2½ cups tomatoes
1 6-ounce, ⅔ cup tomato paste
1 package noodles
2 12-ounce cartons, 3 cups large curd cream style
   cottage cheese
2 beaten eggs
1 teaspoon salt
½ teaspoon pepper
2 tablespoons parsley flakes
½ cup Parmesan cheese, grated
1 pound Mozzarella cheese sliced very thin

Brown meat in hot oil. Add next 6 ingredients. Simmer uncovered until thick about one hour, stirring occasionally.
Cook noodles in boiling salted water until tender, drain,
rinse, in cold water. Meanwhile combine cottage cheese
with next five ingredients. Place half the noodles in 13×9×2
baking dish. Spread half of the cottage cheese mixture
over. Add half of the Mozzarella cheese half the meat mixture. Repeating layers.
Bake in moderate oven 375 degrees for 30 minutes.

ADRIANNE DALTON

LASAGNA II

Butter baking dish 13x9x2 inch. Preheat oven 375°

Tomato Sauce:
  ¼ cup, ½ stick butter
  ½ pound beef, ground
  ½ pound pork, ground
  1 cup onion, chopped
  1 clove garlic, minced
  3¼ cups tomatoes
  2 cups tomato paste
  2 cups water
  2½ teaspoons salt
  1 teaspoon pepper
  1 teaspoon oregano
Lasagna:
  1 pound lasagna noodles
  2 pounds Ricotta cheese
  6 cups shredded Mozzarella cheese
  1½ cups grated Parmesan cheese
  Paprika

To prepare Tomato Sauce: In a large skillet melt butter; slowly brown meat. Add onion and garlic; sauté until tender. Stir in tomatoes, tomato paste, water, salt, pepper and oregano; simmer over low heat 45-60 minutes.

To Prepare Lasagna: Cook noodles according to package directions. Drain. Handle noodles carefully to keep from tearing. Place a layer of noodles in bottom of baking dish; top with layer of tomato sauce. Sprinkle over ⅓ each of the Ricotta, Mozzarella and Parmesan cheeses; repeat 2 more times, reserving a small amount of sauce to spread in center of top layer of cheeses for a colorful casserole. Sprinkle with paprika. Bake about 30 minutes. Allow to set 10-15 minutes before cutting into squares for serving.
12-15 servings.

MARY FLOWERS
AUCTION SALES

SPAGHETTI

1 pound ground lean beef
½ medium onion, chopped
1 clove garlic, minced
3 8-ounce cans tomato sauce
4½ cups water
1 teaspoon salt
½ teaspoon pepper
1 teaspoon sugar
¼ teaspoon sweet basil
1 tablespoon parsley flakes
Pinch of thyme
Pinch of oregano
1 8-ounce package uncooked spaghetti
2 tablespoons Parmesan cheese, grated

In Dutch oven, sauté beef, onions, and garlic until meat is brown and onion soft. Add remaining ingredients, except spaghetti and cheese. Bring to boil, add spaghetti. Stir with fork to keep from sticking together. Return to boiling, boil for 18 minutes, stirring frequently. Stir in cheese, turn off heat and let set on burner for 10 minutes, before serving.

Pass grated Parmesan.

IN MEMORY OF MARVIN BEAM

NOODLES

Mix:
1 egg, lightly beaten
2 tablespoons milk
1/2 teaspoon salt

Add: Enough sifted all purpose flour to make stiff dough — about 1 cup. Roll very thin on well floured board, let stand 20 minutes. Roll up loosely and slice very thin — let dry two hours and then drop by handsfull into stock (chicken or beef).

IN MEMORY OF MARVIN BEAM

LORI'S LASAGNA

1½ pound of hamburger meat, browned with:
¼ medium onion, minced
4 cloves garlic, minced
Salt and pepper to taste

Add:
1 16-ounce jar of spaghetti sauce with mushrooms
1 16-ounce can of tomato sauce
Let simmer:
1 15-ounce package dumplings

When tender stir sauce and dumplings together
Pour ½ of mixture back into skillet.

Mix:
1 16 ounce carton cottage cheese with 6 ounces of
   Parmesan
2 eggs
3 tablespoons parsley flakes

Pour on top of skillet mixture and top with remaining dumplings. Top with Mozzarella cheese (8 ounces grated). Put lid on skillet and heat at low heat for 20 minutes.

NINA COWAN
INTERNATIONAL/MEXICO DAY

International Mexico Day

The International/Mexico Day Committee was formed in 1965 to promote our Livestock Show throughout Mexico. The opening day of stock show has been designated as International/Mexico and is celebrated as such hosting many international guest from Mexico and abroad at a "fiesta." This committee promotes the sale of more than $8,000,000 worth of purebred livestock and farm equipment each year making this committee a vital part of the San Antonio Livestock Show Rodeo.

Robert Yturri
Chairman

TEXAS RANCH HOUSE BEANS

4 cups dried pinto beans
8 cups water
½ pound salt pork
2-4 tablespoons chili powder, depending on taste
¼ -½ teaspoon hot pepper sauce, depending on taste
Salt to taste

Bring beans and water to a boil. Remove from heat, cover and let stand for 1 hour. Add salt pork and simmer, covered for 1½ to 2 hours or until beans are tender and water is almost absorbed. While beans are cooking, stir in enough chili powder, hot pepper sauce, and salt to give beans a spicy flavor. Beans can be prepared ahead of time and reheated. Makes 10 to 12 servings.

*BETTIE RUTLEDGE
WESTERN COOKBOOK*

GOLDWATER BEANS

2 pounds pinto beans
2 large onions, sliced
4 cloves garlic, diced
2 or more teaspoons salt
½ teaspoon pepper
½ teaspoon cumin
1 can taco sauce
1 large can tomatoes
1 can diced green chilies

Soak beans in cold water overnight. Drain, wash, and cover with 2 inches water. Add salt and boil over moderate heat about 1 hour. Add remaining ingredients. Cook over low heat until tender.

These beans may be frozen and reheated.

ANNE FLEENOR

M.D. SMITH AND LAND CO. OLD FASHION BAKED BEANS

1 can pork and beans
¼ cup catsup
½ cup brown sugar
1 tablespoon onions, chopped
2 teaspoons prepared mustard

Combine all ingredients and place in baking dish. Bake at 325 degrees for 25 minutes.

Top with bacon if desired.

M.D. SMITH

DUDLEY'S CAMP GRUB

6-8 slices bacon
6 eggs
1 can pork and beans

Fry bacon until crisp, remove and drain. Scramble eggs until almost done, add pork and beans and bacon (break in small pieces). Let simmer for a few minutes. Serve hot.

SANDRA SESCILA

WRANGLER'S GREEN BEANS

1 can, 2 cups, cut green beans
2 tablespoons butter or margarine
2 teaspoons prepared mustard
1 teaspoon Worcestershire
½ teaspoon salt
½ teaspoon pepper, black
2 tablespoons Parmesan cheese, grated

Reduce liquid from beans to one-third by boiling. Add beans and heat through; then drain. Melt butter with mustard sauce, salt and pepper in small pan. Pour over hot beans and stir gently. Sprinkle Parmesan cheese over dish.

RE-FRIED BEANS

Mash pinto beans with fork in bean liquid, cook until liquid has evaporated. Cook one minced small onion in 2 tablespoons bacon fat for 5 minutes, add ½ cup tomato puree. Add beans, season. Makes 4 servings.

BETTIE RUTLEDGE
COOKBOOK COMMITTEE

RANCH BEANS

12 cups water
4 cups dried pinto beans
2 large onions, coarsely chopped
½ teaspoon garlic powder
2 bay leaves
2 pounds thick sliced bacon, cut in ½ inch long pieces
2 16½-ounce cans of canned tomatoes, chopped in blender
4 teaspoons chili powder
1 teaspoon dry mustard
½ teaspoon crushed oregano
Salt to taste with onion salt

Pour water over beans, cover and soak for 12-15 hours. Add onion, garlic, and bay leaf. Cover and bring to a simmer. Add meat to beans. Bring to a rapid boil; reduce heat to a slow simmer. Cover tightly and cook for 1 hour and 30 minutes. Stir in remaining ingredients. Bring to a rapid boil; reduce heat to a slow simmer. Add onion salt to taste if needed. Cover; simmer for 2 hours. Makes 12+ servings.

A.J. KALLUS
CALF SCRAMBLE,
HALLETTSVILLE, TX

RANCH STYLE BEANS AND MEAT

5 cans pork and beans
5 cans ranch style beans
4 onions, chopped
1 bottle catsup
2 pounds ground meat
½ cup maple syrup
½ cup mustard
½ cup brown sugar

Brown meat — add onions — then other ingredients. Simmer 1 hour. Serves 10-12. Double recipe for 20 people.

PEGGY AND JIM DOCKERY
JUNIOR STEER RIDING

FRIED BEANS

2 cups cooked pinto beans, drained
3 tablespoons onion, chopped
1 medium tomato, chopped
2 tablespoons celery, chopped
2 tablespoons ketchup
2 tablespoons mayonnaise

Sauté onion, tomato, and celery in a small amount of bacon drippings in an iron skillet. Add beans and mash them. Add ketchup and mayonnaise. Stir and cook slowly for a few minutes. Makes a good dip, sandwich, and good with bacon and eggs.

ROSALINE CARTER
LIFE MEMBER

BOOTLEGGER BEANS

Dice up three strips of bacon and fry. When half done, add a small chopped onion. When the onion is slightly browned, pour off most of the grease and add one can of pork and beans packed in tomato sauce, one tablespoon brown sugar, two tablespoons vinegar, and two tablespoons catsup; stir well and cover. Let this simmer for at least 30 minutes. The longer you let it simmer, the better it is. Or else bake slowly at 300 degrees for a couple of hours.

IN MEMORY OF MARVIN BEAM

CHARRO BEANS

Water
½ pod of garlic
3 cups pinto beans
½ cup raw pork skins or ½ package of bacon, cut into
  small pieces
1 large tomato, chopped
1 medium onion, chopped
5 small green peppers, chopped
½ cup cilantro leaves, chopped
1 can beer

Cook beans in water with ½ pod of garlic. Add salt to taste, always keep covered. While beans are cooking, cut bacon into small pieces and fry (not crisp). When beans are half cooked, add bacon. Chop onions, tomatoes, peppers, and celantro leaves, and fry in 1 tablespoon of oil. When all fried together, add to cooked beans and add beer. Cook additional 15 minutes. Serve in bowls.

COL. MAXIMO VIRGIL
INTERNATIONAL/MEXICO DAY COMMITTEE

"RODEO" EGGPLANT CASSEROLE

1 medium eggplant, chopped and peeled
1 medium white onion, chopped
1 or 2 whole garlic cloves
1½ cups fresh mushrooms, chopped
1 medium bell pepper, chopped
2 cups zucchini, chopped
2 cups yellow squash, chopped
1 can Rotel Tomatoes and Green Chilies
2 cans tomatoes, peeled or stewed
Ground comino, sweet basil, salt, pepper and tomato
    paste to taste

Using a large skillet or dutch oven, heat garlic cloves in oil over medium heat. Add salt and pepper, onion and green pepper, and cook until transparent. Add peeled and chopped eggplant and cook until transparent, stirring over slightly higher heat. The eggplant will absorb oil rapidly, so a little more may be needed to prevent sticking. Add squash and mushrooms, Rotel Tomatoes and Chilies, canned tomatoes and seasonings to taste. Simmer over low to medium heat for 45 minutes, stirring occasionally. To this point, recipe may be prepared a day ahead (and is usually better that way).

Preheat oven to 350 degrees. In deep casserole, layer eggplant mixture and bread-crumb-cheese mixture. Bake until thoroughly heated and bubbly, about 30 to 45 minutes.

ROBYN MERCHANT
AUCTION SALES COMMITTEE

BLACK EYED PEAS

2 packages onion soup
8 cups of water
1 pound of ham
1½ cups celery diced
4 chilipiquin
TABASCO sauce to your liking
3 20-ounce packages frozen black eyed peas
6 tablespoons butter or oleo
4 cups cooked Rice

Cook peas until tender, according to directions on package with the above seasonings. Add rice or serve over rice.

EMMA BLAKEWAY

BLACK EYED PEAS

2 cups blackeyed peas
1½ quarts cold water
1 pound bacon or salt pork
1 large bay leaf
2 cloves
1 clove garlic, minced
1 medium-sized onion, chopped
10 peppercorns, grind
½ teaspoon salt

Pick over and wash peas and soak overnight in cold water. Put on to cook in same water, adding bacon or salt pork, and all the other ingredients. Simmer covered, until tender which will take about 2 hours. Add hot water as it is necessary during the cooking as they absorb a lot of water.

CALISTA MARSHALL
AUCTION SALES

SICILIAN BROCCOLI

1 large bunch broccoli
3 tablespoons oil
1 large onion, sliced
Pitted black olives
Fresh mushrooms 15-20
Anchovies
1 cup dry red or white wine
1 cup Parmesan cheese, grated

Clean broccoli and cut into slices 3-4 inches long. In a skillet, pour 1 tablespoon oil. Make a layer of broccoli, a layer of onions, and mushrooms, and drizzle with oil. Sprinkle with cheese and anchovies. Continue this process until all are used. Pour the wine over above ingredients. Cook slowly until tender, about ½ hour. Add salt and pepper and garlic powder to taste. Green pepper may also be added.

LIBBY JONES
AUCTION SALES

BROCCOLI CASSEROLE

2 10-ounce packages chopped broccoli
½ cup onions, chopped
¼ cup butter, melted
2 tablespoons flour
3 eggs, beaten
1 16-ounce jar Cheez Whiz
½ cup cracker crumbs
½ cup water

Cook broccoli and drain; sauté onions in ¼ cup butter; blend in flour; stir in water and cook until smooth and thick. Remove from heat and stir in eggs and cheese. Add broccoli. Put in casserole dish and bake at 325 degrees for 30 to 40 minutes.

SHIRLEY AND LARRY SIMPSON
WESTERN COOKBOOK

BROCCOLI-CHEESE CASSEROLE

2 medium onions, chopped
1 cup melted butter or margarine, divided
2 10¾-ounce cans cream of mushroom soup, undiluted
2 4-ounce cans chopped mushrooms, drained
2 6-ounce rolls garlic cheese, chopped
2 teaspoons chopped parsley
Salt and pepper to taste
½ cup slivered almonds
4 10-ounce packages frozen chopped broccoli, partially
   cooked and drained.
4 cups herb-seasoned stuffing mix.

Sauté onion in ½ cup butter until tender. Combine onion, soup, mushrooms, cheese, parsley, salt and pepper, almonds and broccoli. Mix well. Spoon into two lightly greased 2 quart casseroles. Combine stuffing mix and ½ cup butter; spoon over broccoli mixture and bake at 350 degrees — 20 to 30 min. Serves 12-14

CHARLYNE WILLIAMS AND JOHN J. WILLIAMS
DIRECTOR

BROCCOLI SUPREME

1 slightly beaten egg 10-ounce package frozen chopped
   broccoli, partially thawed
1 8½-ounce can cream style corn
1 tablespoon onion, grated
¼ teaspoon salt
Dash pepper
3 tablespoons butter
1 cup herb-seasoned stuffing

In mixing bowl, combine egg, broccoli, corn, onion, salt and pepper. In small saucepan, melt butter. Add stuffing, tossing to coat. Stir ¾ cup of the buttered stuffing into vegetable mixture. Turn into ungreased 1 quart casserole. Sprinkle with remaining ¼ cup stuffing mix. Bake uncovered at 350 degrees for 35-40 minutes. Serves 4-6

JAMIE BROWN
CALF SCRAMBLE

BROCCOLI AND RICE

½ cup chopped celery
1 tablespoon margarine or butter
2 10-ounce frozen chopped broccoli packages
1 cup cooked Rice
1 can cream of mushroom soup
1 can cream of chicken soup
1 8-ounce jar Cheez Whiz (jalapeño)
Salt, pepper, paprika

Sauté celery in butter. Cook broccoli as directed. Combine cooked rice, vegetables, soups, Cheez Whiz, salt and pepper in 2½ quart casserole, sprinkle paprika on top.

Bake in 350 degree oven 30 minutes.

12 servings (freezes well)

RICHARD WILLIAMS
CALF SCRAMBLE

BROCCOLI-RICE CASSEROLE *& good*

⅔ cup onion, diced
⅔ cup celery, diced
3 tablespoons cooking oil
1 package frozen chopped broccoli
1 can cream of chicken soup
½ soup can milk
1 cup water
1½ cup Minute Rice
1 8-ounce jar Cheez Whiz
Paprika

Sauté onions and celery in cooking oil. Add broccoli and simmer for 10 minutes. Mix soup, milk, water, rice and cheese. Add to above mixture and bring to a boil. Pour in buttered 1½ quart casserole and garnish with paprika. Bake at 350 degrees for 25 minutes. Serves 6.

MARY ELLEN PENWELL
AUCTION SALES

Pasture Pickins

OKRA — CRUMRINES' FAVORITE

2 pounds fresh okra — young — tender
6 slices bacon, sliced thin
1 medium onion, chopped
1 bunch green onions, chopped
1 large green pepper, chopped
1 No. 2½ can tomatoes or fresh peeled tomatoes
Sprinkle oregano
Sprinkle Italian red pepper or minced jalapeño

In dutch oven pan:
Brown bacon. Remove from pan and save. Leave bacon grease in pan and sauté onions and green pepper until soft — not brown. Add okra (washed with water — patted dry — and sliced thin). Remove the top and tip off okra. Stir over medium heat until the okra "goo" is sealed. Add canned tomatoes broken into small pieces and seasonings. Cook over low flame until okra is tender. Stir frequently, about 45 minutes. Add salt and pepper to taste and bacon peices.
Serves 10

Hint: If mixture is too thick after adding tomatoes, add small amount of water.

EILEEN/ELMER CRUMRINE
RURAL YOUTH

BROCCOLI WITH RICE CASSEROLE

1 large onion, chopped
2 tablespoons oil
2 packages broccoli, chopped
1 can cream of chicken soup
1 can water
1 small jar Cheese Whiz
1 cup Rice, cooked
Cracker crumbs
Salt

Chop onion — sauté in oil. Add 2 packages broken broccoli. Add 1 can cream of chicken soup, 1 can water, and 1 jar Cheez Whiz. Add broccoli and onion to 1 cup cooked Rice. Top with cracker crumbs. Bake in 350 degree oven for 30 minutes.

CALISTA MARSHALL
AUCTION SALES

EGGPLANT CASSEROLE

2 medium eggplants, remove seeds, peel and dice
1 pound pork sausage (Owens or Jimmy Dean hot or plain)
1 large onion, diced
1 clove garlic, minced
½ cup celery, diced
½ cup green pepper, diced
1 16-ounce can of tomatoes, break into small pieces
1 teaspoon salt
Dash of black pepper
½ cup Parmesan cheese, grated
½ cup bread crumbs
½ teaspoon sugar

Brown sausage: Remove all but 2 tablespoons fat. Add onion, green pepper, celery and sauté until tender. Add diced eggplant, tomatoes, salt, pepper, and sugar. Simmer until eggplant is tender. Pour into greased baking dish and top with cheese and bread crumbs. Bake at 375 degrees for 45 minutes. Serves 8 amply.

EILEEN/ELMER CRUMRINE
RURAL YOUTH

POTATO CASSEROLE

1 large package hash browns (frozen potatoes, partially
 defrosted)
1 pint sour cream
2 cups Cheddar cheese, shredded
½ cup butter
1 can cream of chicken soup
½ cup onion, chopped
¼ teaspoon salt
1½ cups corn flake crumbs
½ cup butter

Mix all ingredients together. Pour in greased casserole. Mix corn flakes and butter, put over top and bake in medium oven for 45 minutes. Serves 16. Easily put into 2 casserole dishes and one frozen.

BUTCH ROBERSON/DOROTHY ROBERSON
CALF SCRAMBLE

POTATOES MICROWAVE

2 baking potatoes, scrubbed, and sliced 3/16″ thick
 (leave peeling on)
3 carrots cut ⅛ thick
4 celery stalks, sliced ¼″ thick
1 small can mushrooms
1½″ slice of Velveeta
Salt and pepper to taste
Enough milk to cover bottom of baking dish

Cover baking dish with saran wrap. Cook 20 to 25 minutes in microwave (May vary depending on type of Microwave)

WALLACE L. BOLDT

PARTY CORN CASSEROLE

3 cans cream corn
3 eggs, well beaten
3 small jars pimiento, diced
3 heaping tablespoons flour

2¼ cups milk
3 tablespoons butter
Salt and pepper to taste
Paprika, sprinkle on top

Mix all ingredients well. Pour into 2 quart casserole. Dot with butter, sprinkle top with paprika. Bake 1½ hours at 375 degrees. Should form pudding-like dish. Remove when bubbling and brown.

Can also use diced green peppers for variation or together with pimientos. Serves 12

JEWEL "JUDY" BRYANT

OKRA CREOLE

6 slices bacon
1 cup green onions, thinly sliced
⅓ cup green pepper, chopped
⅔ cup celery, chopped
2 cans (1 pound each) stewed tomatoes
1 bay leaf
1½ teaspoons salt
¼ teaspoon pepper
10 drops TABASCO sauce
2 cups okra, thinly sliced
Dash of gumbo filé
4 cups white Rice, cooked

Cook bacon until crisp. Remove, crumble and set aside. In bacon drippings, sauté onion, green pepper and celery until tender, about 5 minutes. Add tomatoes, bay leaf, salt, pepper and TABASCO. Simmer 10 minutes. Add okra and filé. Cook 5 minutes more or until okra is done. Sprinkle with bacon. Serves 8

LARRY BROWN
JUNIOR STEER RIDING

CORN CASSEROLE

1 can whole kernel corn
1 can cream style corn
1 stick margarine
1 cup saltine crackers, crumbled
3 eggs
1 cup Longhorn cheese, grated
¾ cup milk
½ onion, shredded
1 medium green pepper, diced
1 jar pimientos

Mix together and bake in oven 350 degrees for 1 hour.

MRS. RUBY PIRCHER
AUCTION SALES-BUYER

FRIED CORN

10 ears fresh corn (prefer white)
2 sticks butter
3-4 ounces cream or evaporated milk
Salt and pepper to taste
Pinch sugar

Cut corn off cob, take several passes with knife, cutting kernels several times. Then scrape cob with spoon. Melt butter in large skillet. Combine corn, salt, etc. Heat over low to medium heat. Mixture must be moist, add more cream if necessary (or water). Cook 20 to 30 minutes stirring often. This mixture freezes well.

GEORGE B. WOODS
AUCTION SALES

TEXAS FRIED CORN

1 pound salt pork, cut into pieces
12 ears fresh corn
Cream
Salt and pepper to taste

Shuck the corn. Put salt pork into skillet and fry. Cut tips of corn off, then scrape the cobs. Add corn to pork and fry over low heat until thickened. Add cream and simmer, allowing liquid to cook down. If cooking ahead of time, add more cream before serving and cook down.

MARY ELLEN PENWELL
AUCTION AND PROGRAM

FIESTA CORN

2 eggs
1 cup cornmeal, preferably fresh
1 16-ounce can cream style corn
¼ cup milk
⅓ cup butter, melted
½ teaspoon soda teaspoon salt
Dash of pepper
1 4-ounce can green chilies, chopped
½ pound Cheddar cheese, grated

Mix all ingredients except, cheese. When well blended, add cheese and bake in greased casserole dish at 350 degrees for 45 minutes.

J.R. HARTMAN/JENNIFER HARTMAN
CALF SCRAMBLE

CORN ON THE COB — CAMPFIRE STYLE

Brush each ear of corn with softened margarine. Wrap each piece of corn in a lettuce leaf and place on foil rectangles. Wrap tightly, twist foil at each end and grill on hot coals turning occasionally until tender.

CREAMY CORN

1 3-ounce package cream cheese, softened
¼ cup milk
1 tablespoon butter or margarine
½ teaspoon onion salt
1 16-ounce can whole kernel corn, drained

Combine cream cheese, milk, butter, and onion salt in a small sauce pan; cook over low heat, stirring often, until cheese melts. Stir in corn; cook stirring constantly until thoroughly heated. I have used frozen corn cooked according to package. Add the cheese, milk, butter, and onion salt. Mix gently until hot.

MRS. NAT V. (WINONA) PRASSEL

SWEET POTATO CASSEROLE

2½ cups sweet potato, mashed
1 cup sugar
2 beaten eggs
½ cup milk
¼ teaspoon nutmeg
½ teaspoon cinnamon
1 teaspoon vanilla

Mix together and pour into greased casserole dish. Bake 45 minutes at 300 degrees.

TOPPING:
¾ stick butter
½ cup sugar
½ cup nuts
¾ cup crushed corn flakes

Mix and sprinkle over potatoes. Put back in oven for 20 minutes longer.

SANDRA NAGEL
AUCTION SALES

SWEET POTATO PONE

3 cups raw sweet potatoes,
   cut up in small pieces (5 potatoes)
¾ cup brown sugar
⅓ cup molasses or dark corn syrup
3 eggs
¼ teaspoon salt
¼ -½ each, teaspoon cinnamon, cloves, all
   spice, nutmeg, depending on taste
1 stick butter softened
½ can evaporated milk

Put cut up potatoes in blender and combine with milk slowly, combine remaining ingredients with potatoes in blender.
Blend thoroughly. Grease 1½ to 2 quart pyrex dish. Bake
325 degrees for 2 hours.

GEORGE B. WOODS
AUCTION SALES

SWEET POTATO-COCONUT DISH

1 cup sweet potatoes, cooked and mashed
1 cup liquid from cooking potatoes
1-2 eggs
½ cup sugar
¼ cup milk
½ teaspoon salt
1 teaspoon vanilla
½ teaspoon lemon extract
½ cup coconut
2 tablespoons butter

Peel and cook sweet potatoes. Add eggs and beat. Add
sugar, butter, vanilla, and lemon extract, milk, salt, and
potato liquid. Mix well. For a smooth pudding, strain. Add
coconut and mix well. Place in a buttered baking dish. Bake
at 350 degrees about 45 minutes or until center is firm.

KATHY BENDER
AUCTION SALES
COORDINATOR

KBUC'S JALAPEÑO STUFFED POTATOES

4 large baking potatoes
4 jalapeños
¼ cup sour cream
4 ounces cream cheese
3 tablespoons jalapeño juice
¼ cup shredded mild Cheddar cheese
Salt and pepper to taste
1 cup sharp Cheddar cheese

Scrub potatoes and rub skins with cooking oil. Wrap in foil and bake at 425 degrees for 1½ hours or until done (if using microwave oven bake 4 minutes on each side). Slice potatoes lengthwise, use small spoon to gently scoop potatoes from skin being careful not to tear the skin. Place in mixing bowl. Slice jalapeños in half and remove all the seeds, dice finely and add to potato mixture; add sour cream, cream cheese, jalapeño juice and shredded mild cheddar cheese, salt and pepper to taste and mix well. Stuff potato skins with potato mixture. Top each potato with generous amount of sharp cheddar cheese. Bake at 350 degrees for 35 to 40 minutes or until cheese is melted.

Variations:
*If you desire a milder taste use less jalapeños.
*1 tablespoon freeze-dried finely chopped chives may be added to potato mixture.
*Use more sour cream if you desire a thinner consistency.
Serves 8.

HARRELL BANKS
VICE PRESIDENT AND GENERAL MANAGER
KBUC RADIO
LIFE MEMBER

POTATOES CAMP FIRE STYLE ౷

Wash potatoes and brush with oil. Wrap in two pieces of foil paper and place directly on coals, roast for approximately 40 minutes or until soft to the touch turning frequently.

LYONNAISE POTATOES

6 medium new potatoes   **2 tablespoons cooking oil**
4 tablespoons butter   **½ finely sliced onion**

Drop new potatoes into enough boiling water to cover. Cook covered until tender from 20 to 30 minutes. Remove skin while still hot, slice thinly. Sauté slices in two tablespoons butter and cooking oil until evenly browned. Sauté onions in remaining butter. Mix onions and potatoes gently. Season with salt, pepper, and parsley.

THOMAS REAVIS
INTERNATIONAL/MEXICO DAY

COWBOY TATORS

Irish potatoes, onions, salt and pepper, garlic salt. In skillet add ¼ inch cooking oil. Slice potatoes ⅛ inch thick, slice onions same way. Add to hot oil, brown for about 2-5 minutes, stirring constantly until a little brown. Add water,about 2 cups, and simmer on low heat until done — amount of each depends on how many people you want to serve.

NORMAN HITZFELDER
INTERNATIONAL/MEXICO DAY

BUFFET POTATOES

2 pounds frozen hash brown potatoes
½ cup melted margarine or butter
¼ cup onions, chopped
1 10¾-ounce can condensed cream of chicken soup
1 pint or 2 cups dairy sour cream
10 ounce grated Cheddar cheese
Bread crumbs

Thaw potatoes about 45 minutes. before assembling. Combine potatoes in a 3 quart 13x9x2 inch baking dish with butter, onion, soup, sour cream and cheese. Sprinkle with bread crumbs. Bake 1 hour at 350 degrees. Serves 8 to 10. If using Potatoes O'Brien, omit onions.

SWEET POTATO CASSEROLE

3 cups cooked mashed sweet potatoes
½ stick oleo
1 cup sugar
½ teaspoon salt
2 eggs
½ cup sweet milk
1 teaspoon vanilla

Whip with mixer and pour into greased baking dish. Top with the following mixture:

Topping:
1 cup brown sugar
⅓ cup flour
⅓ stick oleo
1 cup nuts, chopped (pecans, peanuts or coconut — I find that you can use less nuts than called for)

Blend above mixture and spread on potato casserole and bake in oven at 350 degrees for approximately 35 minutes. (I use less sugar).

MR. AND MRS. ELMO J. BOUCHILLON
GREENVILLE, MISSISSIPPI

SWEET POTATO CRISP

1 large sweet potato, 2 cups
1 cup sugar
½ stick butter
½ cup evaporated milk
¼ teaspoon salt
¾ teaspoon cinnamon
Dash nutmeg
Marshmallows

Butter baking dish (not with butter above). Shred sweet potato, spread in dish. Pour butter and milk over potato. Sprinkle salt, cinnamon and nutmeg over potato. Bake in 350 degree oven for 30 minutes, then put marshmallows on top of potato and bake in oven at 400 degrees for 10 min.

MRS. AL SODERSTROM
GO WESTERN

NEW ENGLAND YAM BAKE

1 20-ounce can pineapple slices
2 17-ounce cans yams, drained
¼ cup flour
3 tablespoons brown sugar
½ teaspoon cinnamon
⅛ teaspoon salt
¼ cup nuts, chopped
3 tablespoons margarine
1 cup miniature marshmallows

Drain pineapple, reserving ¼ cup syrup. Line sides of 10 x 6 inch baking dish with pineapples slightly overlapping and arrange yams in center. Pour pineapple syrup over yams. Combine flour, brown sugar, cinnamon, and salt. Cut in margarine until mixture resembles coarse crumbs, stir in nuts. Sprinkle over yams. Bake at 350 degrees for 25 minutes. Top with marshmallows; broil until lightly browned. Yield 6 to 8 servings.

MARY ELLEN PENWELL
AUCTION AND PROGRAM

CHEESE GRITS

Bring 3 cups of water to boil
Add:
¾ cup grits and cook 4 minutes
½ pound pasteurized process cheese spread
¾ stick oleo
2 eggs, well beaten
¾ teaspoon salt
1 tablespoon hot sauce

Bake for 45 minutes at 350 degrees. Serves 4-6.

SHERI/TERRY LOPER
ENTERTAINMENT

CHEESE GRITS

1½ cup grits
6 cups water
1½ sticks oleo
1 pound Velveeta
3 eggs beaten
11 drops TABASCO sauce

Add grits to boiling water. When thick, remove from heat and add butter, cheese, eggs, and TABASCO. Pour into baking dish and bake one hour at 250 degrees. This recipe also freezes well. Serves 12.

JIM TOBE ATKINSON
STEER RIDING

GARLIC GRITS

1 cup grits
4 cups water
1 teaspoon salt
1½ rolls garlic cheese
½ stick margarine
2 well beaten eggs

Cook grits until done. Add cheese and margarine and stir until cheese is melted. Fold in beaten eggs and pour into buttered casserole dish 9 × 13 × 2. Bake at 325 degrees for one hour.

MARY ELLEN PENWELL
AUCTION AND PROGRAM

SAVORY CABBAGE ROLLS

1 pound ground beef
1 cup cooked Rice
¼ cup onion, chopped
1 1-pound can tomatoes, cut up
10 cabbage leaves
1 tablespoon cornstarch
1 tablespoon cold water
Salt and pepper

Combine rice, beef, onion, salt, and pepper and ¾ cup of tomatoes; mix well. Steam cabbage leaves for 3 minutes or until just limp; drain. Spoon meat mixture onto leaves; roll each leaf around meat turning ends under. Place in large saucepan or Dutch oven. Pour remaining tomatoes over rolls. Cover, and simmer 30 minutes. Remove rolls to warm platter. Combine cornstarch and cold water; stir into liquid in saucepan. Cook and stir over medium heat until mixture thickens and boils. Serve with cabbage rolls.

ROBYN MERCHANT
SOUVENIR PROGRAM

SKILLET CABBAGE

1 large cabbage, coarsely shredded
3 large tomatoes, sliced
1 large onion, sliced
1 large green pepper, sliced
1 cup chopped celery
3 tablespoons butter
1 tablespoon sugar
1 teaspoon salt
½ teaspon pepper
¼ cup water

Combine all ingredients in a large skillet. Cover and simmer 30 minutes or until tender.

10-12 servings.

MARY FLOWERS
AUCTION SALES

STUFFED CABBAGE

1 large cabbage with nice leaves
2 sticks butter
1 clove garlic, minced
1 onion, chopped
1 stalk celery, chopped
1 teaspoon salt
2 packages RITZ crackers, crushed
6 eggs, beaten

Remove leaves (5 or 6) set aside. Chop remainder and boil in salted water until tender. Remove and drain, add the Ritz crackers. Sauté garlic, onion, and celery in the one stick of butter; add to the cooked cabbage. Add the 6 eggs and mix thoroughly. Arrange the leaves to where it looks like a cabbage head and fill it with the mixture. Place the cabbage in a cloth and tie. Place in pot with water to cover and boil it for 1 or 2 hours. Remove from water, slice and pour melted butter over top.

PATRICIA GARZA
INTERNATIONAL/MEXICO DAY

CABBAGE CASSEROLE

1 head of cabbage
Velveeta or American cheese (amount desired for layers)
1 can cream of chicken soup
1 can french fried onion rings

Dice cabbage in bite size pieces, steam 10 minutes. Layer cheese and cabbage alternately in buttered casserole ending with cheese. Mix soup with ¼ cup water, stir well, heat if desired and pour over casserole. Cover with onion rings, bake 350 degrees for 30 minutes.

Note: (Delicious and un-detectable as cabbage)

MICKEY HUBER
CALF SCRAMBLE

CREAMED CABBAGE WITH WALNUTS

1 medium head cabbage, shredded
¼ cup margarine
2 tablespoons corn starch
1 teaspon salt
¼ teaspoon pepper
2 cups milk
½ cup walnuts, chopped
1 cup cheese, shredded
2 tablespoons fine dry (toasted) bread crumbs

Cook cabbage in 1 quart boiling water with 1 teaspoon salt for 7 minutes. Meanwhile, melt margarine in saucepan over medium heat. Remove from heat. Blend in corn starch, salt, and pepper. Gradually blend in milk. Cook over medium heat, stirring constantly until mixture thickens and comes to a boil. Drain cabbage well. Arrange alternate layers of cabbage, walnuts, cheese, and sauce in greased 1½ quart casserole ending with layer of cheese. Sprinkle with bread crumbs. Bake at 450 degrees (very hot) oven about 10 minutes or until heated through and crumbs are lightly browned. Serves 6.

CALISTA MARSHALL
AUCTION SALES

"LAURAS WESTERN ONIONS"

2 cups sliced onions
½ cup water
1 tablespoon sugar
Enough vinegar to cover

Let stand in ice water or refrigerate 3 or 4 hours. Drain, add 1 cup mayonnaise, 1½ tablespoons celery seed and salt to taste.
This goes great with Barbecue.

FRITZ AND EMILIE TOEPPERWEIN
WESTERN PARADE

PEPPERS, ONIONS, AND TOMATOES

3 tablespoons olive oil
2 medium onions, chopped
1 clove garlic, finely chopped
4 green peppers, seeded and cut in strips
6 large tomatoes, cut up
1 teaspoon salt
½ teaspoon pepper
4 basil leaves, finely chopped

Put oil in saucepan and cover. Heat until hot. Add onions and garlic and sauté until golden brown. Add pepper strips; cook briskly until mixture begins to boil; lower heat and simmer for ½ hour. Serve hot as a side vegetable with any meat.

ANNE FLEENOR

ARTICHOKES

4 artichokes
½ cup water

Clean artichokes and cut the stalks short. Put ½ cup water and artichokes in pressure-cooker. Seal with lid and set top on 15 pounds pressure. Cook over medium heat until top jingles and then turn heat down and cook for 15 minutes. Remove from heat immediately and place sealed pot under cool water to slowly reduce the pressure. Remove top, to allow more pressure to be released. Then you may remove the lid. Serve with mayonnaise dip as an appetizer or vegetable for a meal.

Mayonnaise Dip:
1 cup mayonnaise
Lemon juice to taste
Garlic powder to taste

Let set in refrigerator while artichokes are cooking.

RITA WOLMA
AUCTION SALES

SWEET AND SOUR CARROTS

5 cups carrots, 2 bunches
Cook for few minutes, keep crisp, drain.
1 green pepper, diced
1 onion, chopped
1 can tomato soup
Heat next 5 ingredients until boil.
1 cup sugar
½ cup vinegar
½ cup salad oil
Dash of pepper
1 teaspoon Worcestershire

Turn off heat. Add all vegetables; pour into 2 quart bottles. Refrigerate. Will keep for a long time.

ELIZABETH JACOBS
INTERNATIONAL/MEXICO DAY

ORANGE GLAZED CARROTS

2 pounds carrots, sliced
1½ cups water
1 teaspoon salt
1 teaspoon orange rind, grated
¼ cup butter
¼ cup brown sugar
½ teaspoon cardamon

Boil sliced carrots in water and salt until tender. Add remaining ingredients. Stir until carrots begin to glaze. Serves 8.

CHERI HUGHES/BOBBY HUGHES
HORSE SHOW

BAKED SQUASH

8 to 10 small yellow squash
1 onion, chopped
1 teaspoon salt
½ teaspoon pepper
½ teaspoon oregano
Garlic salt to taste
3 tablespoons butter
1 egg beaten
¼ cup milk
½ cup bread crumbs
1 cup grated sharp cheese
¼ cup buttered bread crumbs

Cook squash with salt in small amount of water. When soft —drain off all water. Sauté onions in butter. Mash squash, add onions, egg, crumbs, and pepper. Top with cheese and buttered crumbs after pouring into baking dish. Bake at 350 degrees until set and lightly browned.

LIBBY JONES
AUCTION SALES

RECIPE FOR SOUTH TEXAS SQUASH

1½ pounds yellow squash, seeded and coarsely chopped
1 cup water
½ teaspoon salt
1 package medium sharp yellow cheese
3 teaspoons picante sauce

Put squash, water and salt in medium sauce pan. Cover and bring to boil for 15 minutes until tender. Pour squash in collander to drain. Put squash back in pan and mash to pulp. Add cheese and picante sauce. Place back on low heat and stir until cheese is melted.
Serves 4.

WYNN D. MILLER
AUCTION SALES

ITALIAN ZUCCHINI CRESCENT PIE

4 cups zucchini, thin sliced
1 cup onion, chopped (or less)
½ cup margarine/butter
2 tablespoons parsley
½ teaspoon salt
½ teaspoon pepper
¼ teaspoon oregano
¼ teaspoon garlic powder
¼ teaspoon basil
2 eggs, beaten well
8 ounces or more Mozzarella, shredded
8 ounce package crescent rolls
2 teaspoons prepared mustard

Preheat oven to 375 degrees (350 degree for glass). Cook squash and onion in margarine until tender, about 10 minutes. Stir in seasoning. In large bowl, blend egg and cheese. Stir in vegetable mix. Spread dough in ungreased 11 inch pie pan. Press over bottom and up the sides to form crust. Spread mustard on crust. Pour vegetable mix into crust. Bake 18-20 minutes at 375 degrees. Cover if crust gets too brown. Cool 10 minutes before serving.

STEVE SCHULTZ
AMBASSADORS

SQUASH

3 zucchini squash
3 yellow squash
Velveeta cheese

Cut the squash and put in a pan full of water. Cook until tender and drain. Add salt and pepper. Pour melted cheese over squash and serve.

RHONDA WOLFE
WESTERN COOKBOOK

PUERTA VALLARTA MEXICAN SQUASH

2 medium tomatoes, fresh
1 medium onion, chopped
Garlic salt
Oregano
Pepper
5 medium Mexican squash
1 package Provolone cheese
Butter

Sauce: Boil tomatoes until peels split. Put in blender with one medium chopped onion. Add garlic salt, oregano and pepper to taste. Blend for several minutes. (Keep it as crisp as possible). Layer in casserole dish, squash, sauce, and provolone cheese. Dot with butter. Bake 20 minutes at 350 degrees.

MARY ELLEN PENWELL
AUCTION SALES

GREEN BEANS WITH CHEESE

2 16-ounce cans whole beans green, drained
2 slices bacon, diced and cooked crisp. (reserve
    drippings)
2 tablespoons pimiento, chopped
½ teaspoon sweet basil
2 cups milk
2 tablespoons cornstarch
1 teaspoon chicken soup base
1 cup Monterrey Jack cheese

In saucepan bring milk to a slow boil. Add the cornstarch and soup base stirring constantly with a wire whisk until the mixture thickens. Add the cheese and simmer until cheese has melted. Pour ½ of the bacon drippings over the beans. Add the remaining ingredients, including the cheese sauce. Salt and pepper to taste and simmer until heated through. Serves 8.

EMMA BLAKEWAY

DILLY GREEN BEANS

2 packages frozen French-style green beans
3 ribs celery, chopped
2 tablespoons butter
2 tablespoons pimientos, chopped
4 ounce can mushrooms, sliced
1 can cream of mushroom soup
¼ cup almonds, sliced
1 package green onion dip mix
½ teaspoon dill seed

In saucepan cook beans, leaving a little crisp and drain. In a skillet sauté celery until soft. Add the remaining ingredients and simmer for 4 minutes. Pour over the beans and toss with a fork until heated through. Serves 8.

EMMA BLAKEWAY

BUTTER BEAN CASSEROLE

2 packages frozen butter beans
6 slices of bacon
⅓ cup celery, chopped
½ cup onion, chopped
2 tablespoons sugar
Salt and pepper to taste
¼ cup green pepper, chopped
2 cloves garlic, minced
2 tablespoons flour
1 cup or little more of canned tomatoes

Fry bacon — remove and cook chopped vegetables in bacon drippings. Add flour, tomatoes, salt and pepper and sugar. Add cooked butter beans, pour into casserole, heat 30 minutes in 350 degree oven. Can be prepared ahead of time and refrigerated.

EMMA BLAKEWAY

BEETS IN ORANGE SAUCE

½ cup butter or oleo
⅓ cup sugar
½ cup orange juice
2 teaspoons grated orange rind
1 teaspoon vinegar
1 tablespoon cornstarch
2 tablespoons cold water
3 cups cooked beets cubed or sliced

Combine butter, sugar, orange juice, rind and vinegar — bring to boil. Reduce heat and cook 5 minutes. Blend cornstarch with cold water and stir into sauce. Cook until thick, add beets and simmer 5 minutes. 6 Servings

EMMA BLAKEWAY

JALAPEÑO CHEESE SPINACH

3 packages frozen chopped spinach
4 tablespoons butter or oleo
2 tablespoons flour
2 tablespoons onion, chopped
½ cup canned evaporated milk
½ cup spinach liquid
½ teaspoon pepper
¾ tablespoon celery salt
¾ teaspoon garlic salt
½ teaspoon salt
6 ounce roll jalapeño cheese
1 teaspoon Worcestershire
½ teaspoon cayenne pepper if desired

Cook spinach until done, save liquid. Melt butter, then add flour, milk, and spinach liquid. Cut cheese in small pieces, stir until melted. Add spinach and put in buttered casserole and refrigerate overnight. Before baking, top with buttered bread crumbs. Cook at 350 degrees 20 or 30 minutes. Serves 6 to 8. Take out of refrigerator a couple of hours before cooking to get to room temperature.

EMMA BLAKEWAY

SPINACH GOURMET

1 pound fresh spinach
1 4-ounce can mushrooms, drained
1 teaspoon onion, minced
1 small clove garlic, minced
½ teaspoon salt
⅓ cup sour cream
1 tablespoon light cream
2 tablespoons butter

Cook spinach until done in salt water, chop and drain thoroughly. Blend spinach, mushrooms and seasonings in sauce pan. Blend sour cream, light cream and pour over spinach. Heat just to boiling point. You may use frozen spinach or substitute swiss chard.

EMMA BLAKEWAY

BAKED SPINACH

2 packages frozen spinach
2 cans cream of mushroom soup
½ cup sesame seeds
1½ teaspoons lemon juice
1 cup sour cream
½ teaspoon black pepper
1 can water chestnuts, sliced thin

Mix all together, put in casserole, pour Croutons on top and bake in oven for 30 or 40 minutes.

EMMA BLAKEWAY

SPINACH WITH HARD BOILED EGGS

2 pounds of fresh spinach
4 hard boiled eggs
¼ cup butter or oleo
3 tablespoons flour
½ cup coffee cream

Cook spinach in salt water until done, remove from fire and drain well. In sauce pan melt butter or oleo. Add flour and cream and cook until thick. Add spinach and mix well. Pour on to platter and slice hard boiled eggs on top.

EMMA BLAKEWAY

SPINACH CASSEROLE

2 10-ounce packages spinach, cooked

Then butter a 1½ quart casserole dish. Beat 2 eggs (in dish) and add:

1 cup milk
1 cup biscuit mix
½ teaspoon salt
1 cup cheese, Cheddar or Longhorn, grated

Beat all ingredients until smooth. Stir in cooked spinach and 1 cup grated Cheddar or Longhorn cheese. Bake at 325 degrees for 1 hour. Makes 6-8 servings.

ROBERT AND SHIRLEY WAGNER
GENERAL LIVESTOCK

GREEN VEGETABLE CASSEROLE

1 10-ounce package frozen baby lima beans
1 10-ounce package frozen green beans
1 10-ounce package frozen tiny peas

Cook lima beans in 1½ cups water for 10 minutes. Add green beans and cook 5 minutes, then add peas and cook until done. Drain.

Sauce:
1 cup mayonnaise
2 hard cooked eggs, chopped
1 small onion, chopped
1 teaspoon prepared mustard
2 tablespoons cooking oil
1 teaspoon Worcestershire
Dash of liquid hot sauce

Mix all ingredients and combine with vegetables. Better if left to marinate for several hours in refrigerator.

HENRY BEKEN, JR.
CALF SCRAMBLE

HOLE-IN-ONE-PEPPERS

Pre-cook 3 green pepper shells in boiling salt water, 5 minutes, drain. Mix can pork and beans, 3 wieners cut thin, 1 tablespoon grated onion, 2 tablespoons brown sugar, ¼ cup catsup, and 1 teaspoon mustard. Fill shells. Bake for 20 minutes.

LUCILLE JOHNSON
MORRIS JOHNSON'S MOTHER

POT LUCK VEGETABLE CASSEROLE

1 17-ounce can whole kernel corn
1 10-ounce package frozen cauliflower, cooked
1 10-ounce package frozen broccoli, cooked
1 4-ounce can sliced mushrooms
1 17-ounce can cream style corn
2 cups Swiss cheese, shredded
1 10¾-ounce can condensed cream style celery soup
2 tablespoons butter or margarine
1½ cups soft rye or white bread crumbs

Drain whole kernel corn, cooked cauliflower, cooked broccoli, and mushrooms. (Cut up large pieces of cauliflower).
Combine cream style corn, cheese, and soup. Fold in
drained vegetables. Turn into a 12x7x4-2 inch baking dish.
Melt butter, toss with crumbs. Sprinkle on top of mixture.
Bake uncovered in 375 degree oven for 35 minutes or until
hot.

JAN STANZESKI
JUNIOR STEER RIDING

CUCUMBERS-N-CREAM

3 medium cucumbers, peeled and sliced
1 pint sour cream
½ onion, chopped
3 tablespoons vinegar
Salt, pepper, buttermilk

Peel and slice cucumbers. Salt heavily and let set for at
least 30 minutes. Rinse well with cold water. Drain, add
chopped onion, pepper, vinegar, and sour cream. Add
enough buttermilk to make sauce smooth and creamy.

BETTY SMITH
AUCTION SALES

HERB STUFFED MUSHROOMS

16 large fresh mushrooms
½ cup butter
3 tablespoons shallots, chopped fine
1 cup fresh bread crumbs
½ cup parsley, chopped
1 teasoon salt
½ teaspoon pepper

Wipe mushrooms, remove stems and chop fine. Melt ¼ cup butter in skillet. Sauté mushroom caps briefly on both sides only until well coated. Remove to a flat pan. Melt remaining butter in same skillet and sauté mushroom stems and shallots a short time. Remove from heat and add remaining ingredients. Spoon mixture into mushroom caps. Bake at 350 degrees for 20 minutes. May be prepared early in the day, covered and refrigerated.

DEBBIE KANE
GO WESTERN

MARINATED CHERRY TOMATOES

1 pint cherry tomatoes, halved
1 bunch green onions, sliced
1 cup salad oil
⅓ cup vinegar
½ teaspoon basil leaves, dried
½ teaspoon oregano
½ teaspoon salt
¼ teaspoon pepper

Place tomatoes in bowl, sprinkle with onion. Combine remaining ingredients in a jar. Shake well, and pour over vegetables. Cover and chill 3 to 4 hours.

Serves: 6-8

Auction Sales

A highlight of the annual Livestock Show and Rodeo is the Auction Sale, held the last Friday of the ten-day event.

Each year this Sale offers citizens of our community an opportunity to encourage our youth to produce quality animals.

It also helps develop the interest of our youth in agribusiness, thus insuring the continuation of the basic principals on which our great country was founded.

"THEY ARE THE PRODUCERS OF TOMORROW"

JOHN A. BITTER, III
CHAIRMAN

OVEN BAG BRISKET

4-5 pounds boneless brisket
1 envelope dry onion soup mix
Garlic powder
Pepper
Worcestershire
2 cups beef bouillon

Place 1 tablespoon flour in bag. Add soup mix. Rub both sides of meat with garlic, pepper, and Worcestershire. Place bag in 2 inch deep pan. Pour broth on both sides of meat. Seal bag. Cut 6 slits on top. Roast at 300 degrees about 4 hours. Serves 12 to 15.

MRS. BOB FLOWERS
CALF SCRAMBLE

OVEN BAKED BRISKET

6-7 pounds brisket
Unflavored meat tenderizer
Seasoned salt
Garlic salt
Celery salt
¼ cup Worcestershire
3 tablespoons liquid smoke

Sprinkle both sides of brisket with meat tenderizer. Then shake liberal amounts of the seasoned salt, garlic salt, and celery salt on both sides of meat. Place in a shallow pan and pour over the Worcestershire and liquid smoke. Seal tightly with foil and bake 6-8 hours at 225 degrees. Cool slighlty and slice. Makes 6-8 servings.

ROBERT AND SHIRLEY WAGNER
GENERAL LIVESTOCK

OVEN BARBECUED BRISKET

5-8 pound brisket, market trimmed
Lemon pepper
Barbecue sauce

Season brisket generously with lemon pepper and wrap in foil. Let stand overnight. Bake in 225 degree oven (in foil) for 5 or 6 hours. Let cool slightly and slice. Mix 1 to 1½ cups barbecue sauce with 1 to 1½ cups liquid from brisket. Pour over sliced brisket, cover with foil and return to oven for 1 to 1½ hours. Serves 4 to 6 people.

RON SNOWDEN
JUNIOR STEER RIDING

OVEN BARBECUED BRISKET

1 6-7 pound brisket
Unflavored meat tenderizer
Seasoned salt
Garlic salt
Celery salt
¼ cup Worcestershire
3 tablespoons liquid smoke

Sprinkle both sides of meat with meat tenderizer. Then shake liberal amounts of seasoned salt, garlic salt and celery salt on both sides. Place meat in shallow baking dish and pour Worcestershire and liquid smoke over meat. Seal tightly with foil. Bake at 225 degrees for 6 to 8 hrs.

MRS. BILLE F. BUSBY
BOERNE, TEXAS

STEAK AND RICE

Round steak
Salt
Pepper
Garlic salt
Mazola Oil
Rice

Cut round steak into small strips, season to taste. Fill bottom of skillet and brown evenly on both sides. Remove meat. Drain all but about 2 tablespoons of oil and replace meat. Add 1 cup of water and bring to boil. Turn fire on low, cover, and simmer for 30 minutes. Occasionally check and make sure there is enough gravy, if not add a little more water. Serve with a bed of rice. Serves 4.

RHONDA WOLFE
WESTERN COOKBOOK

BEEF FUIJI

1 pound beef steak, sliced thin (slice while partly frozen)
    1 small onion, sliced
    2 tablespoons cooking oil
    ½ cup strong beef broth
    1 tablespoon cornstarch
    ¼ cup teriyaki sauce
    1 tablespoon cool water
    1 8-ounce can mushrooms sliced
    1 8-ounce can bamboo shoots (drained)
    1 8-ounce can water chestnuts, sliced
    ½ cup sliced green onions
    1 6-ounce package chinese peapods (thawed)
    1 1-pound can sliced peaches

Cook beef and onions in oil in skillet until meat browns (about 5 minutes). Add beef broth, cook about 5 minutes more. Combine cornstarch, teriyaki sauce, and water, stir in vegetables and peaches. Heat until hot. Serve with cooked rice. Egg rolls would add to meal.

HARRY BOGGESS

SHISHKABOB

1 cup of water
¼ cup red wine vinegar
1 tablespoon tomato paste
1 teaspoon garlic salt
½ teaspoon salt
1 teaspoon pepper
1 bay leaf
½ cup jalapeño peppers, chopped
1½ pound sirloin tip, cubed
2 tablespoons margarine

In a shallow dish prepare marinade by blending together water, vinegar, tomato paste, garlic salt, salt, and pepper. Add bay leaf and jalapeño peppers. Place meat in marinade, cover and refrigerate overnight. Remove meat from marinade and place on skewers. Cook until done, basting frequently with melted margarine. Serves six.

KENNETH/GLORIA WAGNER
AUCTION SALES

BEEF BURGUNDY

3 pounds beef tenderloin (sirloin)
1 cup burgundy wine
3 cups water
1 6-ounce can mushrooms Dash of garlic salt
10 beef bouillon cubes
1 tablespoon dry onion soup mix

Remove all fiber from meat and cut into link strips. Place beef in a preheated skillet 375 degrees and stir the meat until browned on all sides. Add ½ cup wine, water, bouillon cubes, onion soup mix, and ½ can mushrooms. Simmer the mixture until meat is tender (about 45 minutes, maybe even an hour). Just before serving, add ½ cup wine and ½ can mushrooms.
Serve in toasted bread cups or over rice. Serves 6 to 8.

PRISCILLA MALONE
INTERNATIONAL/MEXICO DAY

LONE STAR ROLLATINE OF BEEF

2 pounds sirloin steak, cut thin
1 cup dry bread crumbs
6 slices bacon — half cooked drained and crumbled
1 teaspoon prepared mustard
2 tablespoons butter, melted
1 tablespoon parsley, minced
1½ cups Lone Star Beer
¼ cup flour
1½ teaspoon salt
½ teaspoon pepper
2 tablespoons salad oil
2 onions sliced
¼ teaspoon thyme

Pound meat as thin as possible. Cut in six oblong pieces. Mix bread crumbs, bacon, mustard, butter, and parsley. Add enough beer to moisten mix. Spread on steak. Roll up tightly. Tie with thread. Mix flour with a little salt and pepper. Flour steak rolls. Heat oil in skillet. Brown onions and rolls. Add remaining Lone Star, salt, pepper and thyme. Cover. Cook one hour on low heat, or till tender. Turn rolls twice. Serves six.

BILL ROTH
AUCTION SALES

MEXICAN STEAK

1-2 pound round steak
2 tablespoons oil
2 large tomatoes, sliced
4 chilies, chopped
1 medium onion, sliced
1 can tomato sauce
Salt, pepper, garlic to taste

Cut steak into serving pieces, heat oil, sear steak on botn sides. Drain oil. On top of steak pour tomato sauce, and layer tomatoes, chilies and onions, add seasonings. Cover and simmer slow for about 45 minutes or until steak is tender. Serve with rice.

JAMES SMITH
GO WESTERN

QUICK AND EASY PEPPER STEAK

1½ pounds sirloin steak, ½″ thick
½ teaspoon salt
2 medium onions, chopped (about one cup)
1 cup beef broth
3 tablespoons soy sauce
1 clove garlic, minced
2 green peppers, cut into 1″ pieces
2 tablespoons cornstarch
¼ cup cold water
2 tomatoes, peeled and cut into eighths
3 to 4 cups hot cooked rice

Trim fat and bone from meat; cut meat into 4 to 6 serving pieces. Grease large skillet lightly with fat from meat. Brown meat thoroughly on one side, turn and season with ¼ teaspoon salt. Brown other side of meat; turn and season with remaining ¼ teaspoon salt. Push meat to one section. Add onion; cook and stir until tender. Stir in broth, soy sauce and garlic. Cover; simmer 10 minutes or until meat is tender. Add green peppers. Cover; simmer 5 minutes. Blend cornstarch and water; stir gradually into meat mixture. Cook, stirring constantly, until mixture thickens and boils. Boil and stir 1 minute. Add tomatoes; heat through. Serve over rice. 4 to 6 servings.

ROBYN MERCHANT
AUCTION AND PROGRAM

16Hoofbeats

Hoofbeats

ANTICUCHOS

1 cup water
¼ cup red wine
1 tablespoon tomato paste
1 teaspoon garlic salt
½ teaspoon salt
1 teaspoon pepper
1 bay leaf
½ cup chopped jalapeño peppers
1½ pounds cubed sirloin tip (or any tender cubed cut of meat)
2 tablespoons oleo

In a shallow dish prepare marinade by blending together water, vinegar, tomato paste, garlic salt, salt and pepper. Add bay leaf and jalapeño peppers. Place meat cubes in marinade. Cover and refrigerate overnight. Remove meat from marinade and thread on skewers. Broil approximately 20 to 30 minutes or until meat is cooked to taste. Baste frequently with melted oleo. Serves six.

DOTTI BIEDIGER
AUCTION SALES

DONALD DHU'S FAJITAS (GREEK ORIGIN)

2-3 pounds of fajitas
1 stick of margarine
2-3 tablespoons lemon juice
3 cloves garlic, minced
¼ medium size onion, minced
Oregano leaves sprinkled on top
Salt and pepper to taste
4-5 sliced potatoes (if desired)

Bake in covered dish for 1 hour at 350 degrees. Add sliced potatoes and continue cooking until potatoes are done.

NINA COWAN
INTERNATIONAL/MEXICO DAY

ANTICUCHOS

1 cup red wine vinegar
3 cups water
2 to 3 serrano peppers
Salt to taste
Whole black peppercorns to taste
2 to 3 cloves garlic
Generous pinch oregano
Generous pinch cumin
2 pounds cubed beef
Bacon drippings

Combine first eight ingredients in blender and blend thoroughly. Place meat in glass dish and cover with marinade. Marinate several hours or overnight. Place beef cubes on skewers. Add bacon drippings to taste to remaining marinade and use to baste meat while it is cooking over hot coals. Bacon drippings add flavor and make the meat smoke.

ESTER GEORGES

FAJITAS

2 pounds skirt steak
Marinade:
1 can Salsa Verde
1 bottle zesty Italian dressing
1 small onion, chopped
1 clove garlic, chopped
1 Jalapeño, optional

Cut meat into 2 inch slivers. Marinate overnight. Cook on Bar-B-Que grill basting often. Serve taco style in warm flour tortillas. Top with avocado and picante sauce.

DOROTHY FERGUSON/MONTY FERGUSON
ENTERTAINMENT

BEEF ROLL-UP

6 beef cube steaks
1 teaspoon salt
¼ teaspoon pepper
¾ cup French dressing
1½ cup carrots, shredded
¾ cup onion, finely chopped
¾ cup green pepper, finely chopped
¾ cup celery, finely chopped
¼ cup water
6 slices bacon

Sprinkle meat with the salt and pepper. Marinate in french dressing for 30 to 60 minutes at room temperature. In saucepan, simmer vegetables, covered, in the water until tender and crisp, about 7 to 8 minutes; drain. Drain steaks. Place about ⅓ cup vegetable mixture on each steak. Roll up in jelly-roll fashion. Cut bacon slices in half crosswise. Wrap two half-pieces bacon around each roll-up; secure with wooden picks. Grill steaks over hot coals, or broil 3 to 4 inches from heat for 20 to 25 minutes, turning steaks occasionally. Makes 6 servings. Great for outdoor picnic. Can be prepared early and cooked later.

BEVERLY ADAMS GRAY
QUEENS CONTEST
CHAIRMAN

CARNE QUISADA

2 tablespoons bacon grease
1 large onion, chopped
1½ pounds of cubed beef
2 tablespoons flour
1 tablespoon chili powder
1 jalapeño pepper, chopped
1 clove garlic
1 teaspoon cumin powder
Salt and pepper to taste

Brown beef in bacon grease, add chili powder, jalapeno pepper, garlic, cumin powder, onion and flour, mix. Add enough water to cover and cook till tender on low heat (I cook in a crock pot)

KAYE BOWIE
JOHN H. SAVAGE III
AUCTION SALES

STEAK DIANE

1 clove garlic, minced
3 tablespoon oil
4 ribeye steaks
3 tablespoons butter
½ cup green onions

6 tablespoons brandy
5 tablespoon Worcestershire
2 teaspoon mustard
1 box fresh mushrooms, sliced

Heat oil in electric skillet, chafing dish or wok at the table. Saute garlic quickly. Discard. Brown the steaks in the oil. Remove steaks and add the butter saute the green onions lightly. Return the steaks to the skillet and on high heat add the brandy and light. When the flame dies down add remaining ingredients and simmer for about 5 minutes. Serve over wild rice.

PATRICIA AND JESSE GARZA

CARNE GUISADA

2 to 3 pounds round steak, cubed
1 tablespoons vegetable oil (small amount)
1 tablespoon flour
2 tablespoons bell pepper, chopped
2 tablespoons onions, chopped
1 to 2 cloves garlic, chopped
¼ to ½ teaspoon cumin
⅛ teaspoon pepper
Salt to taste
½ can tomato sauce (or enough to color)
½ can Ro-Tel Tomatoes with Green Chilies

Brown the round steak in a small amount of cooking oil. After the meat is browned, coat with flour and add the remaining ingredients with about ½ cup of water. Cook about 30 to 45 minutes or until the meat and other ingredients are done and the sauce becomes thick.

MARY ELLEN PENWELL
AUCTION SALES

BARBECUED PINWHEELS

2½-3 pound round steak, ½ inch thick, trimmed and
   boned
Salt and pepper
8 bacon slices
*Barbecue sauce

Sprinkle meat with salt and pepper, pound into meat with
mallet. Lay bacon slices on meat along short side. Roll up
starting at long side. Tie with string at each bacon strip. Cut
into 8 pieces. Place 2 pinwheels on each skewer. Broil 25-30
minutes or until desired doneness, turning and brushing
after with sauce.

*Barbecue sauce
½ medium onion, chopped
2 tablespoons butter
¼ cup brown sugar
1 tablespoon dry mustard
½ or 1 tablespoon Worcestershire
Ketchup, salt, pepper

Saute onion in butter until tender; add remaining ingredients and enough ketchup to make a sauce, about a cup or
more. If necessary, thin sauce with beer.

JAMES SMITH
AUCTION SALES

BEAN BURGERS

1 pound ground beef
1 can 8½ ounces refried beans
½ cup shredded Cheddar cheese
1 package taco seasoning
¼ cup water

Mix. Shape into 8 patties and saute in butter for about 8 to
10 minutes per side.

SHIRLEY AND LARRY SIMPSON
WESTERN COOKBOOK

BEEF STROGANOFF

2 pounds sirloin tip (cut into cubes of about ½ to 1" thick)
(Meat may also be cut into strips about 2" long cut
across the grain)
½ teaspoon salt
½ teaspoon pepper
1 stick butter
4 green onions, chopped
5 tablespoons flour
1 can beef broth
1 teaspoon Dijon Mustard
1 box fresh mushrooms, sliced
⅓ cup dairy sour cream
⅓ cup sauterne

Cut meat across the grain in strips about 2 inches long.
Sprinkle ½ teaspoon salt and pepper. Heat skillet, add butter let melt, saute meat, push to one side add onions, cook
until transparent. Add five tablespoons flour in drippings
then add the can of beef broth, bring to boil stirring constantly. Stir in 1 teaspoon Dijon Mustard, turn heat down,
cover and simmer one hour until meat is tender. Five
minutes before serving, add sliced mushrooms, sour cream,
and sauterne.

PATRICIA AND JESSE GARZA
INTERNATIONAL/MEXICO DAY

TEXAS RANCH POT LUCK

Saute in oleo a large onion and green pepper, chopped.
Brown two pounds of ground beef.

Add:
2 cans whole kernel corn
2 cans chili with beans or plain
2 cans tamales (cut into fourths)
2 cups cheese, shredded
1 small can ripe olives

Put in casserole dish and sprinkle cheese and olives between layers. Heat in oven until bubbly. (Also freezes well.)

TRAIL RIDERS

PEPPER STEAK AND RICE

1 pound lean beef round steak, cut ½ inch thick
1 tablespoon paprika
2 tablespoons butter or margarine
2 cloves garlic, crushed
2 large fresh tomatoes, cut in eighths
1½ cup beef broth
1 cup green onions, sliced, including tops
2 green peppers, cut in strips
2 tablespoons cornstarch
¼ cup water
¼ cup soy sauce
3 cups hot cooked rice

Pound steak to ¼ inch thickness. Cut into ¼ inch wide strips. Sprinkle meat with paprika and allow to stand while preparing other ingredients. Using a large skillet, brown meat in butter. Add garlic and broth. Cover and simmer 40 minutes. Stir in onions and green peppers. Cover and cook 15 minutes more. Blend cornstarch, water, and soy sauce. Stir into meat mixture. Cook, stirring, until clear and thickened — about 2-5 minutes. Add tomatoes and stir gently. Serve over beds of fluffy rice. Makes 6 servings.

ROBERT AND SHIRLEY WAGNER
GENERAL LIVESTOCK

HOBO STEAKS

4 chopped sirloin or ground beef patties, 1 inch thick
1 medium onion, diced
1 jar mushrooms, sliced
1 small bell pepper, diced
4 medium potatoes, diced
Salt and pepper

Tear 4 large pieces heavy duty aluminum foil. Place one meat pattie in center of each foil piece. Evenly divide remaining ingredients on top of meat patties. Salt and pepper to taste. Wrap each hobo steak in tent fashion. Place on bar-b-que grill for 1 hour or bake in oven at 350 degrees for 30 to 45 min.

LYNNE BRIGGS

ROUND-UP TIME STEAK AND CHILI GRAVY

2 pounds round steak (cut in pieces)
1 teaspoon salt — pepper
1 egg beaten with 2 tablespoons water
1 cup corn flakes, finely crushed
¼ cup vegetable oil
1 medium onion, slice
1 small green pepper
2 8-ounce cans tomato sauce
¾ cup water
1 teaspoon chili powder

Pound steak with mallet (or saucer). Sprinkle with salt and pepper. Dip in egg, then into crushed corn flakes mixed with chili powder. Heat oil in skillet and brown meat on both sides. Add onion and green pepper, pour in tomato sauce mixed with water. Cover and simmer 1½ hours until tender.

BETTIE RUTLEDGE
SOUVENIR PROGRAM

ROUND STEAK AND GRAVY

1 large round steak
3 tablespoons flour
1 large onion, sliced
1 bell pepper, sliced thin
1 pod of garlic, minced
1 can tomatoes
Salt to taste
Pepper to taste
Worcestershire to taste
1 cup water

Cut round steak and brown in Wesson oil. When brown, add flour and brown. Add water, tomatoes, and other ingredients. Cover and simmer until meat is tender.

PAT McGUIRE
JUNIOR STEER RIDING

JALAPEÑO CORNBREAD W/GROUND MEAT

1 cup yellow cornmeal
1 cup milk
2 eggs
¾ teaspoon salt
½ teaspoon soda
½ cup bacon drippings

1 1-lb, 1-ounce can
  cream style corn
1 pound ground beef
1 large onion
1 pound yellow cheese
5 canned jalapeños

Combine cornmeal, milk, beaten eggs, salt, soda, bacon drippings, and cream style corn. Mix well and set aside. Brown ground beef until crumbly and drain well on paper towels. Pour half of cornbread batter into well greased cast iron skillet or baking dish that has been dusted with cornmeal. Sprinkle grated cheese evenly over batter. Sprinkle chopped onion and jalapenos evenly over meat. Top with remaining cornbread batter. Bake at 350 degrees F. about 50 minutes. Serve hot. Serves 6 to 8.

VIVION COLLIER
SOUVENIR PROGRAM

QUICK COWBOY MEAT PIE

1 pound ground meat
⅓ onion, chopped
1 teaspoon salt
⅛ teaspoon garlic salt
⅛ teaspoon pepper
1 can cream of mushroom soup
10 biscuits (homemade or canned flakey)

Brown onions and meat in 10 inch iron skillet, mixing in salt, garlic salt, and pepper. Add mushroom soup and water (as directed on the can); let simmer for five minutes. Place biscuits on top of meat and bake at 400 degree oven for 10 minutes or until biscuits are brown on top. Can be cooked in dutch oven on the trail.

JIM DOCKERY
JUNIOR STEER RIDING
CHAIRMAN

TAMALE PIE

1 pound ground beef
1 medium onion, chopped
1 can of tomatoes
1 small clove of garlic, minced
1 green pepper, chopped
1 8-ounce can tomato sauce
Salt and pepper
1 12-ounce can whole-kernel corn
1 4½ ounce can taco sauce
2 teaspoons chili powder
1 cup pitted black olives
6 tablespooons yellow cornmeal
1 cup sharp cheddar cheese, diced

Put first 7 ingredients in large skillet, cover and simmer 10 to 15 minutes. Add corn and next 3 ingredients. Gradually stir in cornmeal, bring to boil and cook, stirring until thickened. Simmer, uncovered about 15 minutes. Stir in cheese and add salt and pepper to taste. Serve with lettuce salad.

BETTIE RUTLEDGE
AUCTION SALES

JACK SELLER'S SPECIAL

1 pound of ground meat
1 pound of Hot Owens Country style sausage
⅓ pound of Velveeta cheese
1 box of white melba rounds

Cook meat and sausage together, drain grease, let stand for a few minutes. Add Velveeta cheese and mix well. Spread on white melba rounds, and put them on a cookie sheet and freeze.

When ready to use, heat at 350 degrees for 10 minutes, top with a slice of jalapeño on each round, Yummy! Yummy!

JACK SELLERS
WESTERN PARADE

OVEN PORCUPINES

1 pound ground beef
½ cup rice, uncooked
½ cup water
⅓ cup onion, chopped
1 teaspoon salt
½ teaspoon celery salt

⅛ teaspoon garlic powder
⅛ teaspoon pepper
1 15-ounce can tomato sauce
1 cup water
2 teaspoons Worcestershire

Heat oven to 350 degrees. Mix meat, rice, water, onion, salts, garlic powder and pepper. Shape mixture into balls. Place in ungreased baking dish. Stir together remaining ingredients; pour over meatballs. Cover with aluminum foil and bake 45 minutes. Uncover and bake 15 minutes longer.

BARBARA SIMON
JUNIOR STEER RIDING

SMOTHERED STEAK — ROAST

1 boneless round steak (2½ pound), cut into serving pieces
Seasoned salt to taste — pepper to taste
All-purpose flour
¼ cup vegetable oil
1 teaspoon garlic salt
1 tablespoon Worcestershire
Dash of hot sauce
2 tablespoons red wine vinegar
2 cups plus 2 tablespoons of beef bouillon
4 green pepper rings

Sprinkle steak with seasoned salt and pepper; dredge in flour. Heat oil in a large heavy iron skillet; brown meat on both sides. Combine 3 tablespoons flour, garlic salt, Worcestershire, hot sauce, wine vinegar, and 1 tablespoon beef bouillon; stir until smooth. Add remaining bouillon stir until well blended. Pour mixture over steak, and top with green pepper rings. Cover and cook over low heat 50 to 60 minutes or until tender. Yield: 6 to 8 servings.

MRS. NAT V. (WINONA) PRASSEL

PICADILLO

1 pound ground beef
2-3 new potatoes
1 16-ounce can tomatoes
3 green onions
½ cup pimiento
2½ cloves of garlic
1 6-ounce can tomato paste
2 jalapenos (with seeds)

1 small box raisins
½ teaspoon oregano
½ teaspoon chili powder
¼ teaspoon cumin
¼ cup green olives, sliced
¼ cup cocktail onions
1 package sliced almonds

Simmer ground beef in electric skillet. Cover with water for 30 minutes at 250 degrees. Chop other ingredients very fine, add to simmering ground beef and cook 2 hours with cover

Serve warm with tostados or any chips.

GEORGE HAYS
GO-WESTERN
CHAIRMAN

SWISS STEAK

¼ cup all-purpose flour
½ teaspoon salt
¼ teaspoon pepper
2 pounds beef round steak
  1" thick
2 tablespoons shortening

1 8-ounce can tomatoes
½ cup onion, minced
¼ cup green pepper, minced
½ teaspoon salt
⅛ teaspoon pepper

Stir together flour, salt and pepper. Sprinkle one side of meat with half the flour mixture; pound in. Turn meat and pound in remaining flour mixture. Cut meat into 6 serving pieces. Melt shortening in large skillet; brown meat over medium heat, about 15 minutes. Cover tightly; simmer 1 hour. Add small amount of water if necessary. Mix remaining ingredients; pour over meat. Cover tightly; simmer 30 minutes or until tender.

6 servings.

ROBYN MERCHANT
SOUVENIR PROGRAM

TAMALE PIE

2 tablespoons salad oil
2 medium onions, chopped
2 cloves garlic, chopped
1½ pounds hamburger
Cook 15 minutes.

Add:
1 2½-pound can whole tomatoes
1 2-pound can whole kernel corn
4 teaspoons chili powder, dissolved in water
1 cup milk
1 cup cornmeal
1 can pitted olives
1 tablespoon salt
Grated cheese

Cook mixture together until cornmeal is done, about 15 minutes. Bake at 300 degrees ½ hour. Cover with grated cheese and bake 10-15 minutes longer or until cheese is metled.

KEN LANGHAM
ENTERTAINMENT

WATSATTA

2 pound ground meat
2 onions, chopped
Brown together and drain.

Add:
1 can tomato soup
1 can mushroom soup
1 pound mild Cheddar, grated
Salt and pepper to taste
¼ pound egg noodles, cooked

Combine all ingredients with the cooked egg noodles. Put in casserole dish and top with buttered cracker crubms. Bake in 350 degree oven for 30 minutes.

LAURIE LEA GULLEY
JUNIOR STEER RIDING

STUFFED BELL PEPPERS

6 medium green peppers
3-4 tablespoons shortening
¼ cup onion, finely chopped
¾ or 1 pound group beef
2 slices bread
1 teaspoon salt
¼ teaspoon black pepper
¼ teaspoon celery seed
1 teaspoon Worcestershire
Tomato sauce over top, optional

Cover peppers with boiling water and simmer about 5 minutes. Drain and remove caps and seeds from peppers. Melt shortening in pan and fry the onions until lightly brown. Meanwhile, salt and pepper the meat and when onions look browned, add to pan and cook meat until it loses its color. Break up the bread in small bits and add with the rest of the seasonings and stir a couple of times. Cook just a bit more. Cup of rice may also be added. Set the pepper cups upright in a pan or casserole dish and fill with the meat mixture. Put about 2 tablespoons water in pan or casserole dish. Bake in moderate oven for about 45 minutes at 350 degrees.

Variation: When meat is being cooked, boil some rice and if you want just add to the mixture.
The tomato sauce makes it tasty when putting in the oven; just pour over tops of peppers.

LUCILLE JOHNSON

STUFFED BEEF LOG (MEATLOAF)

2 pounds hamburger
½ cup onion, chopped
1 egg beaten
½ cup oatmeal, uncooked
½ cup milk
Salt and pepper

Mix well and shape into rectangle on wax paper (approximately 1 inch from edges of paper, ½ inch thick by approximately 10 inches.)

½ pound bulk pork sausage
1 cup bread crumbs
¼ cup onion, minced
1 medium potato, grated
1 egg, beaten
Salt

Mix well and spread over beef in thin layer. Roll up and place (seam side down) in loaf pan. Bake at 300 degrees for 1½ hours. Serves approximately 8.

CHERI HUGHES/BOBBY HUGHES
CHAIRMAN
ENTERTAINMENT

S.O.S.

1 pound hamburger meat
Milk
Flour
Bread

Brown hamburger meat, drain grease. Cover meat with flour, add about ¼ cup of milk. Mix all together to make gravy. If too dry add small amounts of milk. Serve on toasted bread.

RHONDA WOLFE
WESTERN COOKBOOK

SOMBRERO PIE

½ **pound ground beef**
½ **pound ground lean pork**
1 **large onion, thinly sliced**
2½ **cups tomato juice**
1 **10-ounce package frozen whole kernel corn**
1 **to 2 tablespoons chili powder**
1 **teaspoon salt**
¼ **teaspoon pepper**
Cornmeal pastry (below)

Cook ground beef, pork, and onion in large skillet until meat is browned, stirring often to crumble meat; drain. Add tomato juice, corn, chili powder, salt, and pepper; mixing well. Bring to a boil — reduce heat and simmer for 10 minutes. Spoon mixture into a greased 12x8x2 baking dish. Top with cornmeal pastry, sealing and fluting edges. Bake at 400 degrees for 30 to 35 minutes or until golden brown. Yields: 6 servings.

Cornmeal Pastry:
1 **cup flour**
¼ **cup cornmeal**
½ **teaspoon salt**
⅓ **cup, plus 1 tablespoon shortening**
3 **tablespoons cold water**

Combine flour, cornmeal, and salt. Cut in shortening until mixture resembles coarse meal. Sprinkle evenly with cold water and stir with a fork until dry ingredients are moistened. On a lightly floured surface, roll pastry to a 12x8 inch rectangle. Yield: pastry for one 12x8x2 inch casserole dish.

BETTIE RUTLEDGE
WESTERN COOKBOOK

MEXICAN CASSEROLE

2 pounds hamburger meat
1 can cream of mushroom soup
1 can cream of chicken soup
1 can evaporated milk
1 can enchilada sauce
1 pound Velveeta cheese
1 large package soft corn tortillas
2 jalapeños

Brown meat, then add other ingredients. Tear tortillas in little strips. Cook in oven at 350 degrees for 20 minutes.

MRS. AL SODERSTROM
GO WESTERN

BAR-B-QUE MEAT BALLS

Season 2 pounds ground chuck with onion powder, garlic salt, salt, and pepper to taste. Grate 2 potatoes and add to meat. Form into small balls and brown in butter or margarine. Drain well.

Add: 1 cup grape jelly
1 bottle chili sauce

Simmer on stove or bake in oven until thick. These can be made ahead and frozen for a month. Thaw and serve with picks.

SHIRLEY SCHREIBER
AUCTION SALES

MEAT BALLS CON QUESO

1½ pounds ground beef
1½ cups fresh bread crumbs
⅓ cup onion, minced
⅓ cup milk
3 tablespoons parsley, chopped
¼ teaspoon pepper
1 egg
3 tablespoons salad oil
1 16-ounce package Velveeta cheese, cubed
1 4-ounce can green chilies, minced
1 1¼-ounce package taco seasoning mix

In medium bowl mix ground beef, bread crumbs, onion, milk, parsley, pepper and egg. Shape into 1-inch balls. In skillet, over medium-high heat, in hot salad oil, cook meat balls, a few at a time, until well browned. Remove them as they brown. Spoon off fat and wipe skillet clean. In same skillet, over low heat, stir cheese, green chilies with their juice, taco seasoning mix and ¾ cup water, until cheese is melted. Return meat balls to skillet; cover and simmer until heated thoroughly.

ROBYN MERCHANT.
SOUVENIR PROGRAM

HARD TIMES — BEEF AND BEANS
(Born out of necessity)

1 pound dried pinto beans
3 medium onions, chopped
2 green peppers, chopped
1 pound ground meat
¼ pound oleo
1 teaspoon chili powder
1 teaspoon garlic salt
1 tablespoon Worcestershire
½ teaspoon mustard powder
½ teaspoon TABASCO sauce

Soak beans overnight. Cook until barely tender. Saute onions, green pepper, and meat in oleo. Add to beans. Add seasoning, simmer 4 hours. Serve with tortillas.

BETTIE RUTLEDGE
GO WESTERN

BURGER STACK UPS

1½ pounds ground meat
2 eggs, slightly beaten
¼ cup chopped onion
¼ cup catsup
1½ teaspoons salt
Dash pepper
1 3-ounce can, broiled, sliced, mushrooms, drained
Melted butter
6 thin slices onion, centers removed
6 thin slices tomato
6 slices process American cheese

Combine meat, eggs, onion, catsup, and seasonings. Mix thoroughly. Form in 12 thin patties. Place mushrooms on half the patties leaving border on meat. Top with remaining patties, sealing edges well. Place on grill and top each with onion and tomato slices. Brush well with butter. Add dampened hickory to coals and close smoker hood. Smoke-cook about 45 minutes. Add cheese last 8 minutes. Serve on toasted buns. Makes 6 servings.

RICKY WARE, SR.
KBUC — LIFE MEMBER

POLISH SAUSAGE N' BEER ℘

1 tablespoon flour
1 pound Polish sausage
4 peppercorns
1 can beer

Preheat oven to 350 degrees. Shake 1 tablespoon flour in small size oven cooking bag and place in two-inch deep roasting pan. Put sausage into bag add peppercorns and beer. Close bag with twist tie and make six half-inch slits in top. Cook 45 minutes. Serves 4.

PORK CHOPS MEXICANA

6 lean pork chops
1 teaspoon salt
¾ cup rice, uncooked
½ package taco seasoning mix
1 can tomato sauce
1½ cups water
1 cup Cheddar cheese, shredded
1 medium green pepper, cut into rings

Brown chops and arrange in pan. Salt. Sprinkle rice around chops. Combine taco seasoning with tomato sauce and water and pour over chops. Cover tightly with aluminum foil and bake at 350 degrees for 1¼ hours. Remove from oven 10 minutes before done and sprinkle with cheese and green pepper rings. Cover and continue cooking until cheese melts.

ANNE FLEENOR

UPSIDE DOWN SUPPER

1½ cup cooked ham, cubed
1 cup cooked lima beans
1 8-ounce can cream-style corn
1 cup shredded Cheddar cheese
2 tablespoons onion, minced
1 teaspoon Worcestershire
⅔ cup biscuit baking mix
⅓ cup cornmeal
1 egg
¼ cup milk

Heat oven to 400 degrees. Mix ham, beans, corn, cheese, onion, and Worcestershire. Turn into greased 1½ quart casserole dish. Cover, bake 15 minutes. Mix remaining ingredients; spoon over hot meat mixture, spreading batter evenly to edge of casserole. Bake uncovered 20 minutes or until lightly browned. Cut into wedges; invert each onto plate. Serves 4 to 6.

GERTRUDE BURRIS

FIESTA

Meat Sauce:

1 large onion	2 teaspoons chili powder
2 pounds ground meat	2 teaspoons oregano
2 cloves garlic, minced	2 teaspoons salt
15 ounces tomato sauce	2 teaspoons accent
2+ 8-ounce cans water	4 tablespoons sugar
3 small cans tomato paste	

Brown onion and meat, drain, and add other ingredients. Simmer 40 minutes.

Rice cooked according to directions.

Following goes on plate in this order

4 packages regular size cornchips (crushed in sack)

Meat sauce

1 pound mild cheddar cheese, grated
1½ heads lettuce, chopped
5 tomatoes, chopped
1 green bell pepper, finely chopped
2 onions, chopped
2 avocados (or guacamole)
1 picante sauce
2 large sour cream

PEGGY AND JIM DOCKERY
JUNIOR STEER RIDING

PORK CHOP CASSEROLE

6 or more pork chops (½ inch thick)
2 cans tomato sauce, small
2 cloves garlic, pressed
5 large potatoes, cut as for french fries
1 large onion, chopped

Arrange ingredients in oblong casserole in this manner. Lay pork chops in bottom, put onions, garlic and potatoes over them and sprinkle with salt and pepper. Pour 2 cans tomato sauce over top. Refill cans with water and pour over top. Bake at 400 degree oven 1 hour, or more, until potatoes pierce easily with fork.

CREOLE EGG PLANT AND GROUND BEEF CASSEROLE

1 egg plant
1 tablespoon chili powder
1 small can tomato sauce
1 pound ground meat
1 cup Cheddar cheese, shredded

Fry floured egg plant in oil. Put each piece as they are fried in a small loaf pan. In another skillet fry ground meat until brown, and drain. Add salt and pepper to taste, chili powder, and tomato sauce. Pour over egg plant in the loaf pan. Add the shredded cheese over top. Bake at 375 degrees for 20 minutes.

MRS. MARVIN COOK, SR.

COWBOY CASSEROLE

1 8-ounce package spaghetti
1 onion, diced
Butter
1½ pounds ground meat
Salt and pepper to taste
Garlic powder, chili powder, seasoned salt, or all 3.
1 can mushroom soup
1 can tomato soup
Worcestershire, dash
Grated cheese

Cook spaghetti until tender; drain; brown onion in butter, add ground meat and brown. Add seasonings and soups. Add and mix in spaghetti. Cover and simmer 15 minutes. Pour in casserole dish, top with cheese and heat in oven to melt.

Serves 6

JOHN J. WILLIAMS
CO-CHAIRMAN — CALF SCRAMBLE

HAM AND RED-EYE GRAVY

Slice ham, preferably well aged, into ¼ inch steaks. Soak in milk overnight. Put just enough ham fat into skillet to keep ham from sticking. Have skillet hot. Slowly brown ham evenly on both sides. When done, remove to hot platter. For gravy, add 1 cup strong black coffee to ham drippings in skillet; sprinkle with a bit of pepper and let come to a boil. Stir well and serve piping hot. Fine over hot biscuits or grits.

MARY FLOWERS
AUCTION SALES

JUICY PIG

4 pounds beef, cubed
2 pounds pork
1 bottle catsup
2 tablespoons Worcestershire
2 tablespoons lemon juice
2 tablespoons prepared mustard
2 cups hot water
1 cup pickles

Sear meat; add water and other ingredients. Bake in a 250 degree oven until very tender. Shred. Serve hot on hamburger buns. Top with sauce made of 3 grated onions; 1 cup pickles; 1½ cups mayonnaise.

PEGGY DOCKERY
JUNIOR STEER RIDING

DEVILED HAM ROLLS

4 4½-ounce cans deviled ham
¾ cup olives, finely chopped
4 3-ounce packages cream cheese softened
1 tablespoon + 1 teaspoon prepared mustard

Mix deviled ham and olives. Chill until firm. Shape mixture into four rolls. Blend the cream cheese and mustard; spread over rolls. Cover. Chill at least 2 hours before serving.

RHONDA WOLFE
WESTERN COOKBOOK

LAMB CHOPS IN WINE

6 lamb chops
1 large clove of garlic
Salt and pepper to taste
4 tablespoons butter
2 tablespoons olive oil
8 scallions, chopped
1 tablespoon parsley, chopped
2 tablespoons flour
1½ cup dry white wine

Rub chops with garlic, season with salt and pepper. Heat 2 tablespoons butter and olive oil in large skillet, add chops. Brown on both sides, remove to baking dish. Add remaining 2 tablespoons butter to skillet, saute scallions and parsley until scallions are soft. Stir in flour, blending well, add wine gradually. Cook, stirring constantly until mixture begins to thicken. Pour over lamb chops. Cover. Bake in preheated 350 degree oven for 20 to 25 minutes. Remove cover, continue baking 10 minutes longer. Yields: 3 servings.

BETTIE RUTLEDGE
AUCTION SALES

ROAST LEG OF LAMB

1 leg of lamb
½ clove garlic
1 onion, sliced
1 fresh basil leaf or ½ teaspoon dry
1 slice Romano cheese, (optional)
Salt and pepper to taste

Make deep slits in leg of lamb and put a mixture of last 4 ingredients in each slit. Sprinkle with salt and pepper and cover. Bake in 350 degree oven until meat is tender. Remove cover last ½ hour of cooking to brown. Allow ½ hour for every pound.

JERRY AND LINDA ANOOSHIAN
BUYER — AUCTION

SHISH KEBOB

Allow one pound boned leg of lamb per person. Have butcher remove leg bone, tissue and fat, and cut meat into 2 inch cubes. Marinate in following mixture for 24 hours.

2 medium onions, minced
¼ cup parsley, chopped
2 teaspoons black pepper
2 teaspoons salt
1 clove garlic, crushed (optional)
1 cup burgundy wine

Thread meat on skewers and barbecue over hot coals or broil in oven for 20 minutes.

Note: Use a glass or enamel container (not metal) for marinating. Mix occasionally. This amount of marinade is sufficient for 2 or 3 pounds of meat.

JERRY AND LINDA ANOOSHIAN
BUYER — AUCTION

BRAISED CABRITO

5-pound cabrito roast
2 tablespoons oil
2 teaspoons salt
1 teaspoon pepper, freshly ground
1 large onion, sliced
6 carrots, sliced
2 teaspoons paprika
1½ jiggers vodka

Preheat oven to 275 degrees. Heat oil in dutch oven and brown meat on all sides. As meat browns, sprinkle it with salt and pepper. Remove meat and set aside. Add onion and carrots, sprinkle vegetables with paprika and brown them. Return meat to pot. Pour vodka over meat and cover immediately. Finish cooking in oven, turning meat and vegetables once. Cooking time will be about 2½ to 5 hours.

MR. AND MRS. ALLEN G. BODE

LENGUA

Beef Tongue
2 tablespoons shortening
1 onion, chopped
1 can of Rotel Tomatoes
Salt and pepper to taste
Dash Chili powder
1 clove garlic, minced
1 to 2 cups potatoes, cubed
Dash of comino
1 bay leaf

Boil the beef tongue until tender, approximately two hours. Remove skin and slice into bite size pieces. Combine the remaining ingredients and add the tongue. Cover with water and cook until all tender.

GREEN TACOS

¼ cup cooking oil
1 pound ground meat
1 large green pepper, chopped
1 medium onion, chopped
2 tablespoons flour
1 can cream mushroom soup
1 soup can of milk
Salt and pepper
1 package corn tortillas

Fry meat in oil add onion and pepper, cook slow until done. Add flour, milk and soup, heat until bubbly. In large casserole put one layer of mixture, 1 layer cut tortillas and cheese. Repeat until all used. Top with shredded cheese, cook moderate oven 30 minutes.

Serve with hot bread and salad.

FROM THE KITCHEN OF
EMMA BLAKEWAY

BEEF JERKY

Flank steak
Soy sauce
Garlic salt
Lemon pepper

Slice flank steak with the grain as thick or as thin as you like it. In a colander, coat it with soy sauce and generously sprinkle garlic salt and lemon pepper over all the meat. Line the oven with foil paper. Place the meat in a 140 degree oven directly on the oven rack. Taste after 10 hours to see if it is dry enough. if not continue cooking until it reaches the desired dryness you like.

"Great treat for a long day's ride"

JESSE F. GARZA
WESTERN COOKBOOK

FRIED BOLOGNA

Heat 2 inches shortening in skillet (preferably a throw-a-way skillet). *You definitely will need to throw the skillet away.* Heat shortening as hot as you can get it without causing a 3 alarm fire. Drop slices of bologna into hot grease and fry until crispy and curled.

Hint: You may want to drop your eggs into this same grease. It gives them a nice bologna flavor.

JOE KAUFMAN (TIMID)

FAJITAS WITH PICO DE GALLO

Skirt steak
Garlic pepper
Flour Tortillas

Sprinkle skirt steak with garlic pepper. Marinate for several hours in refrigerator. Grill over charcoal to desired doneness. (Rare is tastier). Slice across the grain and serve on warm flour tortillas with Pico de Gallo.

Pico de Gallo:
Tomatoes, chopped   **Lime juice**
Green onions, chopped   **Salt to taste**
Garlic, minced   **Avocado, chopped (optional)**
Cilantro, chopped

Combine the above ingredients add an avocado chopped if you desire. Delicious. Do not make Pico de Gallo too far ahead of time.

MRS. JACK PITLUK

OXTAILS IN WINE

2 oxtails — disjointed, dipped in flour, salt, and pepper.
Brown in small amount of oil.

Add:
1 large can tomatoes
1 cup dry wine (burgundy)
½ teaspoon lemon pepper
½ teaspoon garlic powder (not salt)
2 tablespoons paprika

Cover and simmer 2 hours (add water and wine as needed).
Add any or all of the following:

2-3 carrots, cut in pieces
2-3 potatoes, quartered
1 small green pepper, chopped
1 cup green beans
3 small white turnips, halved
2-3 stalks, celery, cut in 1 inch pieces.

Simmer cover ½ hour or until vegetables are tender. If necessary, add a little water when adding vegetables. Thicken liquid with a little flour or cornstarch before serving.

EILEEN STEWART
INTERNATIONAL MEXICO DAY

MEAT JERKY
(Apache-Pueblo-Navajo)

Lean venison, lamb, mutton or beef can be sued. Be sure to use only lean meat without any fat.

Slice meat into thick, ½ inch slices. Salt moderately well on both sides. Hang meat on line in full sun to dry. Turn from side to side frequently as sun starts to go down, bring meat indoors to hang in dry place. Return out doors the next day in full sun. Depending on climate and humidity, meat will dry in a few to several days. Store in dry place in covered container. Jerky can be eaten as is or used in stews.

BETTIE RUTLEDGE
AUCTION SALES

COMPUESTO

1st layer —
1 can refried beans
1 can bean dip
1 small onion, chopped
2nd layer —
2-3 avocados, mashed
lemon juice
3rd layer —
3 oz. sour cream
½ cup mayonnaise
1 package taco seasoning mix
4th layer —
8 ounces Monterrey Jack cheese, grated
8 ounces Cheddar cheese, grated
5th layer —
1 can ripe olives, sliced
6th layer —
2 or 3 dice fresh tomatoes, diced and drained
7th layer —
3 or 4 green onions, chopped — (blades also)

Put into 2 by 13 dish — Serve at room temperature with tostados

EMMA BLAKEWAY

CORNDOGGIES

½ cup yellow cornmeal
½ cup flour, sifted
1 teaspoon salt
½ teaspoon black pepper

1 egg
½ cup milk
1 tablespoon oil
12 weiners

Sift together cornmeal, flour, salt and pepper into bowl. Stir in egg, milk and shortening. Dip weiners into batter, drain and fry in hot fat 375 degrees until cooked and golden brown.

CHILDREN'S BARNYARD

Ready-to-Cook Poultry

One of the nation's premiere poultry raising centers is a vast geographic area to the east and south of San Antonio. Based on the importance of the poultry industry to Texas, it is now included in the San Antonio Stock Show.

All contestants are FFA and 4-H members. Each may enter chickens and turkeys in the Ready-to-Cook Poultry Show. The birds are first judged live to determine their live market quality. Those passing this rigorous judging are then processed and judged again on the basis of meat quality. The San Antonio Show is the only one to feature "Ready-to-Cook" poultry, rather than live.

D. W. "TWIN" RENEAU
CHAIRMAN

CHICKEN SAUTÉ WITH HERBS

2 broiler fryers (about 2½ pounds each, quartered)
6 tablespoons unsalted butter
Salt and pepper to taste
½ cup dry white wine, divided
3 tablespoons each,
  chopped parsley, chives and dill
Few drops lemon juice
Lemon slices

In large deep skillet with tight fitting lid brown chicken well on all sides in butter. Reduce heat; season with salt and pepper. Cover and cook gently five minutes; add ¼ cup wine, cook 10 minutes. Move white meat pieces to top, leaving dark meat which takes long to cook on bottom. Sprinkle chicken with herbs, cover and cook 5-10 minutes longer or until just tender but juicy. Remove to hot platter. Add remaining ¼ cup wine and lemon juice to skillet, bring to a boil, scraping up brown glaze from bottom of pan until juices are reduced by half. Pour over chicken, garnish with lemon slices. Serves 4 generously.

BETTY SMITH
GO WESTERN

GARLIC CHICKEN

1 medium fryer cut up or parts to equal
6 to 8 slices of white bread
1 small can Parmesan cheese
1 teaspoon garlic powder
1½ sticks oleo
Salt and pepper

Place slices of bread in blender until crumb consistency. Add cheese and garlic powder. Season chicken with salt and pepper and roll in melted oleo. Then roll in crumb mixture.
Bake on cookie sheet at 325 degrees for one hour.

DOTTI BIEDIGER
AUCTION SALES

CHICKEN-BROCCOLI AND RICE CASSEROLE

1 fryer 2½ pounds
½ cup rice, cooked
1 package frozen broccoli pieces
1 stick oleo
1 medium onion, chopped
½ cup celery, chopped
½ cup green pepper, chopped
1 can cream mushroom soup
1 small jar Cheez Whiz — plain or jalapeño
1 small can evaporated milk

Boil chicken pieces until done — Boil ½ cup rice in boiling water — Put broccoli pieces in boiling water for 15 minutes. When chicken is done, remove from bone, makes 2 cups of chicken. Put oleo in skillet, add chopped onion, celery, and bell pepper; cook until tender. Put rice in 2½ quart casserole. Add cut up chicken, vegetables, and broccoli. Mix mushroom soup with milk, pour over ingredients in casserole. Salt and pepper to taste. Bake in 350 degree oven 35 minutes. Then add jar of cheez whiz spread on top of casserole. Return to oven for 5 minutes — Serve hot.

MRS. MARVIN COOK, SR.

CHICKEN ITALIANO

2 pounds chicken parts
2 tablespoons shortening
1 can golden mushroom soup
⅓ cup canned tomatoes, drained, chopped
½ cup onions, sliced
⅛ teaspoon basil leaves, crushed

In skillet brown chicken in shortening; pour off fat. Add remaining ingredients. Cover; simmer 45 minutes or until done. Stir occasionally. Serve with cooked rice. Makes 4 servings.

ROBYN MERCHANT
AUCTION SALES

CHICKEN ARTICHOKE

3 pounds chicken breasts cut in pieces
1½ teaspoon salt
½ teaspoon paprika
¼ teaspoon pepper
6 tablespoons butter
1 pound mushrooms, cut in pieces
12-15 ounce can artichoke hearts
2 tablespoons flour
⅔ cup consommé or bouillon
3 tablespoons sherry wine

Salt and pepper chicken pieces. Brown in 4 tablespoons butter and place in casserole. Put other 2 tablespoons butter in frying pan and sauté mushrooms for 5 minutes. Arrange artichokes between chicken pieces. Pour mushrooms and sherry over and bake at 375 degrees for 40 minutes. Can be fixed in morning and baked later. Serves 6.

SHIRLEY SCHREIBER
AUCTION SALES BUYER

BAKED CHICKEN BREASTS

4 to 6 chickens breasts
Salt and pepper to taste
Garlic powder
Parsley
1 can cream of mushroom soup
1 can cream of chicken soup
1 cup sour cream
½ cup white wine

Place 4 to 6 breasts (whole or split) in a shallow baking dish. (I take the skin off, but it can be left on.) Sprinkle with the salt and pepper, garlic powder and parsley. Combine the soups, sour cream and white wine. Pour over chicken. Sprinkle with paprika. Bake 1½ hours at 325 degrees. Serve over rice.

MARY ELLEN PENWELL
AUCTION SALES

CHICKEN AND SQUASH

1 chicken, cut up
3 tablespoons fat
1 can whole kernel corn, drained
4 medium Mexican squash
1 can tomatoes
½ teaspoon comino
½ teaspoon garlic salt
¼ cup tomato paste
½ teaspoon salt
¼ teaspoon pepper
½ teaspoon chili powder
1 medium onion, chopped

Brown chicken in fat about 20 minutes, cooking over medium heat. Add remaining ingredients and simmer about 30 minutes or until done.

MARY ELLEN PENWELL
AUCTION AND PROGRAM

KING RANCH CHICKEN

1 fryer — stewed, boned and cut into bite-sized bits
Mix the next four ingredients and set aside:

1 can cream of chicken soup
1 can cream of mushroom soup
½ can (soup can) chicken broth from fryer
½ can Rotel Tomatoes and Green Chilies
1 medium onion, chopped
1 package corn tortillas, cut into 6ths
½ pound Cheddar cheese, grated

In a greased casserole, mix the ingredients in layers in the following order: chicken, tortillas, onion, soup mixture, and cheese. Repeat until all ingredients are used, cheese on top. Bake at 350 degrees for 1 hour.

GAYLE HARRIS   *BUTCH GARAHAM*
ENTERTAINMENT   *AUCTION SALES*

CALABAZITA CON POLLO

1 fryer, cut up
½ cup flour
½ cup olive oil
1 8-ounce can tomatoes
½ cup onion, chopped
½ cup green bell pepper, chopped
½ teaspoon cumin
½ teaspoon garlic powder
1 teaspoon salt
1 teaspoon black pepper
4 cups sliced green Mexican squash
1 cup fresh corn or frozen corn

Lightly coat chicken in flour and brown in olive oil on both sides. Add tomatoes, onion, green pepper, cumin, garlic powder, salt, pepper and sauté. Add squash, corn and mix thoroughly. Cover and let simmer for 30 minutes.
Serves four.

DORA SALINAS
INTERNATIONAL/MEXICO DAY

MRS. DEARINGS CHICKEN

1 package long grain and wild rice mix
1 can celery soup
½ cup mayonnaise
1 can French green beans, drained
1 cup slivered almonds
1 can water chestnuts, chopped
¼ cup pimientos, chopped
2 cups cooked chicken, chopped

Mix all ingredients and serve hot or cold

JAMIE BROWN
CALF SCRAMBLE

CHICKEN AND BEANS CASSEROLE

1 can French style green beans
1 can French fried onions
2 cans boned chicken
1 can cream of chicken soup
¼ cup mayonnaise
¼ teaspoon curry powder

Butter a casserole dish. Layer dish with half the can of green beans, drained. Sprinkle half the can of fried onions over beans. Spread one can of boned chicken over onions. Melt 1 can of cream of chicken soup, and mix with ¼ cup mayonnaise and ¼ teaspoon curry powder. Spread half over chicken and repeat layers using the rest of ingredients, adding the other can of boned chicken.

(Sliced water chestnuts on top of beans are optional). Sprinkle top with paprika. Cook at 325 degrees for 30 to 40 minutes.

ROBYN MERCHANT
SOUVENIR PROGRAM

CHILI TILLAS

1 chicken — boiled and boned
2 cans tomatoes
2 4-ounce cans chopped green chilies
1 package Longhorn cheese, grated
2 medium onions, chopped
1 dozen corn tortillas, cut up
Salt and pepper to taste

Sauté onions until tender. Add tomatoes and chilies. Simmer to reduce liquid. Salt and pepper to taste. Add rest of ingredients. Place in 350 degree oven until cheese melts. Serves 4-6 persons.

JAN HERRINGTON
AUCTION SALES

ENVUELTOS

1 large onion, chopped
1 green pepper, chopped
1 carton half and half
2 8-ounce cans tomato sauce
1 chicken, boiled and de-boned
2 packages corn tortillas
½ cup Cheddar cheese, grated

Sauté ½ onion and ½ green pepper in oil. Add ½ carton of half and half and ½ can tomato sauce. Add chicken (torn into pieces). Set aside for filling. In another pan, sauté rest of onion and green pepper. Add remainder of half and half and tomato sauce. Heat tortillas in oil. Use 1 teaspoon of filling to stuff each tortilla. Roll and place in baking dish. Pour sauce over all and top with grated Cheddar cheese. Bake 15-20 minutes or until hot at 350 degrees.

CHARLES "SEB" ALLEN
CALF SCRAMBLE

CHICKEN WELLINGTON

½ breast of chicken per person
Bone chicken — take skin off

In a skillet put ½ inch sauterne wine and cook chicken 2 minutes on each side — no more. Cool — refrigerate

Cook:
½ pound fresh mushrooms
1 bunch green onions in
¾ stick of margarine.

Add wine and flour to thicken, seasoning to taste. Cool. Roll out Pepperidge Farm puffed pastries, put slice swiss cheese, slice of ham, chicken and then spoon mushroom mixture on top. Fold up and put on ungreased cookie sheet (fold side on bottom). Chill ½ hour. Before baking brush with egg white. Bake in 350 degree oven 30 minutes.

FRANCES CARTER

GOLDEN HARVEST CHICKEN

2 fryers (about 2½ to 3 pounds, each), cut up
¾ cup all-purpose flour
3 teaspoons salt
1 teaspoon pepper
¾ cup shortening or oil
2 cloves garlic, minced
1 large onion, diced (1 cup)
1 cup celery, sliced
1 small green pepper, halved, seeded and cut into strips
½ pound mushrooms, sliced (canned may be used)
1 teaspoon leaf thyme, crumbled
¼ teaspoon cayenne pepper
1 bay leaf
1 1-pound 1 ounce can Italian plum tomatoes
1 cup dry white wine or dry rosé
2 tablespoons tomato paste
½ pound shrimp, frozen or fresh, uncooked, peeled and
 deveined

Shake chicken pieces, a few at a time, in a plastic bag with flour, 1½ teaspoons of the salt and ½ teaspoon of the pepper; reserve left over seasoned flour mixture. Brown chicken, a few pieces at a time, in oil, in a large skillet. Place browned chicken in 10-cup casserole. Remove all but 2 tablespoons of the oil from skillet. Sauté garlic and onion until soft; add celery, green pepper and mushrooms; sauté until tender-crisp. Add remaining 1½ teaspoons salt, ½ teaspoon pepper, 2 tablespoons of the reserved seasoned flour mixture, thyme, cayenne, and bay leaf; toss to coat vegetables. Add plum tomatoes with can liquid, wine and tomato paste; stir just to mix. Bring to boiling. Pour over chicken in casserole, cover. Bake in a moderate oven (350 degrees) for 25 minutes. Uncover; add shrimp, pushing them down into liquid. Cover, bake an additional 35 minutes until chicken and shrimp are tender.Uncover, gently stir to mix ingredients.

Serve over steamed rice. Garnish with chopped parsley if you wish. Makes 6 generous servings.

Note: The shrimp is optional, but it does add to the dish, especially for company fare, since it gives an elegant look and taste.

ROBYN MERCHANT
AUCTION SALES

CHICKEN "N" VEGIES

3 whole chicken breasts, skinned and boned
½ teaspoon garlic powder
3 tablespoons peanut oil, divided
2 tablespoons soy sauce, divided
3 tablespoons cornstarch, divided
½ teaspoon salt
¼ teaspoon pepper
2 bell peppers, cut into 1 inch pieces
1 cup celery, diagonally sliced, (1 inch pieces)
8 green onions, cut into ½ inch slices
1 6-ounce package Chinese peas, fresh or frozen
¼ teaspoon sugar
⅛ teaspoon ground ginger
¾ cup chicken bouillon, cooled

Cut chicken into 1 inch pieces and set aside. Combine garlic powder, 1 tablespoon oil, 1 tablespoon soy sauce, 1 teaspoon cornstarch, salt, pepper, and chicken. Mix well, and let stand 20 minutes. Pour remaining oil around top of preheated wok, coating sides. Allow to heat at medium high for 2 minutes. Add green pepper and stir-fry 4 minutes. Add celery, onions, and pea pods, stir-fry 2 minutes. Remove vegies from wok, and set aside. Combine remaining soy sauce and cornstarch, stir in sugar, ginger, and chicken bouillon. Set mixture aside. Add chicken to wok and stir-fry 3 minutes, add stir-fried vegies, and bouillon mixture. Stir over low heat for 3 minutes or until thick. Serve over rice. Serves 6.

LINDA AND JOE RAY ACKERMAN
AUCTION SALES

CHICKEN CROQUETTES

3 tablespoons shortening
1 teaspoon salt
⅓ cup flour
1 cup milk
2 cups cooked chicken, chopped
2 tablespoons parsley, minced
1 tablespoon onion, minced
2 eggs
2 tablespoons lemon juice
⅓ cup fine bread crumbs

Make a cream sauce by melting shortening and blending in flour and salt. Add milk gradually. Cook over low heat until smooth and thick, stirring constantly. Add chicken, onion and parsley. Spread in shallow greased pan. Chill thoroughly. Divide into 8 portions. Shape into logs. With a fork lightly beat eggs and lemon juice. Dip croquettes, first in egg mixture, then in crumbs. Fry in deep shortening heated to 365 degrees until golden brown (about 3-5 minutes). Drain on absorbent paper.

LYNDA VYVLECKA

CHICKEN MARENGO

3 pounds chicken parts
3 tablespoons shortening
1 can condensed golden mushroom soup
1 can condensed tomato soup
1 medium clove garlic, minced
1 pound (about 16) small whole white onions

In large skillet, brown chicken in shortening; pour off fat. Stir in remaining ingredients. Cover; cook over low heat 45 minutes or until tender. Stir occasionally. Uncover; cook until desired consistency. 6 servings.

ROBYN MERCHANT
SOUVENIR PROGRAM

CHICKEN CASSEROLE

6 slices bacon
1 cup rice
1 fryer, cut up (or favorite chicken pieces)
Pinch garlic salt
1 teaspoon oregano
2 teaspoons dried parsley
Paprika
Nutmeg
1 can cream of chicken soup
⅔ cup water

Line a large casserole with raw bacon. Sprinkle uncooked rice over bacon. Salt, pepper and paprika chicken, and place on top of rice. Thin soup with ⅔ cup water, and pour over it. Sprinkle with garlic salt, pinch of nutmeg, oregano and parsley. Cover tightly and bake 2 hours at 300 degrees.

MR. AND MRS. R. B. "BOB" HARRELL
READY TO COOK POULTRY

CHICKEN ENCHILADAS

1 dozen corn tortillas
2 cans green chilies, chopped
½ pint sour cream
1 can cheddar cheese soup
1 cup cooked chicken, chopped

Fry tortillas, drain on paper towel. Mix soup, chilies and sour cream in sauce pan and heat to boiling point (do not boil). Place a tablespoons chicken and sauce in each tortilla and roll. Place in casserole dish, pour balance sauce on top. Bake at 350 degrees for 15 minutes.

RUTH RENEAU
READY TO COOK POULTRY

FAVORITE CHICKEN CASSEROLE

1 broiler/fryer, cut up
½ teaspoon salt
¼ teaspoon pepper
½ teaspoon celery salt
¼ teaspoon garlic powder
1 tablespoon instant onion flakes
1 medium bay leaf
1 10-ounce package
   frozen Italian vegetables (may substitute broccoli or
   cauliflower)
1 3-ounce jar sliced mushrooms
1 can cream of chicken soup
1 can cream of mushroom soup
1 can water chestnuts, sliced thin
⅓ cup onion, diced
1 cup grated Velveeta Jalapeño cheese
2 cups grated Colby or Cheddar cheese

Simmer chicken in 2 quarts water with next 6 ingredients listed until done, approximately 2 hours. Remove chicken from broth, cool, separate from bone and cut in chunks. (Strain broth and reserve for other recipes, if desired) Cook rice according to package directions; cook vegetables according to package directions and drain. Mix together rice, soups, mushrooms, water chestnuts, ½ cup jalapeño cheese, and 1 cup Cheddar cheese. In 9x13 buttered pan, layer ½ of rice, soup mixture, vegetables, chicken, and then remainder of rice and soup mixture. Top with all remaining cheese. Bake at 350 degrees approximately 20-25 minutes until bubbling.

NINA KAUFMAN
GO WESTERN

CHICKEN ENCHILADAS

2 large chicken breasts
1 cup onion, chopped
1 clove garlic, minced
2 tablespoons butter or margarine
1 16-ounce can tomatoes, cut up
1 8-ounce can tomato sauce
¼ cup green chilies, chopped
1 teaspoon sugar
1 teaspoon ground cumin
½ teaspoon salt
½ teaspoon dried oregano, crushed
½ teaspoon dried basil, crushed
12 corn tortillas, frozen
2½ cups cheese, shredded
¾ cup dairy sour cream

In sauce pan, simmer chicken breasts in water to cover 15 to 20 minutes or until tender. Drain and carefully remove skin and bones. Sprinkle chicken with a little salt, cut into 12 strips, set aside. In saucepan, cook onion and garlic in butter or margarine until tender. Add tomatoes, tomato sauce, chilies, sugar, cumin, salt, oregano, and basil. Bring to boil, reduce heat and simmer, covered for 20 minutes. Remove from heat. Dip each tortilla in tomato mixture to soften. Place one piece of chicken and about 2 tablespoons of shredded cheese on each tortilla; roll up and place, seam side down, in 13½x8¾x1¾ inch baking dish. Blend sour cream into remaining sauce mixture, pour over tortillas. Sprinkle with remaining cheese. Cover and bake in 350 degree oven for about 40 minutes or until heated thoroughly. Makes 6 servings.

PAT MARTIN
GO WESTERN

CHICKEN ENCHILADA CASSEROLE

Stew 1 chicken, save broth
Sauté 1 onion, chopped, in ½ stick butter

Add: 1 can cream of mushroom soup
1 can cream of chicken soup
1 small can chopped jalapeños, or
½ can if you like it mild.
1 can broth from chicken stew

Add pimientos if desired/simmer for 20 minutes

Layer in 2 quart casserole dish:

6 corn tortillas, cut up
½ chicken cubes
½ sauce
¼ pound of Velveeta cheese, grated

Repeat — ending with cheese on top.
Cook 30 minutes in oven at 400 degrees.

FRANCES JOHNSON

CHICKEN IMPERIAL

2 10-ounce boxes frozen green beans
2 cups chicken, cooked and cut into bite-size pieces

Sauce:
1 can cream of mushroom soup
⅔ cup evaporated milk
¼ pound American cheese, diced
⅛ teaspoon pepper

Cook and drain green beans. Place in a greased shallow 1½ quart baking dish and top with the chicken. Mix all ingredients for sauce. Stir over medium heat until cheese melts. Pour sauce over chicken. Sprinkle with paprika and bake at 350 degrees for 15 minutes or until bubbly. Serves 4 to 6.

RUTH RENEAU
READY TO COOK POULTRY

BEBE'S SPECIAL CHICKEN

6 to 8 boned chicken breasts, split
1½ pound cleaned fresh mushrooms
1 bottle capers
⅓ cup white wine

Flour / Celery Salt / Poultry
seasoning / White pepper

Best when prepared in a clay baking dish.

Flour and season the chicken breast. Lay in bottom of baking dish. Top with the capers and about half of the caper juice. Arrange the fresh mushrooms around the chicken. Pour the wine around the sides. Cover and bake at 350 degrees to 375 degrees for 1½ to 2 hours. The time and temperature depends on the baking container. The chicken will brown in the clay container. If another container is used may have to uncover the last thirty minutes to brown.

When serving spoon each piece with the juice and mushrooms.

BEBE JONES
AUCTION SALES

SANDY'S CHICKEN AND RICE

1 chicken (boiled, skinned, and boned)
1 medium bell pepper, diced
1 medium onion, diced
3 celery sticks, diced
1 cup long grain rice
1 can cream of mushroom soup
1 small can pitted black olives
1 small jar Spanish olives, stuffed with pimientos
2½ cups chicken broth

Brown rice in 2 tablespoons butter along with onion and bell pepper. Then add chicken broth, celery salt, and pepper. Let simmer for 10 minutes. Add cream of mushroom soup, sliced olives, and chicken. Simmer another 10 minutes and serve.

SANDRA SESCILA

CHICKEN WITH LONE STAR BEER

1 whole chicken or desired parts
1 envelope dry onion mix or onion, chopped
Celery, chopped
Green pepper, chopped
1 can small orange juice
1 12-ounce can LONE STAR BEER, room temperature
1 can cream of mushroom soup
Splash TABASCO sauce
Salt and pepper to taste

Brown chicken parts in shortening, add envelope of soup mix or onion, celery, and green pepper. Steam a few minutes then add orange juce, Lone Star Beer and cream of mushroom soup, TABASCO and salt and pepper. Cook over medium low heat one hour stirring from time to time. If more liquid is needed add more orange juice and Lone Star Beer. Serve over hot noodles or rice.
Freezes very well.

MICKEY HUBER
CALF SCRAMBLE

BREAST OF CHICKEN ON RICE

1 10½-ounce can condensed cream of mushroom soup or
    cream of chicken soup
1 soup can of milk
¾ cup uncooked white rice
1 4-ounce can mushrooms, sliced
1 envelope dry onion soup mix
2 chicken breasts, split in half

Heat oven to 350 degrees. Blend soup and milk, reserve ½ cup of the mixture. Stir together remaining soup mixture, rice, mushrooms (with liquid), and half the onion soup mix. Pour into ungreased baking dish, 11½ by 7½ by 1½ inches. Arrange chicken breasts on rice mixture. Pour reserved soup mixture over chicken and sprinkle with remaining onion soup mix. Cover, bake 1 hour. Uncover, bake 15 minutes longer. Yields: 4 servings.

CHICKEN PILAF

1 10½-ounce can of cream of mushroom soup
1¼ cup of boiling water
½ cup of dry sherry
½ envelope dry onion soup mix
1½ cups of rice, precooked
2 tablespoons pimiento, chopped
5 small chicken breasts
Butter or margarine melted
Salt, pepper, and paprika

Combine first 6 ingredients in a 1½ quart casserole. Brush chicken breasts with butter. Season with salt, pepper, and paprika. Place on top of rice. Cover and bake in moderate oven 375 degrees for 1¼ hours or until rice and chicken is tender.

RHONDA WOLFE
WESTERN COOKBOOK

CHICKEN RICE CASSEROLE

1 frying chicken cut up and seasoned
1 stick oleo
1 cup uncooked rice
1 can cream of chicken soup
1 can cream of onion soup
1 can water

Melt oleo in pan, pour uncooked rice evenly over oleo, place chicken pieces over the rice (may add chopped green onions, green pepper and fresh mushrooms). Mix soups and water and pour over chicken. Bake 350 degree oven — 1 hour — turn off oven and let stand 15 minutes longer.

BARBARA WILLIAMS AND GEORGE WILLIAMS
CALF SCRAMBLE

ROCK CORNISH HEN WITH WINE SAUCE

Season rock cornish hen or hens with butter and parsley. Roast in 450 degree oven for 10 minutes. Baste frequently with butter or oleo. Lower oven to 350 degrees for 25 minutes. Continue basting. Place under broiler for a few minutes to brown. (Watch under broiler carefully — not over 5 minutes.)

Hot Wine Sauce:

1 tablespoon butter
½ glass currant jelly
Juice of ½ lemon
Pinch cayenne

½ cup port wine
3 cloves
1 teaspoon salt

Simmer together for 5 minutes all ingredients except wine. Strain, add wine and a little pan gravy from rock cornish hens plus 1 tablespoon cornstarch to thicken slightly. Spoon over cornish hens.

Excellent wine sauce will keep under refrigeration in tightly covered jar for couple of weeks.

BUTCH GRAHAM
AUCTION SALES

CHICKEN MACARONI CASSEROLE

1½ cups uncooked elbow macaroni
1 cup shredded Cheddar cheese
1½ cups diced chicken or turkey
1 4-ounce can mushroom stems and pieces drained
¼ cup chopped pimiento
1 10½-ounce can condensed cream of chicken soup
1 cup milk
½ teaspoon salt
½ teaspoon curry powder

Heat oven to 350 degrees. Stir together all ingredients. Pour into ungreased 1½ quart casserole dish, cover and bake for 1 hour.

DEBBIE BEALL

CHICKEN TETRAZZINI

2 frying chickens, boiled until tender, cooled in the broth, boned and cut up.
2 large onions, chopped (I used one)
1 green pepper, chopped
½ pound bacon, diced
2 large cans tomatoes, drained and cut up
1 large package Vermicelli, cooked in chicken broth
1 can whole mushrooms
1 4-ounce jar pimiento, chopped (you may use more if you like)
8 ounces Cheddar cheese, grated
12 ounces Mozarella cheese, grated

In dutch oven, sauté bacon, onion, and pepper. Add tomatoes, salt, and pepper to taste, simmer 5 minutes. Add chicken, mushrooms, and pimiento; then cooked vermicelli. Add cheese, reserving some to put on the top. Remove from fire. Mix and allow to stand 10 minutes to melt cheese. Transfer to oven proof serving casserole, top with reserved cheese, heat at 300 degrees for 30 minutes.

MRS. NAT V. (WINONA) PRASSEL

"THAT" CHICKEN

1 fryer cut up (or use all thighs, breasts, etc.)
Place in baking dish 1½" deep and large enough to place chicken in single layer.
Spread ½ can of cream of mushroom soup over chicken. Fill up can with cream sherry wine, stir until smooth. Add 1 teaspoon curry powder, pour mixture over chicken. Top with ½ cup toasted almonds. Bake in 350 degree oven 1¼ to 1½ hours. Do not salt, turn or cover.

EILEEN STEWART
INTERNATIONAL/MEXICO DAY

TRISHA'S CHICKEN AND DRESSING

1 large chicken (or pieces of your choice)
1 onion, chopped
2 stalks celery, chopped
1 Bouquet garni
Salt and pepper

Boil above ingredients until chicken is tender. Remove meat from bone. Combine the following ingredients:

2 packages corn bread mix
6 eggs
milk
½ cup shortening

Bake in 350 degree oven for about 45 minutes.
Sauté the following:

1 stick oleo
3 stalks celery, chopped
3 medium onions, chopped
1 small bell pepper, chopped

Crumble the cooked corn bread in a large bowl. Add the cooked vegetables and mix well. Add chicken broth to mixture until soft. Add salt and pepper to taste if needed. Place half of the dressing in a baking pan. Adding the chicken on top then add the rest of the dressing. Bake at 350 degrees until set.

PATRICIA GARZA
WESTERN COOKBOOK

CHICKEN AND DUMPLINGS SERVED WITH SAUERKRAUT

Select 3 to 3½ pound chicken, cut into pieces cook slowly in boiling water with 1 large onion, 3 or 4 ribs of celery, 2 or 3 carrots, parsley, salt and pepper until tender or done. When done remove chicken and vegetables from broth, so you may cook dumplings in broth.

DUMPLINGS

2 cups flour
4 teaspoons baking powder
2 tablespoons melted shortening
1 teaspoon salt
¾ cup milk or little more if necessary to blend

Sift dry ingredients twice, add shortening and milk. Stir until blended. Drop by teaspoonfuls into the hot broth. Cover and steam for 12 minutes. Remove dumplings from broth, return chicken to broth to reheat, remove chicken, thicken broth and pour over chicken and dumplings and serve.

SAUERKRAUT

1 can sauerkraut
1 medium onion

Drain sauerkraut, add chopped or sliced onion and chicken broth with chicken fat for seasoning. Let boil for 20 minutes.

EMMA BLAKEWAY

CURRIED CHICKEN

4 tablespoons butter or oleo
3 onions diced
1½ cups fresh sliced mushrooms
4 chicken breasts boned skinned and cut into bite size
  pieces
½ teaspoon thyme; salt and pepper to taste
½ cup chicken broth
⅓ cup vermouth
⅓ cup cream
¼ teaspoon curry powder

Sauté onions in butter, salt and pepper chicken and dredge in flour and add to onions, cook 10 to 15 minutes, add mushrooms cook 5 minutes add remaining ingredients and thicken with flour if needed.

Serve over rice.

FROM THE KITCHEN OF,
EMMA BLAKEWAY
REQUESTED BY,
Mr. "Q"

CHICKEN CRESCENTS

2 cups chicken, cooked and boned
1 can of 8 crescent rolls
3 ounce cream cheese
1 teaspoon lemon pepper
1 tablespoon margarine
1 teaspoon chives

Combine all ingredients and separate rolls. Divide mixture 8 ways and put in rolls. Roll up. Bake until golden brown. Serves 4.

I used this for a luncheon and it went over real well.

BEBE JONES
AUCTION SALES

CHICKEN ITALIAN

1 4 to 5 pound hen
2 cans cream of mushroom soup
1 can tomato soup
1 cup diced celery
2 green peppers, diced
2 medium onions, diced
2 large garlic buds, diced
1 No. 2 can of English peas, drained
1 teaspoon Worcestershire
1 teaspoon TABASCO sauce
2 cans drained mushrooms
1 12 to 16-ounce package wide egg noodles
Salt and pepper to taste

Boil hen. Remove from bones and cube meat. (You will need 2 quarts broth — add water to equal this.) Lightly brown celery, peppers, onions, and garlic in 4 teaspoons oil. Add this plus chicken and simmer a few minutes. Then add noodles to broth and cook slowly until noodles are tender. They should absorb all the liquid. Serve.

HARRY BOGGESS

CHINESE POT-POACHED DUCK

(6 appetizer servings)
1 duck (3½ to 5 lb.) cut into 1½ inch pieces with bones in
1 cup dry white wine
½ cup dark soy sauce
¼ cup dry sherry
4 green onions with tops, chopped
2 teaspoons sugar

Place duck pieces on rack in 4 quart pressure cooker. Pour in wine, soy sauce and sherry. Sprinkle with onions and sugar. Secure lid. Place cooker on high heat to 15 pounds pressure. Reduce heat and cook 25 minutes. Reduce pressure immediately.

BEBE JONES
AUCTION SALES

CHICKEN PARISIENNE

6 medium chicken breasts
½ cup dry white wine
1 10½-ounce can mushroom soup
1 3-ounce can sliced mushrooms, drained
Paprika
1 cup dairy sour cream
Hot cooked rice

Place chicken breasts, skin side up, in 12 by 7½ by 2" baking dish. Sprinkle with salt; blend wine into mushroom soup; add mushrooms and pour over chicken. Bake at 350 degrees 1 to 1¼ hours. Remove chicken to platter; sprinkle with paprika; pour sauce into saucepan; blend in sour cream and heat gently till hot; serve sauce over chicken and hot cooked rice.

Makes 6 servings.

MATT AND MELISSA FATHEREE
ENTERTAINMENT

EASY CHICKEN DIVAN

2 10-ounce packages frozen broccoli
2 cups sliced cooked chicken or 3 chicken breasts,
    cooked and boned
2 cans cream of chicken soup
1 cup mayonnaise
1 teaspoon lemon juice
½ teaspoon curry powder
½ cup shredded sharp cheese
½ cup bread crumbs
1 tablespoon butter, melted

Cook broccoli in boiling salted water until tender; drain. Arrange stalks in greased 11½ x 7½ x 1½ inch baking dish. Place chicken on top. Combine soup, mayonnaise, lemon juice and curry powder; pour over chicken. Sprinkle with cheese. Combine crumbs and butter. Sprinkle over all. Bake at 350 degrees for 25-30 minutes. Serves 6-8.

BEBE JONES
AUCTION SALES

CHICKEN JALAPEÑO

1 cooked chicken, whole (bones and skin removed) cut up
   small
1 can cream of chicken soup
1 can cream of mushroom soup
1 cup milk
3 large jalapeños, seeded and chopped
1 small jar pimientos
1 onion, chopped
1 pkg. tortilla chips) (medium size package)
½ pound Velveeta cheese, grated

Sauté onions in ¼ stick oleo. Mix soups, milk, peppers, pimientos, and onions and heat. Crush chips and line large casserole. Place chicken on top of chips. Pour soup mixture over chicken and top with half pound of grated Velveeta cheese.

Heat in low heated oven until cheese is melted good.

ROBYN MERCHANT
AUCTION SALES

MEXICAN CHICKEN CASSEROLE

1 2⅓ or 3 pound fryer
2 tablespoons shortening
2 tablespoons onion, chopped
8 ounces Rotel Tomatoes and Green Chilies
8 ounces Velveeta cheese, grated
1 pint half and half
1 small bag of dip size corn chips
1 cup Longhorn cheese, grated
1 tablespoon flour or more if needed to absorb Oil

Boil chicken; bone and chop. Sauté onion in shortening. Add flour, green chilies and tomatoes, grated Velveeta cheese, and half and half, then chicken. In casserole dish put layer of corn chips, layer of mixture, until dish is full, ending with chicken mixture. Sprinkle grated longhorn cheese on top. Bake in 300 degree oven until bubbly.

JACK AND BETTYE BRADFORD
AUCTION SALES

CHICKEN KIEV

8 whole chicken breasts, boned
2 eggs
Finely crushed bread crumbs
Salt
White pepper
1 can mushrooms, sliced
2 cups sour cream
2 or 3 tablespoons green onion tops
¾ pound shrimp, boiled but firm
Butter

Wash and dry chicken breasts, split open lengthwise. Dust lightly with paprika. Place a small pat of butter on each and roll, securing with a toothpick. Season with salt and white pepper. Dip in eggs and roll in crumbs twice. Cook in butter until brown. In 2 tablespoons of the butter, sauté mushrooms, then add sour cream and onion tops. Cook these a couple of minutes and pour over chicken breasts in flat casserole. Bake, coverd, at 325 degrees for 45 minutes. Just before serving, snip shrimp in halves and sauté in 1 tablespoon butter. Then sprinkle over each chicken breast in casserole. Serves 8.

BUTCH GRAHAM
AUCTION SALES

UNIQUE TURKEY SEASONING

Before placing turkey on smoker, season as follows: Dry bird and rub with softened butter until completely covered. Season with curry and sprinkle with sesame seeds. Lay slices of thick bacon over the top of the bird, breast up. Follow cooking times as indicated on smoker.

This could also be done on a turkey cooked in the oven.

BEBE JONES
AUCTION SALES

BAKED CHICKEN AND RICE

1 cup rice
(regular, not instant)
1 2½ to 3 pound frying
chicken, cut in pieces
5 or 6 slice bacon

1 can cream of chicken soup
½ teaspoon oregano
1 small can mushrooms
Salt, pepper, and parsley

Line pan with bacon slices and spread with 1 cup uncooked rice. Salt and pepper raw chicken pieces and place on top. Sprinkle with paprika. Drain liquid from small can of mushroom and save liquid. Put mushrooms on top of chicken and sprinkle with oregano. Cover with can of cream of chicken soup, diluted with liquid from mushrooms and enough water to fill can. Sprinkle with parsley and cover with foil.

Bake in 9 by 13 by 2 glass pan at 300 degrees for 1 hour and 45 minutes. If using metal pan, set oven for 325 degrees.

RON SNOWDEN
JUNIOR STEER RIDING

CHICKEN SPAGHETTI

2 10-ounce boxes cut spaghetti
1 cooked chicken, diced
½ cup green peppers, chopped
½ cup onions, chopped
½ stick oleo
1 small can pimientos, chopped
½ can chicken broth
1 pound Velveeta cheese
1 can cream of chicken soup
1 can cream of mushroom soup

Butter 2½ quart casserole (or larger) bowl. Pre-heat oven to 350 degrees. Cook and drain spaghetti. Sauté onions and green peppers in butter. Heat soup and broth until hot, combine all ingredients. Bake 1 hour. After 30 minutes stir. If all is not needed, freeze half unbaked. Yield 8 servings.

ARLINE HARRIS/FRED HARRIS
READY TO COOK POULTRY

SMOKED TURKEY AND HAM AU GRATIN

Bread slice (toasted)
Cream sauce
Ham (sliced)
Smoke turkey (sliced)
Cheddar cheese

On oven-proof plate, place one slice of toasted bread. Cover with sliced ham. Spread a layer of cream sauce over ham. Then put sliced smoked turkey over the ham and sauce. Cover this with cream sauce. Finally cover ham, turkey and sauce layers with Cheddar cheese. Heat thoroughly in moderate oven until cheese is melted.

NEW BRAUNFELS SMOKEHOUSE

CHINESE SUNDAE

8 cups steamed rice
2 large cans chow mein noodles
Cold stewing chicken, chopped
1 can cream of chicken soup, heated
3 tomatoes, sliced thin
4 celery stalks, sliced thin
1 pound shredded cheese
1 can cream of chicken soup, heated
Small bunch of green onions, chopped
Small package of slivered almonds
Large can of crushed pineapple
1 package shredded coconut
Maraschino cherries

Assemble all ingredients in a line in the order they are listed. Have guests begin with the steamed rice and pile all ingredients on top of one another ending with the cherries. Serves 6-8.

DEBBIE KANE
GO WESTERN

CHICKEN MOLE

1 3-pound medium fryer
1 tablespoon shortening
2 tablespoons Dona Maria red mole (dissolved in two cups hot water)
2 tablespoons masa harina (dissolved in two cups hot water)
1 tablespoon salt
1½ cups water

Quick fry chicken in shortening until brown at about 400 degrees in deep skillet. Drain, just leave about 2 tablespoons fat in pot. Pour in mole and masa (already dissolved) into pot and 1½ more cups of water and salt. Reduce to a medium to low or 200 degree heat and cook for about 45 minutes or until chicken is soft. (Do not overcook, chicken will come off bone.)

GEORGE ROBBINS
AUCTION SALES

OVEN BARBECUED CHICKEN

1 3 to 3½ pound broiler or fryer, quartered and skinned
1½ cups tomato juice
¼ cup vinegar
2 medium onions, sliced or diced
1½ tablespoon Worcestershire
¼ cup catsup
1½ or 2 packets sugar substitute
2 teaspoons prepared mustard
1 teaspoon salt
½ teaspoon pepper

Combine all ingredients (except chicken) in saucepan and heat; pour over well seasoned (garlic salt, salt, and pepper) chicken. Bake uncovered 1¼ hours or until tender at 350 degrees. Baste about every 15 minutes. *Optional:* Last 30 minutes add 1 can well drained mushrooms and 1 can sliced water chestnuts.

SHIRLEY SCHREIBER
AUCTION SALES BUYER

CRISPY PARMESAN CHICKEN

1 cup Pepperidge Farm Herb seasoned croutons, crushed
½ cup grated Parmesan cheese
¼ cup chopped fresh parsley
½ cup butter or margarine
⅛ teaspoon garlic powder
1 2½ to 3 pound broiler-fryer, cut up and skinned
Salt and pepper
Paprika
Fresh parsley sprigs (optional)

Combine breadcrumbs, cheese, and chopped parsley in a pie-pan; mix well, and set aside. Place butter in a small glass bowl; microwave at high for 1 minute or until melted. Stir in garlic powder. Sprinkle chicken with salt and pepper, and dip in butter; roll each piece in crumb mixture, and sprinkle with paprika.

Arrange chicken in a 12 by 8 by 2 inch baking dish, placing meatier portions to outside of dish. Cover with waxed paper and microwave at high for 8 to 10 minutes. Rearrange chicken (do not turn) so uncooked portions are to outside of dish. Cover and microwave at high for 9 to 12 minutes or until done. Garnish with parsley, if desired. Yield: 4 servings.

JAMES A. SCHMULEN JR./BETH SCHMULEN

RANCHO CALABASITA con POLLO

Pollo (Chicken)
Calabasita (Squash)
Onions, chopped
Garlic, ground
Comino
Salt
Pepper
Corn (canned or fresh or frozen)
Tomatoes
Bell Pepper

Brown chicken in oil. Add the squash and very little water. Let simmer for awhile until you see the chicken is getting tender. Add the onions, garlic, comino, salt and pepper to taste. Add the corn, tomatoes and bell pepper. Great over an open fire.

MAYO ZUNIGA
Horseshoer
Charlotte, Texas

CHICKEN CURRY

4 tablespoons butter, melted
¼ cup onions, chopped
1 clove garlic, minced
1-1½ teaspoon curry powder
½ apple, pealed, cored and chopped
⅛ teaspoon ginger
3 tablespoon flour
1 cup chicken broth
1 cup milk
2 cups chicken, cooked and chopped
½ teaspoon lemon juice
3 to 4 cups rice.
Salt and pepper to taste

Saute onion, garlic, apple, curry and ginger powder in butter, add flour and seasonings stir until smooth. Stir in chicken broth and milk. Simmer stirring constantly until thick. Add chicken, salt and pepper and lemon juice.
Serve over rice.

TOPPINS'
Almonds, slivered
Avocado, Sliced
Bacon bits
Coconut, flaked
Peanuts
Pineapple chunks.

Souvenir Program

Production of the souvenir program is a complicated and time consuming process.

The program gives information on all of the activities associated with the 10-day event. In this book you will find the answers to any questions you may have concerning judging events, auction sales, the professional cowboys, entertainment, exhibits and the officials of the San Antonio Stock Show and Rodeo.

HOMER WALKER
CHAIRMAN

BAKED BASS

1 5 pound bass (or equivalent)
1 large onion, chopped
1 bell pepper, chopped
½ stick oleo
2 cans tomato sauce
1 can whole tomatoes
Juice of 1 lemon
1 cup cooking wine
½ cup green onions and parsley
Dash TABASCO sauce
Salt, pepper, garlic powder to taste

Sprinkle fish with lemon juice and season generously ahead of time, preferably overnight. Wilt onions, bell pepper in oleo. Add tomato sauce and whole tomatoes and cook over medium heat for 45 minutes in uncovered pot. Add 2 cups cold water and seasoning to taste adding dash of TABASCO sauce. Cook for 25 minutes over medium heat. Add wine and pour mixture over fish and bake in 325 degree oven for 40 minutes. Baste several times. Sprinkle parsley and onion tops over and serve with slices of lemon for garnishment. Serves approximately six.

BUTCH GRAHAM
AUCTION SALES

BAR-B-QUE SHRIMP

Melt ¾ pounds oleo in oblong pan. Add 2 tablespoons Worcestershire. Put shrimp in pan. Squeeze 1 fresh lemon over shrimp. Grind fresh black pepper over shrimp. (heavy) Cook in oven on broil, 11 minutes on each side. (Grind more pepper on shrimp when you turn them) Use shrimp with heads if possible. Just wash and they're ready to cook.

JIM TOBE ATKISON
CALF SCRAMBLE

CLAM PIE

½ package piecrust mix
2 medium potatoes, cooked in skin, peeled, cut into ¼ inch slices
4 slices bacon, cooked and crumbled
1 medium onion, minced
2 8-ounce cans minced clams
½ cup milk
¼ cup butter or margarine
2 tablespoons flour
¾ teaspoon leaf savory, crumbled
½ teaspoon salt ¼ teaspoon pepper

Prepare pie crust mix, following directions. Place in refrigerator until ready to use. Cook bacon, crumble. Set aside. Cook minced onion in bacon fat. Set aside. Drain liquid from clams into a 2 cup measuring cup. Add milk to measure 1¾ cups liquid. Add clams to onions and bacon. Melt butter in small sauce pan. Add flour, savory, salt and pepper. Cook until bubbly — 1 minute. Stir in clam-milk liquid. Cook over medium heat until thickened. Add clam, onion, and bacon mixture. Arrange potato slices over bottom of pie plate. Spoon mixture over top. Roll out pastry to 11 inch round. Place over pie plate. Cut several slits on top to let out steam. Trim overhang. Bake at 450 degrees for 45 minutes or until golden. Let stand 15 minutes before serving.

GENE ROSE
COPY MACHINE

FRIED CLAMS

1 quart shucked clams
1 egg, slightly beaten
1 teaspoon salt
⅛ teaspoon pepper
Dash of paprika
1 cup dry bread crumbs
½ cup butter or margarine

Drain clams, reserving 2 tablespoons liquid. Combine clam liquid with egg, salt, pepper, and paprika. Dip clams in egg mixture; then roll in bread crumbs, coating completely. In hot butter in medium skillet, sauté clams 3 to 4 minutes on each side, or until golden brown. Drain well on paper towels. Serves 4 to 6.

JIMMY WOLFE
ENTERTAINMENT

BOILED CRABS

½ cup salt
16 live-hard-shell crabs

In large kettle, bring 4 quarts water and salt to boil. Place crabs in colander; wash in cold water until crabs seem clean. Holding crab by tongs, plunge head first into boiling water; return water to boiling. Reduce heat, and simmer, covered 12 to 15 minutes. Drain and let cool. To remove meat: twist off claws and legs; crack with hammer; remove meat. Lay crab on top of shell. Insert point of a knife under forward end of flap that folds under body from rear, break it off, and discard. Pick up crab in both hands; pull upper and lower shells part. Discard top shell. Hold crab under running water, remove gills and all spongy material. Cut away any hard membrane along outer edge; carefully remove meat with fork. Makes about 2 cups of crabmeat.

JIMMY WOLFE
ENTERTAINMENT

CRAB AND SHRIMP BOIL 〜

6 quarts cold water
1 lemon, sliced
¼ cup crab or shrimp boil

Combine above ingredients and boil for two minutes. Add crabs and shrimp and cook only until water comes to a boil again. Drain, rinse with cold water. Serve with warm melted butter and lemon, lime or orange wedges. Serve cold with chilled sauces for dunking. French bread, a salad crisp and tender and lots of cold beer. WHAT A PARTY.

OYSTERS ERNIE

Two dozen oysters — browned slightly in butter. Put in flat pan and cover with sauce made of the following:

3 tablespoons melted butter
2 teaspoons lemon juice
2 tablespoons steak sauce
1 tablespoon Worcestershire
1 jigger sherry or madeira

Run under broiler until hot.

ROBYN GLASSCOCK
AUCTION SALES

SALMON CROQUETTES 〜

1 16-ounce can pink salmon
¾ cup dry oatmeal
¼ cup onion, finely chopped
2 eggs
Garlic salt, sprinkle

Combine all the above ingredients and mix well. Drop by spoon into hot oil and fry until golden brown. Drain on paper towel. Great with catsup and french fries.

315

BAKED STRIPED BASS

4 to 5 pounds whole striped bass with head, cleaned
2 teaspoons salt
1 small lemon
Parsley
1 cup onion, thinly sliced
½ cup carrots, thinly sliced
½ cup celery, thinly sliced
½ teaspoon dried thyme leaves
1 bay leaf
1 cup dry white wine
¼ cup of butter or margarine, melted
Lemon butter

Preheat oven to 400 degrees. Lightly grease a shallow roasting pan. Wash fish inside and out under cold running water; pat dry with paper towels. Sprinkle fish inside and out with salt. Slice lemon thinly; cut slices in quarters. With small, sharp-pointed knife, make deep cuts, about 2 inches apart, along both sides of fish. With fingers press a piece of lemon and a small sprig of parsley into each cut. Place fish in prepared pan. Add any remaining lemon slices and parsley, along with onion, carrot, celery, thyme, and bay leaf. Pour in wine and ½ cup water. Pour butter over fish. Bake, basting frequently with liquid in pan, 30 to 40 minutes, or until fish flakes easily when tested with fork. Carefully lift fish to serving platter. Take vegetables and place around fish; vegetables will be crisp. Garnish platter with parsley and lemon if desired. Serve with lemon butter (below).

LEMON BUTTER:
6 tablespoons butter or margarine
2 tablespoons lemon juice

In small skillet, heat butter over medium heat until if foams, and becomes light brown. Remove from heat, stir in lemon juice. Serve at once.

JIMMY WOLFE
ENTERTAINMENT

BAKED WHITE FISH 'A LA BIEDIGER'

2 pounds white fish (boneless cod or trout is best)
½ gallon white wine (believe me, you'll use all of it.)
½ cup Parmesan cheese
3 lemons
¼ cup real butter
½ teaspoon paprika
1 tablespoon of parsley (fresh or dried)
1 teaspoon of coarse ground black pepper
Garlic powder, curry powder, and salt to taste.

When making the market list for this recipe, white wine should be in big bold letters at the top of the list. Any white wine will suffice, as long as it satisfies the chef's palate. Almaden mountain chablis or rhine are my favorites and they're cheaper when bought by the half gallon.

Your white fish should be thawed, and the oven should be set at 375 degrees.

Place the fish in a glass baking dish. Pour one glass of wine and take a sip. Take 2 of the 3 lemons, and juice them, pour the juice over the fish. Pick up your glass and take a drink of wine. Melt the butter, and pour it over the fish. Drink some more wine. Sprinkle paprika, parsley, ground pepper, salt, curry, and garlic to taste, and add Parmesan cheese. Take the last lemon and slice it across to make lemon wheels, and garnish the fish with them. Drink some more wine and pour about 1½ cups of it on the fish. Place a sheet of foil over the fish and cook it for about 30 min. Then take the foil off and cook at the same temperature for another 15 minutes. When the wine in the chef equals the air in the wine bottle, *the fish is ready!* This dish serves about four people, and is delicious with french bread.

CLAUDIA BIEDIGER
AUCTION SALES

SHRIMP WITH PINEAPPLE

2 cups fresh shrimp, peeled and deveined
2 cups fresh pineapple cubes (1 inch square)
Batter:
2 egg yolks
⅔ cup milk
1 cup flour
½ teaspoon salt
1 tablespoon butter, melted
1 tablespoon lemon juice

Fold in 2 egg whites, stiffly beaten. Let stand 1 hour. Dip shrimp and pineapple in batter and fry in deep fat at 375 degrees. Drain and serve hot. (Batter from Betty Crocker Cookbook)

KATHY BENDER
AUCTION SALES COORDINATOR

TUNA OR SALMON BISCUIT LOAF

½ cup mayonnaise
1 cup flaked tuna, or 1½ cup salmon
¼ cup green pepper, chopped
1 cup well-drained cooked lima beans, green beans or
  peas
1 to 1½ teaspoon salt
¼ teaspoon pepper
1 cup diced American cheese
2 tablespoons pimiento, chopped

Blend ingredients. Mix biscuit dough. Roll between waxed paper into 12x10 rectangle. Place on ungreased cookie sheet. Spread filling down the center, covering an area 4 inches wide. Make 7 cuts on each side and cross over filling.

Bake 20-25 minutes in 425 degree oven. Serve with a sauce of cream of mushroom soup heated.

KATHY BENDER
AUCTION SALES COORDINATOR

HUACHINANGO A LA VERACRUZANA
(SNAPPER GARLIC SAUCE OR MOJO DE AJO)

4 fresh filets of red snapper
¼ cup flour
Salt and pepper to taste
¼ cup vegetable oil
½ pound butter
¼ pound margarine (1 stick)
8 fresh cloves of garlic
2 tablespoons parsley, chopped

Dredge snapper filets with flour. Add salt and pepper first, sauté in oil and oleo mixture for 3 minutes on each side. Place on warm serving platter, cover with the sauce. A good serving suggestion is with rice and broiled tomatoes.

Sauce:
Place the butter in a sauce pan. Add the fresh garlic, cook for 3 minutes. Add the fresh parsley and simmer 1 more minute. Serve hot.

ERNESTO'S

SHRIMP-RICE DISH

2 small packages pre-cooked frozen shrimp
5 stalks celery, diced
1 bundle fresh green onion, chopped
1 stick margarine
2 cans cream of celery soup
1 dash of thyme seasoning
Salt and pepper seasoned to taste
1 cup rice

Sauté celery and onions in margarine until tender; add shrimp, dash of thyme, salt and pepper to taste; and cream of celery soup. Simmer for 30 to 45 minutes. Boil rice in salt water until done as per instructions on package. Serve shrimp over the rice.

SONNY HILD
AUCTION SALES

Junior Steer Riding

Junior Steer Riding Competition is provided for boys and girls between the ages of 11 and 15. The competition consists of 14 "go-rounds" made up of seven contestants each. The winner of each "go-round" receives a $500.00 scholarship to the college or university of their choice.

Judges are provided by the Rodeo Producer Association, judging contestants along regular Rodeo Cowboys Association Guidelines. The object of the competition (seldom accomplished) is to try and stay on the steer for 8 seconds.

The Junior Steer Riding Committee is made up of ranchers, former rodeo cowboys, school administrators, students, and business and professional men from the San Antonio and South Texas community.

Crain "Budweiser" Distributing Company, owned by Mr. Bill Crane provides the Committee Sponsorship. Mr Crain also serves as an ex-officio member of the committee.

JAMES "JIM" DOCKERY
CHAIRMAN

COON STEW

4 pounds coon cut in cubes
2 or 3 onions, sliced
Salt and pepper
Bay leaf
Dash Worcestershire
2-3 cups canned tomatoes
Carrots
Onions
Potatoes
Turnips

Brown meat in dutch oven slowly without grease. Add onion slices at end of browning period so as not to scorch. Reduce heat, add canned tomatoes to cover meat, season and cover. Simmer slowly until meat is almost tender, add vegetables and continue to simmer until vegetables are tender. Serve with corn bread or hot biscuits.

BILL HOFFMAN
INTERNATIONAL/MEXICO DAY

DEER STEAK BAKE

Venison steak
Salt
Pepper
1 can celery soup
1 medium onion, if desired
½ can water

Salt and pepper venison steak. Place in a cold iron skillet; add some chopped onion, if desired. Pour 1 can celery soup and ½ can of water over the steak; cover with aluminum foil, sealing the top fairly tight. Place in 350 degree oven for 2 hours. Do not stir, uncover or touch for that time. Steak and gravy will be ready for the table. Simple, good and tender.

MARY ELLEN PENWELL
AUCTION SALES

MEAT BALLS WITH SPAGHETTI
ELK OR DEER HAMBURGER

2 eggs, beaten
2 cans (6-ounces each) or 1 can (12-ounces) tomato paste
1 small onion, minced (¼ cup)
¼ cup grated Parmesan cheese. (I use Romano)
2 tablespoons minced parsley
1 clove garlic, minced (I did not use)
2 teaspoons salt
1 pound elk or deer, ground
¾ cup soft bread crumbs (1½ slices)
3 tablespoons vegetable oil
2½ cups hot water
1½ teaspoon sugar
1 teaspoon leaf basil, crumbled
1 teaspoon leaf oregano, crumbled
¼ teaspoon pepper
1 1-pound package spaghetti, cooked and drained

Combine eggs, 1 tablespoon of the tomato paste, onion, cheese, parsley, garlic, 1 teaspoon of the salt, beef and bread crumbs in a large bowl; mix thoroughly. Form into 20 balls, about 1 inch in diameter. I mix all this together the night before and cover well and make into balls the next day. Be sure to refrigerate. Brown meat balls in hot oil in a dutch oven; drain off fat. Blend remaining tomato paste with hot water, sugar, basil, oregano, remaining 1 teaspoon salt, and pepper in a bowl. Pour over meatballs. Cover; simmer 10 minutes. Uncover; simmer 10 minutes longer. Serve over hot spaghetti. Garnish with chopped parsley, if you wish.

MRS. NAT V. (WINONA) PRASSEL

BARBECUED DOVE OR QUAIL

Quail or Doves (three or four per person, depending on
   appetite)
Italian salad dressing
Bacon slices cut in half
Lemon pepper seasoning (add to taste)

Marinate birds in salad dressing (breast down) 4 hours.
Remove from marinade and sprinkle with lemon pepper.
Wrap each bird with ½ slice bacon and hold with toothpick.
Broil over charcoal until done (can also be smoked.)

RUTH ANN LUCCHELLI
AUCTION SALES

DOVES IN A POT

Doves
Garlic
Salt
Red Pepper
Flour
Water
Sauterne

Prepare: After birds are washed and cleaned, make small
incisions in breast, (four to a bird). Stuff each incision with
½ clove garlic, salt and pepper, then season bird inside and
out with salt and pepper.

Method: Cover bottom of pot with cooking oil and heat on
medium fire. When oil is hot put birds in. Brown on all sides,
then lower heat. Turn birds while sprinkling with flour for
about ½ hour. Add just enough water to make thick gravy
on bottom of pot. Cook, uncovered, about 2 hours. Birds
should be turned often to keep them moist. Add water when
needed to keep same consistency of gravy. Add 2 tablespoons sauterne about 30 minutes before done.

BUTCH GRAHAM
AUCTION SALES

GRILLED DOVE

2 or 3 doves for each person eating (breast only)
1 bottle Italian dressing
½ jalapeño pepper for each dove
1 slice bacon for each dove
Salt and pepper to taste

Salt and pepper each bird and fill cavity with ½ jalapeño. Wrap with strip of bacon and use a toothpick to secure. Place on charcoal grill and baste with Italian dressing. Grill slowly and continue basting with dressing until birds are done.

MARY ELLEN PENWELL
AUCTION SALES

DOVES IN SHERRY

12 doves
Flour, seasoned with salt and pepper
Fat for browning birds
1 cup sherry
2 bunches of shallots
2 small cans diced mushrooms
Slice of bacon

Wash and dry doves. Roll in seasoned flour. Brown in iron skillet in small amount of fat. Place 3-4 shallots in cavity of dove. Wrap strip of bacon around dove and secure with toothpicks. Place in pan, pour sherry and mushrooms over doves. Bake at 350 degrees for 45 minutes to one hour. Serve sauce with doves.

HENRY BEKEN, JR.
CALF SCRAMBLE

FAVORITE FRIED RABBIT

1 large rabbit — cut up
1 cup cold water
½ cup wine or garlic vinegar
1 teaspoon each of the following:
　Parsley
　Sage
　Thyme
　Rosemary
　Sweet Basil
　Marjoram
½ teaspoon coarse black pepper
1 tablespoon onion flakes
½ cup arrowroot
1 tablespoon paprika
Beau Monde seasoning

Blend all together . . . pour over rabbit and let stand in cool place 8 hours. Wipe rabbit clean . . . rub well with Beau Monde seasoning, a little salt and roll in ½ cup arrowroot with 1 tablespoon paprika. Fry in margarine or butter until tender. Make milk gravy from drippings in pan.

EILEEN STEWART
INTERNATIONAL/MEXICO DAY

VENISON CHILI

Brown in ½ cup hot bacon drippings, 2 pounds ground venison. Season with salt and pepper and add: 1 medium onion, chopped fine; 3 tablespoons chili powder; and 3 tablespoons flour. Sear a little longer. Then add 1 cup tomato sauce and enough water to cover. Simmer about 1 hour. Garlic may be added.

JOE L. TATUM
READY TO COOK POULTRY

BEST EVER FRIED VENISON

Venison backstrap or ham steaks, sliced ½" thick from which all bones, fat and membranes have been removed.

1 13-ounce can canned milk
½ teaspoon Worcestershire (optional)
Flour
Salt and pepper, to taste

Soak venison in canned milk at least 4 hours, preferably overnight. (This removes any gamey taste and tenderizes at the same time.) If desired, add Worcestershire sauce to canned milk for a little different taste. Drain milk from steaks and dredge steaks in flour to which salt and pepper have been added. Heat cooking oil or shortening to a high temperature and fry steaks very quickly. (Overcooking causes venison to get tough.)

Drain on paper towels and enjoy!

JOE KAUFMAN
AUCTION SALES
JUNIOR STEER RIDING

DRIED VENISON JERKY
(CHUNK STYLE)

Cut venison in 2-inch chunks, any length. Rub each piece well with salt, using 1 cup of salt to every 20 pounds of meat. Set in a cool place for 2 or 3 days; dip in hot water, drain, string, and sprinkle with coarse black pepper. Hang up and smoke for 2 or 3 days; will be ready to eat in about a week.

JOE L. TATUM
POULTRY COMMITTEE

TEXAS QUAIL

1 cup flour
Salt and pepper to taste
½ teaspoon garlic powder
1 teaspoon lemon pepper
1 teaspoon paprika
2 quail per person
½ cup butter
1 cup dry white wine
1 tablespoon minced parsley
1 tablespoon Fines Herbs
1 teaspoon dill weed
¼ teaspoon curry powder
2 tablespoons cognac
1 cup sour cream

Combine flour, 2 teaspoons salt, garlic powder, lemon pepper, and paprika. Coat quail with flour mixture. Brown in butter in skillet. Combine wine, parsley, Fines Herbs, dill weed, curry , salt, and pepper to taste. Pour over browned quail. Cover; simmer for 20 to 25 minutes, spooning sauce over quail. Do not overcook. Remove quail. Keep warm. Stir cognac and sour cream into pan drippings; blend and heat through. More wine may be added if sauce cooks down too much. Pour part of sauce over quail and serve remaining in gravy boat.

OPEN RANGE COOKING
"COTTONTAIL" IN WINE SAUCE

First, you have to catch 3 cottontail rabbits, clean and cut them up. Next, dip in flour, salt and pepper, and brown in heavy iron skillet with small amount of cooking oil. Set browned rabbit aside in deep cooking pot. Remove almost all oil from skillet and add ½ cup onions. Cook until onions are clear but not brown. Then add 1 cup dry red wine and 1 cup beef stock. Bring to boil, pour liquid with onions over rabbit in deep pot. Cover and simmer for 1 hour or until tender. Thicken sauce with a little flour, add more wine to taste.

SQUIRREL STEW

3 squirrels — cut into pieces
3 quarts water
¼ cup diced bacon
¼ teaspoon cayenne
2 teaspoons salt
½ teaspoon black pepper
1 cup chopped onions
4 cups (two No. 303) cans tomatoes
2 cups diced potatoes
2 cups lima beans
2 cups corn

Place squirrel pieces in large kettle. Add water, bring to boil, reduce flame and simmer 1 to 1½ hours or until squirrel is tender. Remove meat from bones and return to liquid. Add other ingredients, cook 1 more hour.

LIBBY JONES
AUCTION SALES

VENISON JERKY

1½ to 2 pounds venison loin or hindquarter.
McCormicks hickory smoked seasoned salt.
McCormicks seasoned pepper.

Cut venison lengthwise with grain into 6″ long strips 1-1½″ wide, and no more than ¼″ thick. Sprinkle enough seasoned salt on venison to cover well. Sprinkle with seasoned pepper. Arrange strips close together but not overlapping on ungreased cake cooling rack. Place rack in cookie sheet or shallow pan. Bake at 150 degrees for 7 to 10 hrs. Cool, cut or break into bite size pieces and store in tightly sealed container or in your freezer. This is the quick method and is very delicious. You may, if desired smoke for 3 or 4 days in smoke house.

MRS. E. R. LITTLETON
AUCTION SALES

SOUTHERN CANNON BALLS

1 pound hot venison pan sausage or any hot bulk sausage
2 cups sharp Cheddar cheese, shredded
2 cups biscuit mix
1 tablespoon poultry seasoning
2 tablespoons grated onion

Combine all ingredients, mixing well. Roll into walnut size balls. Place on an ungreased cookie sheet and bake at 400 degrees for 15 minutes. Drain on paper towels. Serve hot. Yield about 48 balls.

MRS. E. R. LITTLETON
AUCTION SALES

VENISON PEPPER ROAST

1-4 pound venison roast
1 recipe sherry-pepper marinade
1 package onion soup mix
Red and green sweet pepper slices from marinade

Sherry-pepper marinade:
2 cups sherry
1 chopped onion
1 chopped garlic clove
½ teaspoon black pepper
¼ teaspoon thyme
Red and green sweet pepper slices

Place meat in glass bowl. Add marinade ingredients and let stand for 24 hours. Turn meat four times. (This marinade can be used on all types of game meat.) To prepare for cooking, remove meat from marinade and dry with paper towels. Brown roast on all sides in ¼ cup vegetable oil. Place roast in foil-lined roasting pan. Add onion soup mix and pepper slices from marinade. Seal foil and bake in 300 degree oven for two and a half hours or until tender.

JOELLA SMITH
HORSE SHOW

CHICKEN FRIED VENISON

2 pounds meat (may be nice slice ¼ inch thick, or the small bits you get when trimming out hocks) and then beat flat with board.
13 ounces evaporated milk
Salt
Pepper
Flour
Garlic powder (optional)
Onion powder (optional)

Put the meat in large bowl with the evaporated milk and enough water to completely cover the meat. Allow to stand for 1 hour. Take meat out, drain only slightly and then season to taste and roll in the flour. Drop into hot grease (375 degrees) and fry until brown. Do not over cook or meat will become dry and tough. Serve with gravy made from the flour and milk left over — and hot bread.

PAT HALPIN
TRAIL BOSS
KERR COUNTY TRAIL RIDERS

CHICKEN FRIED VENISON

Cut venison into steaks. Pound to tenderize. Season with salt, season salt, pepper, and cayenne pepper. Dip in flour, then into egg and back into flour. Fry in cast iron skillet. Serve with cream gravy.

JOELLA SMITH
INTERNATIONAL/MEXICO DAY

BAKED JAVALINA

1 package dry onion soup mix
1 cup water
2 tablespoons flour

Season javalina with season salt, pepper, garlic, and cayenne pepper. Dredge meat in flour. Place in cooking bags. To each cooking bag, add 1 cup water, package onion soup and 2 tablespoons flour. Bake at 250 degrees for 4 hours. Debone and serve with rice or flour tortillas.

JOELLA SMITH
HORSE SHOW

COW COUNTRY ROAST JAVALINA

Salt and pepper javalina ham and place in a covered roaster. When meat has cooked slowly for 30 minutes, make a paste of bread crumbs, crushed tortillas (corn or flour) and the liquid in the roasting pan. Add a small amount of dry mustard, a crushed bay leaf, dried celery leaves, about a teaspoon of chopped onion and a pod of red pepper. Cover the roast with the mixture and put the lid over the roast. In about 30 minutes, test the meat for doneness. Remove the crust cover. Cool and slice. Pour the drippings from the pan over the meat.

BETTIE RUTLEDGE
GO WESTERN

ARMADILLO

1 armadillo
1 onion
2 cloves garlic, minced
1 bell pepper
3 carrots
2 potatoes
Oil
Salt and pepper to taste

After you catch the armadillo, carefully remove him from his shell. CLean and wash him very good removing all insides. Stuff him with the remaining ingredients. Close him up after you finish stuffing him. Brush him with oil and sprinkle him with salt and pepper. Wrap him in foil and place on the open coals and let cook.

MAYO ZUNIGA
Horseshoer
Charlotte, Texas

Rural Youth

The Rural Youth Committee is made up of members from the San Antonio Kiwanis Club and educators from The Texas Agricultural Extension Agency, The Texas Education Agency, Texas A & I University, Texas A & M University, San Antonio College, Business Men from San Antonio and the surrounding area and The San Antonio Livestock Exposition.

Each year on the opening night of the San Antonio Livestock Show the Rural Youth Honor Banquet is held in one of the major meeting halls in downtown San Antonio. At this annual banquet, 10 Future Homemakers of America, 20 4-H members, and 10 Future Farmers of America are all individually honored for their achievements in school, civic and organization activities, most of which are oriented with agriculture in some way. These honorees, their parents, organization sponsors, educators, and committee members join together for this banquet. Special guests, including the Mayor of San Antonio, the scheduled entertainer for the opening night, and guest speaker, all take part in honoring these young people who will be the future leaders in all walks of life in this great state of Texas.

C. E. NOONAN
CHAIRMAN

BETTER THAN SEX CAKE

1 package yellow cake mix (with pudding in mix)
1 8-ounce can crushed pineapple
½ cup sugar
Small container Cool Whip brand topping
1 cup chopped pecans

Bake cake according to directions using oblong cake pan (13x9). Allow cake to cool for 15 minutes. Make holes in cake with knife, add topping. Refrigerate for two hours. Add Cool Whip and pecans.

Topping: While cake is in the oven, mix crushed pineapple with ½ cup sugar and bring to boiling point, remove from fire. Pour on cake after cake has been cooled for 15 minutes.

DORA SALINAS
INTERNATIONAL / MEXICO DAY

AMBROSIA ANGEL CAKE

1 Angel food cake mix
Bake angel food cake as directed
Filling and frosting:
4 egg yolks
1 cup sugar
2 oranges, juice and grated rind
14-16 marshmallows
½ cup coconut
slivered almonds
1 pint heavy cream, whipped

Beat yolks slightly, add sugar and orange juice and rind. Cook until thickened, stirring constantly. Add marshmallows and mix in while melting. Cool. Fold in coconut and whipped cream. Split cake in 3 layers and spread filling between and on top. Sprinkle almonds over top. Chill —

SHIRLEY SCHREIBER
AUCTION SALES

SNOW ON THE MOUNTAIN
A "DIFFERENT" CAKE

Cake:
1 cup dates, chopped
1 cup nuts, chopped
1 cup sugar
4 eggs, whole
½ cup plain flour
1 teaspoon baking powder
¼ teaspoon salt
2 teaspoons vanilla

Method: Beat eggs & sugar. Mix flour, salt, baking powder and add to egg mixture. Add chopped dates and nuts (room temp) and lastly the vanilla. Spread in two 8″ or one oblong sheetcake pan that has been well oiled and floured. Bake 30 minutes at 350 degrees.

Ingredients for "mountain":
5 oranges, peeled & cut bite-size
3 bananas, chopped
scant ¼ cup sugar, to cause juicing
1 pint whipping cream, w/ sugar & vanilla or almond
    flavoring to taste
½ cup shredded coconut

Rip cooled cake into bite-size pieces. Form a "mound" of cake, 12″ in diameter, with center being a little higher than rest of mound (I use a large Pyrex bowl.) LAYER AS FOLLOWS:
Cake bits
Orange/Banana/Sugar mixture
Cake bits
Fruit again
End with cake bits
Press together a little as you go so it will stay high. (Excess juice in bottom of fruit mixture bowl will help cake "fuse" together.) Refrigerate at least 2-3 hrs. before inverting onto plate. Cover entire mountain w/ whipped cream & top with coconut.

HARRELL BANKS
VICE PRESIDENT & GENERAL MANAGER
KBUC RADIO

CHOCOLATE POUND CAKE

½ pound butter or margarine
½ cup shortening
3 cups sugar
5 eggs
3 cups flour, sifted
6 tablespoons cocoa
½ teaspoon baking powder
¼ teaspoon salt
1 cup milk
1 teaspoon vanilla
½ teaspoon butter extract
Bundt pan

Cream together in large mixing bowl butter, shortening, and sugar until fluffy. Add eggs one at a time and beat each in thoroughly. In separate bowl, sift together flour, cocoa, baking powder and salt. To large mixing bowl contents, add ⅓ of flour mixture, then ½ cup milk, then ⅓ of flour mixture, then ½ cup milk, and finally, the remaining ⅓ of flour mixture. Add 1 teaspoon vanilla and the butter extract.

Pour into greased and floured bundt pan and bake at 325 degrees for one hour and twenty minutes. Let cool in pan for 25 minutes, then turn out on cake plate.

PEGGY DOCKERY
JUNIOR STEER RIDING

"QUICK" CHOCOLATE UPSIDE-DOWN CAKE

1 tablespoon butter
¾ cup sugar
½ cup milk
1 cup flour
¼ teaspoon salt
1 teaspoon baking powder
1½ tablespoons cocoa
½ cup pecans, chopped
Filling:
½ cup sugar
½ cup brown sugar
¼ cup cocoa

Cream butter and sugar; add milk and stir. Sift dry ingredients and add to mixture. Pour into a greased cake pan. Sprinkle chopped nuts on top. Mix ingredients for filling and evenly sprinkle over top. Pour 1¼ cups boiling water over top and bake 30 minutes at 350 degrees.

BEVERLY ADAMS GRAY
SPECIAL DAYS

BUTTER CAKE

2 sticks oleo, melted
3 cups sugar
3 cups flour
1 cup buttermilk
4 eggs
¼ teaspoon soda
1 teaspoon vanilla
1 teaspoon lemon extract

Cream butter and sugar, add eggs one at a time, beat well after each egg. Add flour and buttermilk, alternating. Start with flour and end with flour. Bake in tube pan 350 degrees for 1 hour or until done.

EMMA BLAKEWAY

HOLIDAY DELIGHT FRUITCAKE 🍃

1 quart pecans
½ pound white raisins
1 pound candied cherries
2 ounces lemon extract, (pure)
6 eggs, separated
5 cups flour
3 cups sugar
1 pound butter
2 tablespoons water
1 teaspoon soda

Cream butter and sugar — add lemon extract and mix. Mix 2 cups flour with fruit and nuts. Add egg yolks to creamed mixture. Add remaining 3 cups flour and soda diluted in water. Mix well. Add fruit mixture and blend. Fold in stiffly beaten egg whites.

Pour batter into a well greased and floured 4 quart tube pan. Bake 3 hours at 250 degrees in preheated oven.

3-DAY COCONUT CAKE

1 box butter flavored or plain yellow cake mix, bake as directed on box or use your favorite recipe for white or yellow cake. Bake in 2-9 inch layer cake pans. When cool split layers and ice with following filling.

Filling:
2 cups sugar
1 16-ounce carton sour cream
1 12-ounce package frozen coconut
1½ cups Cool Whip brand topping

Combine sugar, cream and coconut. Reserve 1 cup of mixture. Spread between layers. Add 1 cup of reserved mixture to Cool Whip and ice top and sides of cake. Put in covered container and refrigerate for 3 days.

FROM THE KITCHEN OF,
EMMA BLAKEWAY

FUDGE CAKE

Fudge Topping Ingredients:
⅔ cup sugar
½ cup milk
1 egg, slightly beaten
3 one ounce squares unsweet chocolate

Cake Ingredients:
½ sup shortening
1 cup sugar
1 teaspoon vanilla
2 eggs
2 cups sifted cake flour
1 teaspoon soda
½ teaspoon salt
1 cup milk

In pan combine fudge topping. Cook and stir over medium heat, until chocolate melts and mix comes to just boiling. Cool! Gradually add 1 cup sugar to shortening: cream until fluffy. Add vanilla. Add remaining eggs, one at a time, beating well after each. Sift together dry ingredients. Add to creamed mix the dry ingredients, with one cup milk, beating just until smooth after each. Blend in cool chocolate.

Bake in 2-greased and floured 9x1 inch round pans at 350 degrees for 25-30 minutes. Cool 10 minutes before removing. Cool! Frost with fudge topping.

YOLI CAMPOS
MISS RODEO TEXAS COMMITTEE
GO WESTERN

SOUR CREAM CAKE

2 cups sugar
½ cup butter or oleo, melted
2 eggs
6 tablespoons cocoa
1 cup sour cream
2 cups sifted flour, level
1 cup boiling water
¼ teaspoon salt
2 teaspoons soda, level
1 teaspoon vanilla

Mix sugar and melted butter, beat in eggs one at a time, beat well after each egg. Add cocoa. Stir soda into sour cream and mix into other ingredients. Add flour with salt sifted 3 times. Last add boiling water and vanilla. This makes a very thin batter. Bake in 2 layers at 350 degree oven approximately 30 minutes or until done. Frost with Chocolate Fudge Filling.

Chocolate Fudge Filling:
3 cups sugar
1 cup milk or half and half
4 tablespoons cocoa
4 tablespoons white Karo syrup

Boil to soft ball stage when tested in cold water or on candy thermometer. Remove from heat. Add 2 tablespoons of butter and ¼ teaspoon salt, and set aside to cool. When cool beat well to spreading consistency.

EMMA BLAKEWAY

HOT MILK CAKE ℰ

1 cup milk
1 stick butter or margarine
5 to 6 eggs
2 cups sugar
2 cups flour
1 teaspoon baking powder
1 teaspoon vanilla

(You may serve this delicious cake as is or use your own imagination.)

In a saucepan heat 1 cup milk with one stick butter or margarine. *Do not boil.* Beat 5 to 6 eggs until foamy and lemony colored. Add two cups sugar and blend. Add two cups flour and blend well. Now add the hot milk mixture and after mixing this, add one teaspoon baking powder and one teaspoon vanilla. Pour into greased and floured tube or angel pan. Bake at 350 degrees for 50 to 60 minutes.
Suggestion: Drizzle chocolate glaze over top letting it run down the sides, then top with chopped nuts.

HUMMING BIRD CAKE

3 cups flour
2 cups sugar
1 teaspoon soda
1 teaspoon salt
1 teaspoon cinnamon
1½ cups oil
3 eggs, beaten

Last add:
1 8-ounce can crushed pineapple
3 cups bananas, chopped
1 cup pecans, chopped

Mix well, pour in greased and floured bundt pan. Bake at 350 degrees for 1 hour and 5 minutes. Cool in pan 10 minutes before removing.
NOBLE J. AND TOPSY TAYLOR
CALF SCRAMBLE

CHARLOTTE RUSSE

Line a cylindrical charlotte mold (angel food cake pan) with wax paper or aluminum foil — cover bottom (radiate from center like petals of flowers) and line sides and cylinder with lady fingers.

Fill mold with sherry-cream mixture and cover top with lady fingers.

Filling:
4 small packages unflavored gelatin in
1 cup cold water — melt over hot water
1 pint cream, whipped stiff
6 egg whites beaten stiff with 1 cup sugar
Pinch of salt
1 teaspoon vanilla
½ to 1 cup sherry

Fold cream into egg whites and add gelatin and sherry. Pour into mold cover lady fingers, top with waxed paper and refrigerate at least 2 hours. FANTASTIC!

SCOTT ABBEY WEST
AUCTION SALES

CHOCOLATE CAKE

1½ cups flour
3 tablespoons cocoa
½ teaspoon salt
1 tablespoon vinegar
1 cup of water

1 cup sugar
1 teaspoon baking soda
½ cup of vegetable oil
1 teaspoon vanilla

Sift all the dry ingredients 3 times and then sift in pan. Do not grease pan. Make 3 holes and put vinegar, vanilla, and vegetable oil in them. Then put the cup of water over it and mix good. Cook about 30 minutes at 350 degrees.

Icing for cake:
5 or 6 tablespoons of brown sugar
3 tablespoons of milk
3 tablespoons of butter

Let cake get cool and then bring all this to a boil and pour on the cake, then pecans.

JIMMY WOLFE
ENTERTAINMENT

CARROT CAKE

2 cups flour
2 cups sugar
4 eggs
3 cups carrots, grated
1 teaspoon vanilla
1½ cups corn oil
½ teaspoon salt
1 teaspoon baking powder
2 teaspoons baking soda
(Add pecans in mix)

Mix all dry ingredients together. Add oil, eggs and vanilla, and blend well. Bake at 350 degrees for 30 minutes or until done.

Frosting:
1 cup chopped pecans
¾ box powdered sugar or to taste
1 8-ounce package cream cheese
1 stick butter or margarine
1 teaspoon vanilla

Cream the cheese and butter. Add sugar, vanilla and pecans. Blend well. Add milk if necessary to spread.

RITA WOLMA
AUCTION SALES

CARROT CAKE

Sift the following ingredients together in a bowl:

3 cups sifted cake flour
2 teaspoons baking soda
2 teaspoons baking powder
2 teaspoons cinnamon
2 cups sugar
½ teaspoon salt

In a separate bowl, mix the following:

1½ cups salad oil
4 whole eggs
2 cups grated carrots
½ cup chopped pecans
1 teaspoon vanilla

Blend all above ingredients together and pour into 10″ ungreased tube pan.

Bake 350 degrees for 1 hour, or until done.

Icing:

1 8-ounce package creamed cheese, softened
1 pound box powdered sugar, sifted
½ stick margarine, softened
1 cup chopped pecans
1 can flaked coconut
1 teaspoon vanilla

Spread icing over cooled cake.

LEE NOONAN
RURAL YOUTH

PRALINE CAKE

1 stick butter, soft (not margarine)
½ cup brown sugar (light)
¼ cup honey
¼ cup water
1 cup pecans, chopped
2 eggs
1¾ cup sifted flour
1 tablespoon baking powder
½ teaspoon salt
½ cup dark rum

Cream butter and sugar. Beat eggs in well, one at a time and add honey, water and rum. In another bowl mix flour, baking powder and salt. Sift into batter and heat until thoroughly moistened. Stir in pecans. Pour into greased and floured 9x5 inch loaf pan. Bake at 375 degrees for 45 to 50 minutes. Cool on rack.

SCOTT ABBEY WEST
AUCTION SALES

RHUBARB CAKE
(don't knock it 'till you've tried it)

5 cups rhubarb, diced (dice small)
1 3-ounce package Strawberry Jello brand gelatin
1½ cups sugar
2 cups miniature marshmallows
1 package (18¾ ounce pudding in the mix)
Strawberry cake mix.

Mix rhubarb, sugar, and Jello in bowl and let set for 15 or 20 minutes. Add 2 cups marshmallows. Mix cake mix according to directions on box. Pour rhubarb mixture into 13½"x9½"x2½" pan. Pour cake mixture over rhubarb mixture and bake according to directions for cake. 350 degrees for 35 to 40 minutes. Caution: Most rhubarb in this area is frozen so it is imperative that your oven has been preheated before placing mixture in to cook. Serve with whipped topping or ice cream. Best when cooled.

MRS. E. R. LITTLETON
AUCTION SALES

BANANA SPLIT CAKE

Crust: Graham Cracker
2 cups graham cracker crumbs
1 stick oleo, melted
2 tablespoons sugar

Put into 9 by 13 cake pan. Bake for about 5 minutes at 350 degrees.

Filling:
2 sticks oleo, softened
2 eggs
2 cups powdered sugar
1 teaspoon vanilla

Beat this mixture for 15 minutes. Pour over crust (Don't Cheat!) Slice five or six bananas over filling (I sprinkle lemon juice over the bananas to keep from discoloring).

1 large can or 2 medium size cans crushed pineapple, drained.

Sprinkle this over the bananas. Spoon 1 large tub Cool Whip over the pineapple. Now sprinkle chopped nuts and cherries (maraschino) on top of Cool Whip. Refrigerate overnight or several hours.

LUCILLE JOHNSON
REBA ROBERSON
AUCTION SALES
MARY ELLEN PENWELL
AUCTION SALES
MONICA GOSE
LIFE MEMBER

ROSALYNN CARTER'S STRAWBERRY CAKE

1 package white cake mix
1 3-ounce package strawberry Jello brand gelatin
¾ cup vegetable oil
1 cup chopped nuts
4 eggs
2 tablespoons flour
1 10-ounce package frozen sliced sweetened strawberries
  — thawed
½ pint heavy cream, whipped
1 tablespoon sugar to serve on top

Preheat oven to 350 degrees and grease and flour 10 inch angel food cake pan or 10 inch bundt pan. Combine cake mix, strawberry Jello, vegetable oil, nuts, eggs, flour, and strawberries in large bowl. Beat with electric mixer at medium-high speed for 3 minutes or until well blended.

Pour batter into pan and bake for 55 to 65 minutes, or until a cake tester poked in center comes out clean. Cool for 10 minutes on rack. Turn out of pan to cool completely. Serve plain or with sweetened whipped cream. Makes 10 to 12 servings.

AS TOLD TO ELIZABETH JACOBS BY
ROSALYNN CARTER
INTERNATIONAL/MEXICO DAY

PAT'S YUMMY STUFF

1 box yellow cake mix

Bake according to directions. While hot, punch holes in cake with handle of wooden spoon (use 9x12 cake pan). Pour 1 can condensed milk over cake and 1 can crushed, undrained pineapple. Sprinkle with pecans. Cover with 9 ounce carton of Cool Whip topping. Sprinkle with coconut. Refrigerate 3 or 4 days.

BILL DUGAT, JR.
CALF-SCRAMBLE

SHEATH CAKE

2 cups sugar
2 cups flour
1 stick butter
½ cup shortening
4 tablespoons cocoa
1 cup water
½ cup buttermilk
2 eggs, slightly beaten
1 teaspoon soda
1 teaspoon vanilla

Sift sugar and flour in a bowl. In a sauce pan add the butter, shortening, cocoa and water bringing it to a rapid boil and pour over the flour mixture and mix. Add the buttermilk, eggs, soda, and vanilla mix well. Pour into greased 9 by 12 pan. Bake at 375 degrees for 30 minutes.

Icing:
1 stick butter
4 tablespoons cocoa
6 tablespoons sweet milk
1 box powdered sugar
1 teaspoon vanilla
1 cup pecans

Five minutes before cake is done mix and bring to a boil the above ingredients. Remove from the heat and add 1 box powdered sugar and 1 teaspoon vanilla and 1 cup chopped pecans. Pour over hot cake.

MARY FLOWERS
AUCTION SALES

OLD FASHIONED POUND CAKE

1 8-ounce package cream cheese, softened
¾ cup butter, softened
1½ cups sugar
1½ to 2 teaspoons vanilla
4 eggs, lightly beaten
2 cups cake flour, sifted
1½ teaspoons baking powder
Powdered sugar, optional

Mix cream cheese, butter, and sugar until creamy. Add vanilla and mix well. Add eggs, blending well. Sift baking powder into flour and gradually add to creamed mixture. Bake in greased and floured 9x5 inch loaf pan at 325 degrees for 1 hour and 20 minutes; or until done. Let cool in pan 5 to 10 minutes then remove. Dust with powdered sugar, if desired.

COMMENTS: This is a delicious rich cake. I prefer to bake the recipe in mini-loaf pans and use them as gifts. It is marvelous with fresh fruit, such as strawberries on top!

J. R. HARTMAN/JENNIFER HARTMAN
CALF SCRAMBLE

CHOCOLATE ORANGE COCONUT CAKE

1 dark chocolate or fudge cake mix
2 cups sour cream
2 cups sugar
2 packages frozen fresh coconut or 1½ cups coconut
1 large Cool Whip brand topping, thawed
2 teaspoons orange flavoring

Prepare cake mix according to directions, adding 1 teaspoon orange flavoring. Bake in two round layers — cool. Mix the sour cream, sugar, coconut and 1 teaspoon orange flavoring. Reserve ¾ cup. When cake layers are cool, cut each layer in two, making 4 layers. Spread sour cream mixture between each layer. Add reserved mix to whipped topping and frost sides and top of cake. Let cake stand in refrigerator at least twenty four hours and it's better after three days.

DOTTIE BIEDIGER
AUCTION SALES

POPPY SEED CAKE

3 cups flour
2 cups sugar
1 cup oil
½ teaspoon salt
½ teaspoon baking soda
4 eggs
1 teaspoon vanilla
1 can milk — evaporated (large size)
1 jar poppy seed mix

In large bowl, combine all above. Mix well with beater until well blended. Bake in tube pan until done — usually 1 hour or longer. Bake at 350 degrees. Grease and flour pan well. Can be baked in a bundt pan, but bakes better in a tube pan. (When mixing, I mix the milk a small amount at a time until blended.)

MARY ELLEN PENWELL
AUCTION SALES

DATE CAKE

3 eggs
1 cup sugar
¾ cup shortening (or 1½ sticks oleo)
1 cup coffee or water
3 cups flour
1 level teaspoon soda
1 teaspoon vanilla
2 teaspoons baking powder
1 teaspoon cinnamon
1 cup raisins
1 cup pecans, chopped
1 large package dates, chopped
2 teaspoons cocoa

In large bowl, have oleo at room temperature and add sugar, beat; add eggs, beat; add coffee a little at a time, and flour a little at a time. In last cup of flour, put cocoa, soda, baking powder and cinnamon. Add dates, pecans and raisins. Bake in tube pan 45 minutes to 1 hour at 325 degrees.

ROSALINE CARTER
LIFE MEMBER

POPPY SEED CAKE

1 package white cake mix
1 large package instant vanilla pudding mix
½ cup orange juice
½ cup water
½ cup cooking oil
5 eggs
2 tablespoons Poppy seed

Mix ingredients in bowl and beat 5 minutes at high speed with mixer. Pour in greased sheet, tube or bundt pan. Bake at 350 degrees for 45 minutes. Cool slightly before removing from pan. Sprinkle with powdered sugar.

ANNE OATES
COMMITTEE SECRETARY

GIRDLE BUSTER CAKE

1 stick butter
1 cup flour
1 cup chopped pecans

Blend together, spread evenly in a 13x9 inch pan, bake 20 minutes at 350 degrees.

8 ounces cream cheese
1 box powdered sugar
½ of a 12 ounce carton Cool Whip topping

Mix together and spread over cooled crust.

1 package instant vanilla pudding
1 package instant chocolate pudding
3 cups milk

Mix together and add as the third layer. Top with remaining ½ of the Cool Whip topping, sprinkle with pecans and drizzle with chocolate syrup. Chill before serving. Serves 20.

REBA ROBERSON
AUCTION SALES

20 MINUTE FUDGE CAKE

2 cups flour
2 cups sugar
2 sticks oleo
1 cup water
4 tablespoons cocoa

½ cup buttermilk
½ teaspoon salt
1 teaspoon soda
2 eggs
1 teaspoon vanilla

Sift together 2 cups flour and 2 cups sugar. Combine in a saucepan the oleo, water and cocoa, stir and cook over medium heat to boiling. Pour over dry ingredients. Stir well and add the remaining ingredients. Mix well, pour into well greased sheath pan. Bake at 400 degrees for 20 minutes. Frost with chocolate icing, mocha whipped cream frosting or chocolate cream cheese frosting (see under frostings).

VERNA SKLOSS

CHEESE CAKE

Crust:
1½ cups vanilla wafer crumbs
½ stick butter melted

Mix crumbs and butter and press into 1½ quart pyrex dish.

Filling:
1 pound cream cheese
3 eggs
⅔ cup sugar
1 teaspoon almond extract

Combine all the ingredients above and beat until smooth, pour over crust. Bake 25 minutes at 350 degrees.

Topping:
½ pint sour cream
3 tablespoons sugar
1 teaspoon vanilla

Beat with wire wisk the above ingredients. Pour over cake and bake 10 minutes at 350 degrees.

GEORGE B. WOODS
AUCTION SALES

RUM CAKE

1 cup pecans
1 box yellow cake mix
1 small box vanilla pudding mix,
  not instant

½ cup water
½ cup light rum
½ cup oil
4 eggs

Prepare tube or bundt pan by grease and flour method or spray. Sprinkle nuts in bottom of pan. Mix remaining ingredients and pour over nuts. Bake at 325 degrees for about 30 to 45 minutes.

Glaze:
1 cup sugar
¼ cup rum

½ cup water
1 stick oleo

Mix all ingredients and cook 1 minute. When cake is done, place on cooling rack and spoon glaze over hot cake. Let set for 30 minutes. Use only ½ of glaze if you do not like cake real moist.

PATRICIA GARZA
WESTERN COOKBOOK
CHAIRMAN

GREAT GRANDMOTHER SCOTT'S POTATO CAKE

2 cups sugar
1 cup cream or milk
1 cup butter
1 cup mashed potatoes
  (cooked & cooled)
½ cup chocolate cocoa
1 teaspoon cinnamon

½ teaspoon nutmeg
½ teaspoon cloves
1 teaspoon baking powder
3 cups flour
4 eggs, separated
1 cup chopped pecans

Cream butter and sugar. Add mashed potatoes and egg yolks, one at a time. Sift chocolate, spices, baking powder, and flour together. Add dry ingredients alternately with cream. Add pecans and fold in beaten stiff egg whites. Batter will be thick. Bake at 350 degrees for 45 minutes in greased and floured angel food cake pan.

SCOTT ABBEY WEST
AUCTION SALES

RUM CAKE

1 cup margarine
2 cups sugar
4 eggs
1 cup buttermilk
3 cups flour

⅓ teaspoon salt
½ teaspoon soda
½ teaspoon baking powder
1 teaspoon vanilla
1 teaspoon rum extract

Glaze:
1 cup sugar
½ cup water
1 teaspoon rum extract

Cream sugar and margarine together. Add one egg at a time, beating well after each. Mix all dry ingredients together in separate bowl. To creamed mixture, add buttermilk, alternately with dry mixture (beginning and ending with buttermilk). Add vanilla and rum extract.

Bake in tube pan at 325 degrees for one hour, or until cake begins to pull from sides.

Bring sugar and water to a boil and remove from heat. Set pan on damp towel. Add rum. While cake is still warm, apply glaze with pastry brush.

CHERI HUGHES/BOBBY HUGHES
HORSE SHOW

APPLESAUCE CAKE

½ cup Wesson Oil
2 cups sugar
2 eggs
1 can applesauce
3 cups flour
1½ teaspoon soda

1½ teaspoon salt
1 teaspoon cinnamon
½ teaspoon allspice
½ cup water
1½ cups walnuts

Mix shortening, sugar, eggs, and applesauce. Add flour, soda, and seasoning and water. Then mix add walnuts. Pour into greased and floured flat pan. Bake 350 degrees for about 45 minutes.

KEN LANGHAM
ENTERTAINMENT

COCONUT LOVERS DELIGHT CAKE

1 package (2 layer size) yellow cake mix
1 package vanilla instant pudding mix (4 servings)
1⅓ cups water
4 eggs
¼ cup oil
2 cups coconut
1 cup nuts, chopped

Blend cake mix, pudding mix, water, eggs and oil in large bowl. Beat at medium speed of electric mixer four minutes. Stir in coconut and nuts. Pour into three greased and floured pans (9"). Bake at 350 for 35 minutes. Cool in pans 15 minutes; remove and cool on rack. Fill and frost with Coconut-Cream Cheese Frosting.

Coconut Cream Cheese Frosting:
4 tablespoons butter or margarine
2 cups coconut
1 8-ounce package cream cheese
2 teaspoons milk
3½ cups sifted confectioners sugar
½ teaspoon vanilla

Melt 2 tablespoons butter in skillet; add coconut; stir constantly over low heat until golden brown. Spread coconut on absorbent paper to cool. Cream two tablespoons butter with cream cheese. Add milk and sugar alternately, beating well. Add vanilla; stir in 1¾ cups of the coconut. Spread on tops and sides of cake layers. Sprinkle with remaining coconut.

ROBYN MERCHANT
AUCTION SALES

BURNT CARAMEL CAKE

1 cup brown sugar, burnt
1 cup boiling water

Burn brown sugar in heavy skillet, add 1 cup boiling water and cook thick as syrup. (Be sure to save 3 tablespoons for icing.)

4 eggs, whites and yolks beaten separately
1½ cups brown sugar
½ cup butter
1 cup cold water
3 cups flour, after sifted
2 teaspoons baking powder, rounded
1 teaspoon vanilla

Cream butter and sugar. Add yolks little at a time, then flour and water. Add burnt syrup, make sure this is cool. Beaten egg whites should be folded in last, add vanilla. Bake at 350 about 35 minutes.

Icing:
2 cups brown sugar
1 cup thick cream
3 tablespoons burnt syrup
2 tablespoons butter
1 teaspoon vanilla
Cook to soft ball. Spread on cake.

TOMMY R. SMITH
HORSE SHOW

LEMON MERINGUE CAKE

1 package Duncan Hines Deluxe II Lemon Supreme cake
  mix
1 package (4-serving size) lemon pudding and pie filling
  mix
2 egg whites
¼ cup sugar

Use two 8-inch round layer cake pans; mix, bake, and cool cake as directed on package. Cook lemon pudding and pie filling mix as directed for pie filling. Cool 30 minutes; stir several times. Beat egg whites until frothy in a bowl; gradually add sugar; beat until stiff but not dry. Split each cake layer into 2 thin layers. Stack on cookie sheets or oven-proof plates. Spread lemon pudding between layers and on top of cake. Spread meringue around sides of cake. Bake at 450 degrees for five minutes, or until light brown. Cool to room temperature before serving. Store cake in refrigerator.

About 16 servings.

MICKEY HUBER
CALF SCRAMBLE

APPLE KUCHEN

½ cup oleo
1 18½-ounce yellow cake mix
½ cup coconut
1 21-ounce can apple pie filling
½ cup sugar
1 teaspoon cinnamon
1 cup sour cream
2 egg yolks

Preheat oven to 350 degrees. Cut oleo into cake mix until crumbly. Mix in coconut. Pat mixture into 13x9 inch pan. Build up edges. Bake 10 minutes. Put apples on baked crust. Mix sugar and cinnamon. Sprinkle on apples. Blend sour cream and egg yolks. Drizzle over apples. Bake 25 minutes.

MRS. BOB FLOWERS
CALF SCRAMBLE

JAMES SMITHS' MEXICAN WEDDING CAKE

2 cups sugar
2 cups flour
2 teaspoons soda
2 eggs, beaten
Dash of salt
1 No. 2 can crushed pineapple
1 cup chopped nuts

Mix ingredients in order given. Bake in greased and floured bundt pan 30-45 minutes in a 350 degree oven.

Frosting:
1 stick softened butter
1 8-ounce package cream cheese
1 box powdered sugar

Cream ingredients and frost cake. Sprinkle with a few chopped nuts.

JAMES SMITH
GO WESTERN

COWBOY COFFEE CAKE

2½ cups flour
½ teaspoon salt
2 cups brown sugar
⅔ cup shortening
2 teaspoon baking powder
½ teaspoon soda
½ teaspoon cinnamon
½ teaspoon nutmeg
1 cup sour milk
2 eggs, well beaten
1 cup chopped pecans

Mix flour, salt, sugar, and shortening, until crumbly. Reserve ½ cup of mixture to sprinkle over top of batter. To remaining crumbs, add baking powder, soda, and spices. Mix thoroughly. Add milk and eggs, mix well. Pour into pan that has been lined with waxed paper. Sprinkle reserved crumbs, nuts, and cinnamon on top. Bake at 375 degrees for 25-30 minutes. Yields 12-15 servings.

OSIE ASHFORD

CHOCOLATE PUDDING CAKE

Layer 1:
1 cup flour
1 stick melted margarine
1 cup chopped nuts

Combine and spread in 13×9 pan, bake 20 min. at 350 degrees. Cool completely.

Layer 2:
1 cup powdered sugar
1 8-ounce softened cream cheese
1 large Cool Whip brand topping

Reserve enough Cool Whip to put thin layer on top. Combine and spread on crust.

LAYER 3: Beat two packages instant chocolate pudding and 3 cups milk. Spread thickened instant pudding over cream cheese layer. Then spread with remaining Cool Whip. Grate small chocolate bar on top. Keep refrigerated.

GAYLE HARRIS
ENTERTAINMENT

FRUIT CAKE

12 ounces candied cherries
12 ounces coconut
½ teaspoon salt
3 cups pecans
12 ounces candied pineapple
1 can sweetened condensed milk
½ teaspoon almond extract

Mix all ingredients together and put in buttered loaf pan. Cook 30 minutes at 300 degrees, then 30 minutes at 275 degrees.

RUTH RENEAU/ D. W. RENEAU
READY TO COOK POULTRY
CHAIRMAN

PUMPKIN CAKE

1 package Pillsbury Plus yellow cake mix
3 eggs
½ cup water
1 cup pumpkin pie filling
2 teaspoons pumpkin pie spice
Glaze:
1 cup powdered sugar
1½ ounces cream cheese, softened
2 tablespoons milk
1 teaspoon vanilla

Preheat oven 350 degrees. Grease and flour a 12 cup fluted tube pan. In large bowl, blend first five ingredients until moistened. Beat 2 minutes at highest speed. Pour into prepared pan. Bake 30 to 40 minutes or until toothpick inserted in center comes out clean. Cool upright in pan 25 minutes; turn onto serving plate. Cool completely. Blend glaze ingredients in small bowl until smooth. If needed add a few more drops of milk to make glaze consistency. Spoon over cooled cake. Refrigerate any leftovers.

MARY ELLEN PENWELL
AUCTION SALES

CHOCOLATE CREAM CHEESE FROSTING

2 3-ounce packages cream cheese
2 tablespoons light cream
2 cups powdered sugar, sifted
¼ teaspoon salt
1 teaspoon vanilla
2 packages sweet cooking chocolate

Place chocolate in small bowl and set over hot water until melted. Cool slightly. Blend in cream cheese and cream add sugar gradually mixing well after each addition. Add salt and vanilla.

VERNA SKLOSS

MOCHA WHIPPED CREAM FROSTING

1½ cups heavy cream
3 tablespoons sugar
1 tablespoon instant coffee
2 teaspoons cocoa
2 tablespoons rum

Whip until soft peaks form.

VERNA SKLOSS

CHOCOLATE ICING

Granny's Sweet Pantry

1 stick oleo
4 tablespoons cocoa
6 tablespoons milk
1 box powdered sugar, sifted
1 teaspoon vanilla
1 cup pecans, chopped

Combine oleo, cocoa and milk into a saucepan. After mixture boils add 1 box powdered sugar and 1 teaspoon vanilla. Mix well, add pecans and put on cake while cake and icing are still hot.

VERNA SKLOSS

UNCOOKED FLUFFY FROSTING

¼ teaspoon salt
2 egg whites
1 cup powdered sugar
1 cup white corn syrup
1¼ teaspoons vanilla

Beat salt and egg whites until peaks form. Add sugar by spoonfuls. Beat until smooth, gradually beat in the syrup and continue beating until frosting holds a peak, then fold in vanilla. You cannot over beat. Enough for 2 layers.

MARY ELLEN PENWELL
AUCTION SALES

PEACH CAKE WITH CREAM CHEESE

Grease bottom and sides of a 9 inch deep dish or 10 inch pie pan for batter, combine:

¾ cup flour
½ teaspoon salt
1 teaspoon baking powder
1 small package vanilla pudding (not instant)
1 egg
3 tablespoons margarine
½ cup milk

Beat 2 minutes and pour in pie pan. Place well-drained peach slices (15-20 ounce can) or pineapple chunks over batter. Reserve juice. Combine in small bowl:

1 8-ounce package cream cheese, softened
½ cup sugar
3 tablespoons reserved juice

Beat 2 minutes at medium speed, spoon on top of peaches to within 1 inch of batter edge. Combine 1 tablespoon sugar and ½ teaspoon cinnamon. Sprinkle over top. Bake 30-45 minutes until crust is golden. Store in refrigerator.

DAVID WEAVER BY MEGAN L. TUTTLE
WESTERN PARADE

MRS. GRAY'S CHOCOLATE CAKE

2 cups sugar
½ cup buttermilk
2 cups flour
2 eggs
1 stick butter
1 teaspoon soda
½ cup shortening
1 teaspoon vanilla
¼ cup cocoa (4 tablespoons)

Sift sugar, flour, and soda together. Set aside. Heat on stove butter, shortening, and cocoa until boil. Pour over flour and sugar and mix. Add buttermilk, eggs, and vanilla. Pour into greased floured pans. Cook at 350 degrees for about 20 minutes.

Frosting:
1 stick butter
¼ cup cocoa
6 tablespoons milk
1 box powdered sugar

Put in saucepan, heat to boil, add sugar and milk.

KEN LANGHAM
ENTERTAINMENT

Horse Show

Every year some of the nation's finest horseflesh can be found among the Paint Horses, Appaloosas, and Quarter Horses, and in the Open Cutting Horse Contest at the San Antonio Stock Show.

Not only are horses judged on breeding and conformation, but also according to various performance classes, including roping, reining, barrel racing, stump racing, pole bending, and western pleasure.

The public may watch all of these fascinating contests in the Horse Arena, and admission is free. At the Horse Show you will find not only examples of the finest in horse breeding, but also superb riders and handlers.

MILROY POWELL
CHAIRMAN & GENERAL
SUPERINTENDENT

FATHEREE'S GRAND CHAMPION COW PATTY PIE

Crust:
1 stick oleo, melted
1 cup pecans, ground
1 cup flour

Mix together and pat in 9x13 pan and slightly up the sides. Bake 12 to 15 minutes in 350 degree oven.

Next layer:
1 8-ounce package cream cheese
1 cup powdered sugar

Fold in 1 cup Cool Whip brand topping. Spread over crust.

2nd layer:
1 package chocolate pudding, instant
1 package vanilla pudding, instant
1½ cups milk per package, 3 cups total

Spread instant pudding mixture on top of the cream cheese layer. Top with Cool Whip brand topping, coconut, and chocolate sprinkles. Chill 2 to 3 hours.

BILL FATHEREE
AUCTION SALES

BUTTERMILK PIE

1 unbaked pie shell
3 eggs, well beaten
2 tablespoons flour
½ teaspoon vanilla
2 cups sugar
1 stick oleo
¾ cup buttermilk

Blend and pour into unbaked pie shell. Bake 325 degrees for 45 minutes.

COLLEEN MOCK
HORSE SHOW

SOUTHERN STYLE CUSTARD PIE

3 eggs
1 13-ounce can evaporated milk
1 cup sugar
3 tablespoons all purpose flour
3 tablespoons melted oleo
¼ teaspoon ground nutmeg
1 teaspoon cinnamon
1 teaspoon vanilla extract

Grease and flour a 9 inch pie pan. Make sure all areas are covered. Combine all ingredients in a blender; blend 30 seconds. Pour into pie pan, and bake at 350 degrees for 40 to 45 minutes, or until a knife inserted in center comes out clean. Pie will rise but will settle as it cools and form a light crust. Yield: one 9 inch pie.

SHA HAYS
GO WESTERN

FROZEN STRAWBERRY PIE

½ pint whipping cream, whipped
2 egg whites
¾ cup sugar
Dash salt
1 tablespoon lemon juice
1 package frozen strawberries, partially thawed

Beat egg whites, sugar, salt, lemon juice, and strawberries together with electric mixer at high speed for 15 minutes. Fold in whipped cream.

Pour into graham cracker crusts. Store in freezer. Yields 2 large pies.

RON SNOWDEN
JUNIOR STEER RIDING

CHERRY CHEESE CAKE PIE

1 8-ounce package cream cheese, softened
1 cup confectioners sugar
1 teaspoon vanilla
1 cup whipped cream
¼ teaspoon almond extract
1 can cherry pie filling
1 baked 9 inch pastry shell

Beat together cream cheese, sugar, and vanilla until smooth. Fold in whipped cream. Pour into shell. Make well in center. Add almond extract to cherry pie filling and place in center of shell. Chill until set.

JAN HERRINGTON
AUCTION SALES

APPLE SOUR CREAM PIE

1 egg
1 cup sugar
1 cup sour cream
2 tablespoons flour
½ teaspoon salt
4 cups sliced apples
9 inch unbaked pie shell

Refrigerate until needed. Preheat oven 400 degrees. Beat egg slightly, add sugar, sour cream, flour and salt. Mix well, add apples, mix until well blended. Bake 30 minutes or until apples are tender.

Topping:
½ cup brown sugar firmly-packed
⅓ cup flour
¼ cup butter or margarine
½ teaspoon cinnamon

Mix brown sugar, flour, butter and cinnamon until crumbly. Sprinkle on pie. Reduce heat to 350 degrees and bake 15 minutes longer.

VIVION COLLIER
SOUVENIR PROGRAM

CHOCOLATE EGGNOG LAYER PIE

1 envelope unflavored gelatin
½ cup water
⅓ cup sugar
2 tablespoons cornstarch
¼ teaspoon salt
2 cups commercial eggnog
1½ squares unsweetened chocolate, melted
1 teaspoon vanilla
1 baked 9 inch pastry shell
1 teaspoon rum
2 cups whipping cream, divided
¼ cup powdered sugar

Soften gelatin in water; set aisde. Combine sugar, corn-starch and salt in saucepan; gradually stir in eggnog. Cook over medium heat, stirring constantly, until thickened — cook 2 minutes. Remove from heat, add gelatin. Stir until dissolved. Divide filling in half; set one half aside to cool. Add melted chocolate and vanilla to other half of filling; stir well and pour into pastry shell. Chill. Add rum to remaining filling. Whip 1 cup whipping cream; add to cooled rum mixture. Spoon over chocolate layer and chill. Whip remaining cream, add powdered sugar and spread over pie.

ANNELLA EGBERT
AUCTION SALES

DREAM PIE

2 graham cracker pie crusts
1 carton (9-ounce) Cool Whip brand topping
1 can (20-ounce) crushed pineapple, well drained
3 tablespoons lemon juice
1 14-ounce can sweetened condensed milk

Mix all ingredients in a large bowl. Stir until well mixed. Chill 30 minutes. Freezes well. Pecans may be added before mixing.

LEE NOONAN
RURAL YOUTH

CHOCOLATE PIE

⅓ cup sifted enriched flour or
¼ cup cornstarch
¼ teaspoon salt
1 cup sugar
3 egg yolks
2 tablespoons butter
½ teaspoon vanilla

Melt one ounce square unsweetened chocolate in 2 cups scalded milk. Mix flour, sugar, and salt gradually adding milk and chocolate. Cook over moderate heat stirring constantly until mixture thickens and comes to a boil. Continue to cook for 2 minutes while slowly adding small amounts of egg yolk into hot mixture, stirring continually. After total egg yolk has been added continue to cook for one more minute stirring constantly; add butter, vanilla and cool. Put on meringue.

KATY "DID"

CHOCOLATE PIE WITH COCONUT CRUST

1 stick oleo or butter
2 cups coconut

Brown coconut in butter in skillet and press in 8 or 9 inch pie pan.

1 8-ounce bar of chocolate with almonds
3 tablespoons pre-made coffee (cooled)

Melt chocolate in pan with coffee and cool.

1 large carton Cool Whip brand topping

Fold cooled chocolate and coffee into cool whip and pour into coconut crust. Optional: Grate additional ½ chocolate bar onto finished pie. Delicious and Fantastic!

SHIRLEY SCHREIBER
AUCTION SALES

EASY MINCEMEAT

1 pound lean ground beef
4 peeled chopped apples
2 cups dark brown sugar
1 cup raisins
1 cup vinegar
1½ teaspoons salt
1 tablespoon cinnamon
1 tablespoon allspice
1 tablespoon cloves

Combine all ingredients in a large pan and mix well. Add one cup of water and boil slowly 2 to 3 hours. Store covered in the refrigerator. Makes two 9—inch pies.

TOMMY REAGAN
GULF COAST CATTLEMAN

EASY PUMPKIN PIE

1½ cups milk
1 package (6 serving size) vanilla instant pudding & pie filling
1 cup canned pumpkin
1 teaspoon pumpkin pie spice
1 cup Cool Whip brand topping
1 baked 9 inch pie shell, cooled

Combine milk, pie filling mix, pumpkin, spice, and whipped topping in a deep narrow-bottomed bowl. Beat at lowest speed of electric mixer for one minute. Pour into pie shell, chill until set at least 3 hours. Garnish with additional whipped topping.

MARY ELLEN PENWELL
AUCTION AND PROGRAM

FRENCH PIE

4 eggs
8 squares soda crackers, rolled fine
1 cup chopped nuts
1 teaspoon vanilla
1 cup sugar

Separate eggs. Beat egg whites stiff. Beat yolks and 1 tablespoon of beaten whites. Add sugar, beating well. Add cracker crumbs gradually while beating. Add chopped nuts and vanilla. Fold in remaining beaten whites. Bake in well buttered glass pan in a 350 degree oven for about 25 minutes. Cool. (Pie will fall slightly while cooling). Top with whipped cream.

SHIRLEY SCHREIBER
AUCTION SALES

GRASSHOPPER PIE

24 cream-filled chocolate cookies, finely crushed*
¼ cup margarine, melted
¼ cup milk
Few drops of food coloring
1 jar marshmallow creme
2 cups heavy cream, whipped
Few drops peppermint extract

*Cookies — Burry's fudge filled shortcake cookies or something similar.

Combine cookie crumbs and margarine. Press into 9 inch spring pan, reserving ½ cup of mixture for topping. Gradually add milk, extract, and food coloring to marshmallow creme, mixing until well blended. Fold in whipped cream; pour into pan. Sprinkle with remaining crumbs. Freeze. Makes 8 to 10 servings.

SHIRLEY SCHREIBER
AUCTION SALES

MY GREAT GRANDMOTHER'S
LOVELY LUSCIOUS LIME CHIFFON PIE

1 9-inch baked pastry shell, cooled
3 eggs, separated
1 can sweetened condensed milk
Green food coloring
½ cup lime juice
2 teaspoons grated lime rind, optional
¼ teaspoon cream of tartar
1 cup (½ pint) heavy cream, chilled
1 tablespoon sugar

In large bowl, beat egg yolks until thick and lemon colored. Continue to beat; gradually add sweetened condensed milk. Add food coloring. Beat until well blended. Add lime juice and 1 teaspoon grated rind. Beat well. Beat together cream of tartar and egg whites until soft peaks form. Gently fold into lime mixture. Pour into baked shell. Refrigerate 5 hours until set. When serving, whip cream until stiff. Fold in sugar. Garnish chilled pie with whipped cream and sprinkle remaining grated lime rind over top.

ELIZABETH JACOBS
INTERNATIONAL/MEXICO DAY

CRUSTLESS PECAN PIE

4 egg whites
1 cup sugar
Pinch of salt
1 teaspoon vanilla
1 cup graham cracker crumbs
1 cup pecans

Beat egg whites until foamy, but not stiff. Add other ingredients and place in a greased pie pan. Bake at 325 degrees for 30 minutes. Delicious served with ice cream or Cool Whip brand topping.

MARY ELLEN PENWELL
AUCTION AND PROGRAM

FRENCH SILK CHOCOLATE PIE

½ cup butter or margarine
¾ cup sugar
2 1-ounce squares unsweetened chocolate, melted and
  cooled
1 teaspoon vanilla
2 eggs
1 8-inch baked pastry shell

Cream butter, gradually add sugar, creaming until light.
Blend in chocolate and vanilla. Add eggs, one at a time,
beating 3 minutes after each addition on medium speed of
electric mixer. Turn into pastry shell. Chill several hours.
Garnish with whipped cream and chocolate curls.

FURNISHED FOR DAVID WEAVER
WESTERN PARADE
BY JANIS R. GRAHAM

PUMPKIN PECAN PIE

1 package pie crust mix
1 1-pound can pumpkin
1 can sweetened condensed milk
1 egg
½ teaspoon salt
½ teaspoon nutmeg
¾ teaspoon cinnamon
½ teaspoon ginger

Combine all ingredients and pour into pie crust (8 inch). Top
with half package pie crust mix, ⅓ cup pecans, ½ cup brown
sugar. Bake at 350 degrees for 50-55 minutes. May be
frozen.

LIBBY JONES
AUCTION SALES

SOUTHERN CHESS PIE

Mix:
1 cup brown sugar, packed
4 cup granulated sugar
1 tablespoon flour
Beat in thoroughly:
2 eggs
2 tablespoons milk
1 teaspoon vanilla
½ cup oleo, melted
Fold in:
1 cup pecans or walnuts

Pour into 9-inch pastry lined pie pan. Bake at 375 degrees 45 to 50 minutes. Just until set.

MRS. BOB FLOWERS
CALF SCRAMBLE

MONA'S PECAN PIE

½ cup sugar
2 tablespoons flour
2 eggs
1 cup white Karo syrup
2 tablespoons butter
1 cup whole pecans
1 teaspoon vanilla

Mix the sugar, flour, butter, eggs, Karo, pecans and vanilla. Pour into uncooked 9-inch pie shell. Cook the first 15 minutes at 400 degrees and turn back to 325 degrees until done.

SAN SABA, INC.
SAN SABA, TEXAS

PECAN PIE

1 unbaked pie shell
3 eggs
½ cup sugar
1 cup corn syrup
⅛ teaspoon salt
1 teaspoon vanilla
¼ cup butter or margarine, melted
1 cup pecans

Beat eggs, add sugar, syrup, salt, vanilla and butter or margarine and nuts. Pour into unbaked pie shell and bake at 350 degrees until crust is brown.

ANNE OATES
SECRETARY

MAW MAW MARTH'S TEXAS PECAN PIE

3 eggs
1 cup white Karo syrup
1 cup pecans
¼ cup butter
1 uncooked pie shell

Beat the eggs, add other ingredients, pour into uncooked pie shell. Bake 45 minutes to one hour at 375 degrees.

DON MARTH
AUCTION SALES

STRAWBERRY DREAM PIE

1 package (4 serving size) vanilla flavor pudding & pie
   filling
1 3-ounce package strawberry flavor gelatin
2 cups water
1 teaspoon lemon juice
1½ cups prepared whipped topping
1 cup sliced strawberries
1 9-inch baked pie shell, cooled

Combine pudding mix, gelatin, water and lemon juice in a
saucepan. Cook and stir over medium heat until mixture
comes to a boil. Pour into a bowl and chill until thickened.
To hasten chilling, place bowl of pudding mixture in larger
bowl of ice and water then stir until thickened. Fold in whipped topping blending well. Stir in strawberries. Pour into pie
shell and chill until set; 1 to 2 hours. Garnish with additional
whipped topping and strawberries.

MARY ELLEN PENWELL
AUCTION AND PROGRAM

LAZY GRASSHOPPER PARFAIT

1 3¾-ounce package vanilla whipped dessert mix
½ cup chocolate wafer crumbs (8 wafers)
2 tablespoons green créme de menthe
1 tablespoon white créme de cacao
Chocolate curls

Prepare whipped dessert mix according to package directions. Fold in créme de menthe and créme de cacao. Chill
about 30 minutes or until mixture mounds when spooned.
Layer in parafit glasses with chocolate crumbs, using about
one tablespoon crumbs between each layer. Chill. Garnish
with chocolate curls. Makes 4 servings.

LYNDA VYVLECKA

PINK ARCTIC FREEZE

8-10 servings:
2 3-ounce packages cream cheese
2 tablespoons mayonnaise or salad dressing
2 tablespoons sugar
1 pound can (2 cups) whole cranberry sauce or
2 cups frozen strawberries
1 9-ounce can crushed pineapple, drained
½ cup chopped walnuts or pecans
1 cup whipped cream
½ cup powdered sugar
1 teaspoon vanilla

Soften cheese, blend in mayonnaise and sugar, add fruit and nuts. Add powdered sugar and vanilla to whipped cream and fold in the cheese mix. Pour into 8½x2½x2½ loaf pan, freeze firm 6-8 hours or overnight. When ready to serve, let stand at room temperature about 15 minutes. Turn out on lettuce slice.

CHARLYNE WILLIAMS
JOHN J. WILLIAMS
CO-CHAIRMAN — CALF SCRAMBLE

PINK FLUFF
(Dessert)

Serves 20

1 can sweetened condensed milk
1 large Cool Whip brand topping
1 can cherry pie filling
1 small can pineapple cubes, drained, no sugar
½ cup nuts

Mix together, stir with spoon — make a day before serving.

For variety you can use: can of pie strawberries or fresh strawberries, unsweetened fruit cocktail or canned whole cranberries.

MICKEY HUBER
CALF SCRAMBLE

PRETZEL STRAWBERRY DESSERT

2 cups pretzels, crushed
¾ cup melted margarine
1 tablespoon sugar
Combine above and put in a 10×14 cake pan
1 package cream cheese, beaten
1 cup powdered sugar
1 cup whipping cream — whipped and chilled
Cover with:
2 3-ounce packages strawberry Jello brand gelatin
2 cups boiling water
2 10-ounce packages frozen strawberries dissolved in
   Jello water

Stir in frozen strawberries until strawberries are separated and start to set. Pour over cheese mixture, refrigerate several hours. Serve with whipped cream. Serves 15-16. Keeps well.

MARGARET AND G. C. WOLFE
G-BAR SIMMENTAL RANCH
LIFE MEMBER

FRIED APPLE RINGS ℰ

¼ cup flour
¼ cup sugar
½ teaspoon cinnamon
½ teaspoon nutmeg
⅛ teaspoon cloves
3 medium unpeeled cooking apples, cored and cut into ½
   inch rings.
¼ cup bacon drippings

Combine first 5 ingredients, mixing well. Dredge apple rings in sugar mixture. Fry in hot bacon drippings, turning once, until golden brown and tender. Yields: 6 servings.

NEW BRAUNFELS SMOKEHOUSE BREAD PUDDING

1 loaf of bread (1pound), cubed
3 ounces raisins
4 eggs
1 cup sugar
4 cups of milk
2 teaspoon vanilla
½ cup brown sugar

In bowl beat eggs and sugar, then add milk and vanilla and beat. Add cubed bread and raisins and mix well. Put in two 9x9x2 cake pans. Sprinkle each pan with ¼ cup of brown sugar. Bake at 350 degrees for 30 minutes or until pudding has risen to top of pans. Cut in 3 inch squares and serve *warm* with *warm* butter sauce.

Butter Sauce:
¾ cup of sugar
3 egg yolks, beaten
2 tablespoons cornstarch dissolved in ¼ cup of water
3 tablespoons melted butter or oleo
2 teaspoons white vanilla
1½ cups of boiling water
⅛ teaspoon of salt

Cream sugar, eggs, and butter. Add cornstarch mixed. Add boiling water slowly. Cook over hot water until thickened; stirring frequently. Add vanilla.

NEW BRAUNFELS SMOKEHOUSE

OLD FARM PUDDING

4 or 5 slices dry, stale, white bread
2 cups applesauce, sweetened to taste
1 teaspoon cinnamon
¼ teaspoon nutmeg
½ cup chopped pecans
½ cup raisins
2 tablespoons butter
2 cups milk
2 eggs, beaten
½ cup sugar
1 teaspoon vanilla extract
Dash of salt

Prepare bread crumbs by breaking into small pieces. Put half in bottom of a buttered deep baking dish (1½ quart). Add cinnamon and nutmeg to applesauce and spread over the bread in dish. Sprinkle with pecans and raisins. Dot with butter. Mix milk, eggs, salt, sugar and vanilla, and pour over the bread and applesauce. Bake at 350 degrees for 45 minutes to 1 hour or until pudding is puffed and set. Serve warm with half and half cream or serve cold with vanilla ice cream. Serves 6 to 8.

GERTRUDE BURRIS

TEXAS BREAD PUDDING

6 slices bread, toasted
2 eggs
1 cup sugar
2 tablespoons butter or oleo
1 teaspoon vanilla
1 cup pecans
1 cup raisins
1 cup coconut
1 teaspoon cinnamon
Milk enough to moisten good

Crumble toast into fine pieces, add milk, sugar, and eggs; beat; add oleo, vanilla. Let set a few minutes. Add pecans, raisins, and cinnamon, and coconut; spread in greased cookie sheet. Sprinkle with a little cinnamon and sugar and bake at 350 degrees until slightly brown. Cut in squares and serve cold.

ROSALINE CARTER
LIFE MEMBER

LEMON ANGEL DESSERT ℰ

1 package lemon Jello brand gelatin
4 egg yolks
4 cups sugar
2 lemons, juiced and rind grated
1 Angel food cake

Cook until thick the eggs, sugar, and lemon juce. Dissolve 1 package lemon Jello brand gelatin in 1½ cups hot water and add to above mixture. Let cook until thick. This must be very cool before the following is added. Beat egg whites and add ½ cup sugar beating well. Fold in cooled lemon mixture. Whip 1 cup cream and add to above mixture. Break an angel food cake in rather small pieces (about half a large cake or a medium size loaf cake.) Place a layer of cake pieces in an oiled pan — then layer of mixture. Continue until all used up. Refrigerate over night and cut in any shape. Serves 12 but keeps a couple of days.

ORANGE ANGEL DESSERT

6 eggs, separated
Juice of 1½ lemons
¾ cup sugar
2 tablespoons gelatin
½ cup water

1 cup orange juice
¾ cup sugar
1 angel food cake
Whipped cream

To well beaten egg yolks, add lemon juice, sugar and ½ cup orange juice. Cook the mixture until thick. Add gelatin dissolved in ½ cup water. Add the remaining cup of orange juice. When cool, fold in beaten egg whites to which ¾ cup sugar has been added. Break angel food cake into small pieces. Put a layer of cake, then a layer of orange mixture into a greased mold. Ice with whipped cream.

HENRY BEKEN, JR.
CALF SCRAMBLE

APPLE CRUNCH DESSERT

½ cup butter or margarine, softened
1 package butter pecan cake mix
2 cans apple pie filling
½ cup walnuts or pecans

Heat oven to 350 degrees. Cut butter into cake mix (dry) until crumbly. Reserve 1½ cups crumbly mixture, pat remaining mixture lightly in ungreased oblong pan, 13x9x2 inches, building up ½ inch edges. Spread pie filling over mixture in pan to within ½ inch of edges. Mix nuts and crumbly mixture; sprinkle over top.

Bake 45 to 50 minutes. Serve warm and if desired with Cool Whip brand topping or ice cream.

Note: For thinner, crisper dessert, use 1 can pie filling and bake 35 to 40 minutes.

ROBYN MERCHANT
AUCTION AND PROGRAM

RED LETTER — DAY TORTE

Crust:
Sift 2 cups sifted all purpose flour and 1 teaspoon salt; cut in 1 cup shortening. Add 1 slightly beaten egg; stir until a soft dough. Pat over bottom of 11½x7½x1½ baking dish. Bake at 425 degrees about 20 minutes.

Filling:
1 1-pound can tart red cherries (water packed)
¾ cup sugar
3 tablespoons tapioca
3 slightly beaten egg yolks
¼ teaspoon red food coloring
2 teaspoons lemon juice

Drain cherries, reserving juice. Add water to juice to make 1 cup. Combine juice with sugar, egg yolks, tapioca, and coloring. Let stand 5 minutes. Cook and stir mixture until it thickens and comes to a boil. Add cherries and lemon juice. Cool slightly.

Meringue:
Beat 3 egg whites with 1 teaspoon vanilla, ¼ teaspoon cream of tarter, dash of salt, until soft peaks form. Slowly add ¾ cup sugar, beating until stiff peaks. Fold in 1 cup walnuts or pecans (chopped). Pour filling over baked crust; top with meringue. Bake in moderate oven at 350 degrees about 20 minutes, or until lightly browned. Cool. Cut into 9 or 12 squares.

SHIRLEY SCHREIBER
AUCTION SALES

CHOCOLATE TORTE

Layer 1:
1 stick oleo
1 cup flour
1 cup finely chopped pecans

Mix and press into 9"x12" pan. Bake 20 minutes at 350 degrees.

Layer 2:
1 8-ounce package cream cheese
1 cup powdered sugar
1 cup Cool Whip brand topping

Mix well and spread over cooled crust.

Layer 3:
2 small packages instant chocolate pudding and 3 cups milk

Mix pudding with milk and pour over layer 2.

Layer 4:
Spread more Cool Whip over last layer, more chopped pecans and a bit of grated chocolate. (like a bar of chocolate candy)

SHARON AND TERRY BISHOP
ENTERTAINMENT

CHOCOLATE DESSERT

1½ cup flour
1 stick melted oleo
½ cup pecans, chopped

Mix above and press down in bottom of 9x13 inch cake pan. Bake at 375 degrees for 10 to 15 minutes.

1 8-ounce package cream cheese
1 cup powdered sugar
1 cup Cool Whip brand topping

Mix these above ingredients and spread over first cooled layer of crust. (I have found this mixture spreads easier if you add a little more Cool Whip as you try to spread it.) Refrigerate for one hour.

3rd layer
2 packages of instant chocolate pudding
3 cups of cold milk

Blend until thickened and spread on top of 2nd layer.

4th layer
Spread remaining Cool Whip (from large carton) over pudding layer. Sprinkle ½ cup of chopped pecans on top. Keep refrigerated.

DOROTHY BOOTH

CHERRY DELIGHT

Crust:
2 cups flour
2 sticks oleo
1 cup pecans, chopped

Mix all together, press into glass pie pan. Bake until slightly brown in 350 degree oven (approximately 20 to 30 minutes)

Middle part:

1 8-ounce package cream cheese
1 9-ounce carton Cool Whip brand topping

Beat the two together, then add 2 cups confectioners sugar. Beat the three together. When crust cools, put the middle layer on crust.

Top:

2 cans of cherry pie filling

Chill. Sprinkle a few chopped pecans on top to look pretty.

FRANCES JOHNSON/MORRIS JOHNSON
STAFF MEMBER

HUNTING CAMP COBBLER

3 cups fresh peaches
1 cup sugar
1 cup flour
4 tablespoons baking powder
1 cup sugar
⅔ cup milk

Combine fruit with 1 cup sugar and simmer 5 minutes. Melt 1 stick margarine in baking dish. Mix balance ingredients into a batter and pour over melted butter. Pour peaches on top, do not mix. Bake 25 minutes at 350 degrees. When crust has risen to the top, sprinkle with sugar and bake 10 minutes more. Serves 6.

RUTH RENEAU
READY TO COOK POULTRY

PAUL'S DEWBERRY COBBLER

Crust:
1½ cups biscuit mix
2 tablespoons sugar
½ cup milk

Filling:
2 pints fresh dewberries cooked, sweetened, and thickened
¼ stick butter
3 tablespoons sugar
½ teaspoon cinnamon (optional)

Mix together first three ingredients. Roll out ⅔ for bottom crust, saving remaining ⅓. Fit into pyrex loaf pan. Pour in dewberries, dot with butter. Roll out remaining ⅓ dough, fit on top of berries. Bring sides of bottom crust over and seal. Sprinkle with sugar and cinnamon. Bake at 400 degrees for 30 or 40 minutes or until golden brown. You may substitute any fresh fruit or berries. Serves six.

PAUL D. SHIRES

HUNTING LEASE QUICK COBBLER

¼ cup butter or margarine
¾ cup flour
¾ cup sugar
¾ teaspoon baking powder
1 teaspoon cinnamon
¾ cup milk
1 can cherry pie filling

Melt butter in 7x11 baking dish. Mix next 5 ingredients together and pour over butter. DO NOT MIX. Pour cherry pie filling over batter. DO NOT MIX. Bake at 325 degrees approximately 35-40 minutes. Serve warm or cold with or without Cool Whip.

NINI KAUFMAN
GO WESTERN

FRUIT COBBLER

1 cup flour
1 cup sugar
2½ teaspoons baking powder
¼ pound margarine or butter
¾ cup milk
1 teaspoon vanilla
1½ cups fruit

Mix flour, sugar and baking powder. Melt butter or margarine and set aside. Add vanilla to milk, then add milk to flour, sugar and baking powder, and mix. Pour mixture in baking dish and pour melted butter over mixture. Put drained fruit over this mixture. (fruit on top) Put in preheated oven and bake at 350 degrees for 50 minutes.

LARRY KELLER
TICKET SALES

GRANDMA'S EASY COBBLER

1 stick margarine
1 cup flour
1 cup sugar
2 teaspoon baking powder
¼ teaspoon salt
⅔ cup milk

Melt margarine in casserole. Mix dry ingredients and milk. Pour mixture into margarine; add 1 large can fruit with juice. Do not stir. Bake at 350 degrees for 45 minutes.

MARY ELLEN PENWELL
AUCTION AND PROGRAM

VANILLA ICE CREAM

4 cups milk
4 eggs
1½ cups sugar
2 tablespoons flour
½ teaspoon salt
4 cups light cream or half and half
4 teaspoon vanilla

Scald milk. Combine beaten eggs, sugar, flour and salt; add to milk. Cook in a double boiler until custard forms, approximately 15 minutes. Cool. Add cream and vanilla. This makes one gallon of ice cream.

MARY ELLEN PENWELL
AUCTION AND PROGRAM

REAL HOME-MADE ICE CREAM

6 eggs, beaten separately
1 cup sugar
1 teaspoon vanilla
½ gallon milk
1 13-ounce can evaporated milk
1 can crushed pineapple

Beat egg yolks, add ½ sugar and vanilla. Beat egg whites until stiff. Add rest of sugar. Combine eggs, add milk, and pineapple, pour into ice cream freezer and turn until stiff.

ROSALINE CARTER
LIFE MEMBER

OLD FASHIONED NO-COOK ICE CREAM

3 eggs
1½ cups sugar
1 tablespoon vanilla extract
½ teaspoon salt
1 can sweetened condensed milk
1 large can evaporated milk
½ gallon whole milk

Beat eggs in electric mixer until they are light in color. Add sugar to eggs and beat at high speed until mixture is thick. Add vanilla extract, salt, and evaporated milk; continue beating until sugar is dissolved. Mix thoroughly into the whole milk. Freeze. (If frozen or canned fruit is added, it must be well drained.) Makes one gallon.

ROBYN MERCHANT
AUCTION AND PROGRAM

HONG KONG SUNDAE

1 11-ounce can mandarin orange slices
1 tablespoon cornstarch
1 8¾-ounce can crushed pineapple
½ cup orange marmalade
1 teaspoon candied ginger, chopped
½ cup sliced preserved kumquats

Drain orange slices, reserving ¼ cup syrup. In sauce pan, blend reserved orange syrup and cornstarch. Stir in undrained pineapple, marmalade and ginger. Cook and stir over medium heat until mixture thickens and bubbles. Remove from heat and stir in orange slices and kumquats. Serve warm or cold over vanilla ice cream.

MARY FLOWERS
AUCTION SALES

FRUIT CUSTARD ICE CREAM

1½ quarts milk
3 or 4 eggs, beaten
1½ cups sugar
1 teaspoon vanilla

Fruit mix:
½ cup chopped nuts
½ cup diced banana
½ cup diced pineapple
½ cup chopped cherries
½ cup chopped fresh strawberries*
¼ cup sugar
2 teaspoons lemon juice
½ teaspoon salt

*You may use frozen; omit ¼ cup sugar for sweetened berries.

Combine cream (milk), eggs, and sugar. Cook over very low heat, stirring constantly, until mixture coats a spoon. Cool, add vanilla. Combine nuts, fruits, ¼ cup sugar, lemon juice and salt. Let stand 5 minutes.

Pour basic mix into freezer can. Add fruit mix. Freeze. Makes 4 quarts.

ED AND DEBBIE BARRON
SOUVENIR PROGRAM

P&M HOME MADE ICE CREAM

1 pint half and half
½ pint whipping cream
1 cup sweetened condensed milk
1 teaspoon vanilla
½ cups sugar
2 junkets

Put junkets in a little water to dissolve. Put milk, sugar, and vanilla in a pan and heat until lukewarm (do not overheat). Add junkets. Put mixture in ice cream can after first putting the paddle in. Let set perfectly still for 15 minutes. Do not move or stir. Then freeze.

PIE CRUST NEVER FAIL

3 cups presifted flour
1½ cups shortening
1 egg
1 tablespoon vinegar
⅓ cup water

Cut shortening into flour until it resembles coarse meal. Beat egg, vinegar, and water; add to flour mixture. Mix lightly with fork until dough clears side of bowl. Chill. Later roll between wax paper.

LAURA McCAULEY

Trail Rides

At one time, not too many years ago, trail riding was a fact of life. Today, things have changed, but each year more than 9,000 riders take to the trails from 11 different locations to converge on San Antonio the day before the Rodeo begins.

The rides are a living memorial to the old pioneer family that settled Texas, and to a way of life that was at once demanding and romantic. Each ride lasts from four to seven days, just long enough for the riders to get a taste of the frontier life, and at the same time have a lot of fun doing it.

Each ride visits numerous cities on its way into San Antonio, and so generates lots of interest and attendance for the show.

The riders are part of the Western Parade through downtown San Antonio. Because of their enthusiasm and the attention they attract, the trail rides are one of the important elements in the success of the San Antonio Stock Show & Rodeo.

A. J. PLOCH
GENERAL TRAIL RIDE
CHAIRMAN

INDIAN BARS (LIKE BROWNIES)

1 cup butter
2 squares unsweetened chocolate
2 cups sugar
4 eggs, beaten
1½ cups sifted flour
1 teaspoon baking powder
2 teaspoons vanilla
1 cup chopped pecans

Melt chocolate and butter over low heat — *Cool.* Add sugar, eggs, and vanilla. Mix thoroughly. Sift flour with baking powder and stir into chocolate mixture. Mix in pecans. Pour into greased and floured 13x9x2 pan. Bake 35 to 40 minutes at 350 degrees. Test for doneness. Set in rack — cool in pan. Cut into bars and wrap individually — Makes approximately 2 dozen.

MARY NAN WEST
VICE-PRESIDENT/SECRETARY
SAN ANTONIO LIVESTOCK EXPOSITION, INC.

JIM'S COOKIES

Measure into deep pot, stir, and bring to boil:

2½ cups sugar
½ cup milk
3 tablespoons cocoa
1 stick oleo margarine (½ up)

Bring to full boil and boil 2 minutes. Remove from heat and stir in, until blended:

½ cup peanut butter (smooth or crunchy)
Pour above mixture over:
3 cups uncooked quick cooking oats
(Optional: 1 cup pecans and/or 1 package coconut
  mixed with dry oats)

Mix well. Drop by spoonfuls on waxed paper.

THURMAN KENNEDY
LIVESTOCK

OATMEAL COOKIES

1 cup shortening
1 cup sugar
1 cup brown sugar
2 eggs, beaten
1 teaspoon vanilla
1 teaspoon soda
1½ cup flour, sifted
3 cups of 3-minute oats

Cream shortening and sugar. Add eggs and vanilla. Stir in sifted soda, flour and oats. Form into small balls and bake on ungreased baking sheet at 375 degree oven for 10-15 minutes. Makes 5 dozen. Optional: ½ cup raisins.

FROM 4th GRADE PARENT
PEGGY & JIM DOCKERY
JUNIOR STEER RIDING

APRICOT NUGGETS

1 pound confectioners ugar
6 tablespoon melted butter or margarine
2 tablespoons orange juice
½ teaspoon vanilla
1 11-ounce package dried apricots, ground
1 cup pecans, chopped

Combine sugar, butter, orange juice and vanilla; add apricots and mix. Then knead in bowl until ingredients are well mixed. Form into 1 inch balls. Roll in chopped nuts. Store in tightly covered container a few days to blend flavors. Flavor improves with storage. May be stored in freezer. Makes about 6 dozen candies.

MARY ELLEN PENWELL
AUCTION SALES

CHOCOLATE CHIP PAN COOKIES

2¼ cups flour, unsifted
1 teaspoon baking soda
1 teaspoon salt
1 cup soft butter
¾ cup sugar
¾ cup brown sugar
1 teaspoon vanilla
2 eggs
1 12-ounce package chocolate morsels
1 cup chopped nuts, optional

Preheat oven to 375 degrees. In small bowl, combine flour, soda, and salt. In large bowl combine butter, sugar, brown sugar, and vanilla; beat until creamy. Beat in eggs. Gradually add flour mixture. Stir in chips and nuts. Spread into a greased 15x10x1 inch pan. Bake for 20 minutes. Cool, cut in squares.

DOROTHY FERGUSON/MONTY FERGUSON
ENTERTAINMENT

CINNAMON STICKS

½ pounds butter
¾ cup sugar
2 cups flour
1 egg yolk
4 teaspoons ground cinnamon
1 teaspoon vanilla
1 cup chopped pecans

Cream butter and sugar. Add flour, egg yolk, cinnamon, and vanilla. Mix. Pat down on buttered cookie sheet to about ¼ inch thick. Put unbeaten egg white all over. Then press chopped nuts down into ¼ inch mixture. Bake in 350 degree oven 30 minutes. Cut in oblongs.

JAMES DOCKERY
JUNIOR STEER RIDING
CHAIRMAN

ORANGE BALLS

¾ cup powdered sugar
16-ounce package vanilla wafers
1 stick margarine, melted
1 6-ounce can frozen orange juice, thawed
1 cup coconut
1 cup nuts, chopped

Crush vanilla wafers. Combine all ingredients. Form into balls, and roll in powdered sugar.

MARY ELLEN PENWELL
AUCTION SALES

COWBOY COOKIES

1 cup shortening
1 cup sugar
1 cup brown sugar
2 eggs
1 teaspoon vanilla
2 cups flour, sifted
½ teaspoon salt
1 teaspoon soda
½ teaspoon baking powder
2 cups oats or cereal mates
1 package chocolate chips
1 cup chopped nuts

Sift together and set aside flour, soda, salt, and baking powder. Blend eggs, shortening, and sugars. Add flour mixture and mix well. Add oats, vanilla, chocolate chips and nuts. Dough will be crumbly. Drop by teaspoon on greased cookie sheet and bake at 350 degrees 15 minutes. Makes 5 dozen.

MRS. BRYAN M. CARTER

PEANUT BLOSSOMS

1¾ cup flour
1 teaspoon soda
½ cup sugar
1 egg
1 teaspoon vanilla
½ cup brown sugar
½ cup shortening
½ cup peanut butter
2 tablespoons milk
48 chocolate candy kisses

Combine all ingredients except candy in large mixing bowl. Mix on lowest speed of mixer. Shape dough into balls, using a rounded teaspoon of each. Roll balls in sugar, place on ungreased cookie sheet. Bake for 10 to 12 minutes. Top each cookie immediately with candy kiss — press down firmly so cookie cracks around edge.

Heat oven to 375 degrees. Makes about 48 cookies.

PAUL DOCKERY
JUNIOR STEER RIDING

CARAMEL BROWNIES

1 package german chocolate cake mix
1½ sticks butter
⅔ cup evaporated milk
12 ounces semi-sweet chocolate chips
1 cup chopped pecans
14 ounces caramels

Mix cake mix with melted butter and ⅓ cup evaporated milk. Put half in 13x9 inch pan. Bake 7 minutes at 350 degrees. Melt caramels with ⅓ cup evaporated milk. Pour over cake; sprinkle with chocolate chips and pecans. Top with remaining batter and bake 18 minutes. Cool before cutting.

RUSSELL ROBERSON/JANET ROBERSON
CALF SCRAMBLE

LEMON BAR

2 sticks butter
½ cup powdered sugar
2 cups flour
4 eggs, well beaten
2 cups sugar
½ teaspoon salt
8 tablespoons lemon juice
½ tablespoon lemon rind, grated
4 tablespoons flour
1 teaspoon baking powder

Cream together the first three ingredients and spread in ungreased cookie sheet with sides (can use a 13x9 cooking pan, but bars will be thicker). Bake at 350 degrees for 15 minutes until lightly brown. Beat eggs and add remaining ingredients. Pour on top of baked pastry and bake at 325 degrees for 30 minutes. Sprinkle with powdered sugar. Cool for 15 minutes. Cut into bars, approximately 32.

COLLEEN MOCK
HORSE SHOW

LEMON SNAPS
(Cookies)

1 package Duncan Hines Deluxe II Lemon
   Supreme Cake Mix
¾ cup shortening
1 egg
¼ cup lemon juice

Stir dry cake mix and shortening together. Add egg and lemon juice, stir until smooth. Drop by teaspoon two inches apart on ungreased cookie sheet. Bake 375 degrees for 10 minutes or until golden brown.

MICKEY HUBER
CALF SCRAMBLE

MISSISSIPPI MUD

4 eggs, beaten
2 cups sugar
1½ cups flour
2 cups pecans

2 sticks butter, melted
⅓ cup cocoa
1 cup coconut
1 teaspoon vanilla

Mix all ingredients. Bake in 13x9 inch pan 30 minutes at 350 degrees. While cake is hot, spread with 7–ounce jar of marshmallow cream. Cool.

Heat in pan over low flame:

1 stick butter
6 tablespoons milk
1 box powdered sugar
⅓ cup cocoa
1 cup pecans
1 teaspoon vanilla

When hot, spread on cooled cake and let all of this cool before slicing. Serves 20.

REBA ROBERSON
AUCTION SALES

3 HUNDRED DOLLAR COOKIES

1 cup sugar
½ can evaporated milk (5⅓ oz.)
½ stick oleo

Bring to a rolling boil, continue cooking and stir 6 minutes. Stir in 1 cup miniature marshmallows, stir until melted. Stir in 1 cup crushed graham crackers, 1 cup nuts, 1 teaspoon vanilla. Drop on wax paper.

COLLEEN MOCK
HORSE SHOW

MISSISSIPPI MUD CAKE

4 eggs
2 cups sugar
2 sticks oleo, melted
1½ cup sifted flour
⅓ cup cocoa
1 teaspoon vanilla
1 cup coconut
½ cups pecans, chopped

Beat eggs and sugar until thick. Combine melted oleo, flour, cocoa, vanilla, coconut, and nuts. Mix well and add to egg and sugar. Pour into a greased, floured 13x9 pan and bake 30 minutes at 350 degrees. When done, remove from oven and spread a jar of marshmallow cream over top of cake. Let set a few minutes and while still warm, put on frosting.

Frosting:
1 stick oleo, melted
5-6 tablespoons milk
⅓ cup cocoa
3 cups powdered sugar
1 teaspoon vanilla
pecans

Melt oleo — remove from heat and add other ingredients, except pecans. Beat well, add pecans. Gently spread over marshmallow cream.

MRS. JAMES S. BOREN (GLENDA)

PUMPKIN BARS

Bars:
4 eggs
1⅔ cups sugar
1 cup oil
1 16-ounce can pumpkin
2 cups flour

2 teaspoons baking powder
2 teaspoons cinnamon
1 teaspoon salt
1 teaspoon soda

Beat together eggs, sugar, oil, and pumpkin until creamy. Mix dry ingredients together and add to creamed mixture, blending thoroughly. Spread in ungreased 15x10x1 inch pan. Bake at 350 degrees for 25 to 30 minutes. Cool, then frost and cut into bars.

Frosting:
1 3-ounce package cream cheese, softened
½ cup butter
1 teaspoon vanilla
2 cups powdered sugar, sifted

Mix all until creamy. Spread on bars.

J. R. HARTMAN/JENNIFER HARTMAN
CALF SCRAMBLE

RUM BALLS

1 cup finely crushed vanilla wafers
1 cup confectioners sugar
1 cup pecans, chopped
2 tablespoons cocoa
2 tablespoons light corn syrup
¼ cup rum
½ cup granulated sugar

Combine crumbs, confectioners' sugar, 1 cup nuts, and cocoa. Add corn syrup and rum; mix well. Shape into 1 inch balls. Roll in sugar.

JIM TOBE ATKINSON
CALF SCRAMBLE

MAGIC COOKIE BARS

½ cup butter
1½ cup graham cracker crumbs
1 can sweetened condensed milk
1 6-ounce package semi-sweet chocolate chips
1 3½ ounce can flaked coconut
1 cup chopped nuts

In 13x9 baking pan, melt butter, remove from the heat. Sprinkle crumbs over the butter. Pour sweetened condensed milk evenly over the crumbs. Top with chocolate chips, coconut, and nuts; press down gently. Bake at 350 degrees for 25 minutes or until golden brown. Cool, cut into 3x½" bars.

STEVE SCHULTZ
SAN ANTONIO CHAMBER OF COMMERCE
AMBASSADORS

EASY BUTTER COOKIES

½ pound butter or margarine
2 cups flour
5 tablespoons sugar
1 teaspoon vanilla

Mix above ingredients together and form into balls. Place on ungreased cookie sheet. Flatten balls with fork.

Bake at 350 degrees about 20 minutes. While warm, roll cookies in granulated sugar.

Note: Chopped pecans can be added to dough before baking. Recipe can be made in food processor.

LEE NOONAN
RURAL YOUTH

PADRE ISLAND SAND DOLLARS

1 cup (two sticks) margarine, soft
½ cup powdered sugar
2 cups all purpose flour
1 teaspoon vanilla
¼ teaspoon salt

Beat together margarine and powdered sugar until creamy and fluffy. Gradually, mix in flour. Stir in vanilla and salt and mix well. Using level tablespoonfuls of dough, shape into balls, press one side of each ball into granulated sugar and place sugar side up on ungreased cookie sheet. Cookies can be rather close together because they do not spread when baking. Bake in preheated oven 400 degrees about 10 minutes or until done but not browned. Remove from cookie sheets and cool completely on wire racks. Makes 3½ dozen cookies. Roll in powdered sugar before cooling, if desired.

PEGGY DOCKERY
JUNIOR STEER RIDING

PEANUT BUTTER/CHOCOLATE BALLS

¼ pound margarine or butter
2 cups chunky peanut butter
1 pound confectioners sugar
3 cups rice cereal

Mix peanut butter and sugar. Blend in margarine. Mix in cereal, but don't press hard. Form into balls (bite size). Drop into chocolate mixture. Place onto wax paper.

Chocolate Mixture:
1 8-ounce plain chocolate bar
1 6-ounce package semi-sweet chocolate chips

Melt slowly in top of double boiler until blended. (Hint: When taking cookies out of chocolate mixture use a spoon and a fork or two forks)

MARCIA WALKER
BANDERA, TEXAS

OATMEAL MACAROONS

½ cup shortening
1 teaspoon salt
1 teaspoon cinnamon
1 teaspoon vanilla
1 tablespoon molasses
1 cup sugar
1 egg, unbeaten

1 cup flour, sifted
¾ teaspoon soda
1 cup rolled oats
⅓ cup raisins
⅓ cup chocolate chips
⅓ cup nut meats

Combine first seven ingredients and beat thoroughly. Sift flour with soda. Add to first mixture; mix well. Add remaining ingredients and mix. Drop level teaspoons of dough on greased baking sheet. Bake at 350 degrees 10 to 15 minutes. Makes 3½ dozen.

MRS. RUBY PIRCHER
AUCTION SALES BUYER

PEANUT BUTTER CUPS

2 cups peanut butter (any style)
½ cup plus 1 tablespoon melted butter
2¾ cups confectioners sugar
1 12-ounce package milk chocolate chips

Stir together peanut butter, ½ cup of melted butter, and confectioners sugar. Press mixture into desired size pan. The smaller the pan the thicker the candy. I prefer a jelly roll pan.

Melt chips and stir together with remaining tablespoons of melted butter. Spread on top. Set in refrigerator for 10 minutes to set chocolate. Cut into small squares. Store at room temperature.

DOROTHY FERGUSON/MONTY FERGUSON
ENTERTAINMENT

PECAN CRISPIES

½ cup shortening
½ cup butter or margarine
2½ cups brown sugar
2 eggs, beaten
2½ cups flour
¼ teaspoon salt
½ teaspoon soda
1 cup pecans

This is a basic recipe, you may add chocolate chips, coconut, or what ever comes to mind. Makes about a hundred cookies. Cream shortening until fluffy. Add brown sugar, beat well. Add beaten eggs, mix well, or beat. Add flour last and drop by teaspoonfuls on greased cookie sheet. Bake 10-12 minutes or until golden brown in 375 degree oven.

MRS. NAT V. (WINONA) PRASSEL

PECAN MERINGUES

2 egg whites
¼ teaspoon ground nutmeg
¼ teaspoon cream of tartar
⅛ teaspoon salt
½ teaspoon pure vanilla extract
½ cup sugar
½ cup pecans

Preheat oven to 250 degrees. Line a baking sheet with aluminum foil. In a large bowl place egg whites, nutmeg, cream of tartar, and salt. Beat until foamy. Add vanilla. With beater set at highest speed beat until stiff peaks form. Gradually add sugar. Fold in pecans. Drop by rounded teaspoons onto prepared pans about one inch apart.

Bake until crisp about 50 minutes. Turn off oven. Leave cookies in oven for *three* hours without opening oven door. Makes 4 doz. Store in airtight containers.

LEE NOONAN
RURAL YOUTH

PECAN PIE SURPRISE BARS

1 package yellow cake mix
½ cup butter or margarine, melted
1 egg
1 cup chopped pecans
½ cup firmly packed brown sugar
1½ cups dark corn syrup
1 teaspoon vanilla
3 eggs

Grease bottom and sides of 13x9 inch baking pan. Reserve ⅔ cup dry cake mix for filling. In large mixing bowl, combine remaining dry cake mix, butter and one egg; mix until crumbly. Press in prepared pan. Bake at 350 degrees for 15 to 20 minutes until light golden brown. Meanwhile, prepare filling. Pour filling over partially baked crust; sprinkle with pecans. Return to oven and bake for 30 to 35 minutes until filling is set. Cool; cut into 36 bars.

Filling: In large mixer bowl combine all ingredients, beat at medium speed 1 to 2 minutes. Bake at 375 degrees as directed above.

ROBYN MERCHART
AUCTION SALES

RANGER COOKIES

½ cup creamy shortening
½ cup sugar
½ cup brown sugar
1 egg
½ teaspoon vanilla

1 cup flour
¼ teaspoon soda
1 cup cornflakes
½ cup oatmeal
¼ cup of coconut

Mix well, drop on greased cookie sheet. Bake 12 to 15 minutes at 350 degrees.

MAJ. RUDY SPANN
NATIONAL GUARD
WESTERN PARADE

POTATO CHIP COOKIES

½ cup sugar
1 cup butter
½ cup crushed potato chips
1 tablespoon vanilla
2 cups flour
1 cup chopped pecans

Cream sugar and butter. Add other ingredients. Mix well and shape in small balls. Roll in sugar. Bake at 350 degrees for 12 minutes. Yields 5 dozen cookies.

LANCE HONIG (AGE 11)
HONDO, TX
ELIZABETH JACOBS
INTERNATIONAL/MEXICO DAY
GEORGE B. WOODS
AUCTION SALES

GRAHAM CRACKER COOKIES

Foil-line a 9 inch wide cookie pan. Cover this with as many graham crackers as it will hold, singular, do not overlap.

Topping:
1 cup butter or oleo
1 cup brown sugar

Bring oleo and sugar to boil. Turn off heat, cool slightly. Add 1 cup chopped pecans. Pour above ingredients over graham crackers in pan. Cover all with one small package chocolate chips. Bake in 350 degree oven for 10 minutes *only*. Chocolate chips will not be completely melted. Smooth out with spatula. Cool for few minutes and slice in squares. These freeze nicely and keep well.

ELIZABETH JACOBS
INTERNATIONAL/MEXICO DAY

PECAN TASSIES

Cream Cheese Crust:
1 3-ounce package cream cheese, softened
1 stick oleo
1 cup flour

Blend cream cheese, oleo and flour. Roll into a ball chill 1 hour or overnight. Pinch out 8 balls. Press balls into muffin tin with fingers, working dough up to the top. Add the following:

Pecan Filling:
1 egg
¾ cup brown sugar
1 teaspoon soft oleo
1 teaspoon vanilla
¼ teaspoon salt
¾ cup pecans (or more), chopped

Beat egg, add brown sugar, mix well. Add oleo, vanilla, salt and chopped pecans. Put 1 tablespoon mixture into each cream cheese cup. Bake at 325 degrees for 25 minutes.

LANIE SING
HARRIS HAWKS (AGE 14)
(FIRST PLACE WINNER)

NUT BALLS

1 cup shortening or butter
4 tablespoons sugar
Dash nutmeg
1 tablespoon vanilla
1 cup chopped nuts
2 cups flour

Put all ingredients into one bowl. Mix together until well blended. Form into small balls and bake on ungreased cookie sheet until light brown at 350 degrees. Approximately 20-25 minutes. When cool, roll in powdered sugar. These cookies are very much like the Mexican wedding cookies.

LIBBY JONES
AUCTION SALES

TEXAS CHEWIES

2 sticks oleo
1 16-ounce box light brown sugar
2 eggs, beaten
1 tablespoon vanilla, that's right
1¼ cup flour
2 teaspoons baking powder
¼ teaspoon salt
1½ cup chopped pecans

Melt oleo and pour over brown sugar. Add eggs and vanilla. Add flour mixed with baking powder and salt. Add pecans, mix well and pour into 11x16 greased and floured pan. Bake 30 minutes at 350 degrees. Cool and cut into squares. Delicious and easy.

MRS. EDNA BLACK, BRACKETTVILLE
SUBMITTED BY SCOTT ABBEY WEST
AUCTION SALES

TRAIL RIDERS COOKIES

2½ sticks oleo
1½ cup brown sugar
1½ cup white sugar
3 eggs
Pinch salt
3 cups flour
1 teaspoon soda
1 teaspoon baking powder
1 teaspoon vanilla
2 cups old fashioned oatmeal
2 cups raisins
2 cups pecans
2 cups chopped dates
1½ cup coconut

Use large bowl, have oleo at room temperature. Add sugar, beat; add eggs, beat. Add 2 cups flour, and vanilla and beat until smooth. Put soda and baking powder in last cup of flour. Stir well and add to mix. Add all fruit, mix. Drop by large spoonfuls on ungreased cookie sheets and bake at 350 degrees until brown.

ROSALINE CARTER
LIFE MEMBER

PINEAPPLE BROWNIES

2 eggs
1¾ cups of brown sugar
1¾ cups of flour, sifted
1 teaspoon of baking soda
1 can of crushed pineapple
   (do not drain)

Mix together, spread on a 12x18 cookie sheet. Bake at 350 degrees for 30 to 40 minutes.

Topping:
1 8-ounce package of cream cheese
¾ cups of powered sugar
4 tablespoons of melted oleo
1 cup of chopped nuts

Mix together, spread on top of brownies while brownies are still warm.

KITTY ALONSO
INTERNATIONAL/MEXICO DAY

CINNAMON CRISPS

1 cup butter or margarine
1 egg — separated
½ teaspoon salt
1 cup sugar
3 teaspoons cinnamon
2 cups flour
1 cup chopped pecans (or almonds)

Cream butter and sugar; add egg yolk and beat; add dry ingredients; press dough out on 12x15 cookie sheet; beat egg white slightly and spread over dough; sprinkle lightly with a bit of sugar; add pecans and press down slightly. Bake at 350 degrees for 15 to 20 minues; cut in squares while hot and remove with spatula.

SHIRLEY & LARRY SIMPSON
WESTERN COOKBOOK

PECAN MUFFINS

½ cup graham flour
2 cups stone ground yellow corn meal
3 teaspoons baking powder
1 tablespoon brown sugar
½ teaspoon salt
1 tablespoon melted butter
1 egg
1½ cups milk

Put graham flour, corn meal, baking powder, brown sugar, salt, and butter in bowl. Beat egg well, add to mixture. Add milk. Fill well greased muffin tins with the batter, sprinkle pecans (chopped) over top of each (or mix in batter). Bake in 350 degree oven 20-25 minutes.

BETTY JACOBS
INTERNATIONAL/MEXICO DAY

ROSIE'S MOLASSES COOKIES

¾ cup shortening
1 cup sugar
1 cup molasses
1 egg beaten
2 teaspoons baking soda
2 cups sifted flour
½ teaspoon cloves
½ teaspoon ginger
1 teaspoon cinnamon
½ teaspoon salt

Preheat oven to 350 degrees.

Melt crisco, let cool, add sugar, egg and molasses, and mix. Add flour and spices, place in refrigerator until dough is stiff. Form dough in small balls (about teaspoon size) roll in sugar. Put on greased cookie sheet, leave space between cookies. Bake 8 to 10 minutes. Do not flatten cookies. They will spread.

ROSIE GRANGER

MICROWAVE PEANUT BRITTLE

1 cup granulated sugar
1 cup raw peanuts
Dash of salt
½ cup white Karo syrup
1 tablespoon margarine
1 teaspoon vanilla
1 teaspoon baking soda

Mix syrup, salt, peanuts and sugar with wooden spoon in 1¾ qt. pyrex pan. Put in microwave for 8 minutes turning 4 times. Leave spoon in the pan while cooking. Take out and add 1 tablespoon margarine and 1 teaspoon vanilla. Put back in oven for an additional 2 minutes. *DO NOT STIR.* Take out and add 1 teaspoon baking soda. Mix in. Pour out onto a GREASED cookie sheet. Cool for 30 minutes.

MRS. AL SODERSTROM
GO WESTERN

AUNT RUBY'S MILLIONAIRES

2 12-ounce packages Kraft caramels
2 tablespoons evaporated milk
Pecans
1 package dipping chocolate*

Place caramels and milk in double boiler and melt. Add nuts and drop by spoon on wax paper. Melt dipping chocolate and dip each cooled caramels in chocolate and let set.

*Dipping chocolate may be purchased through a cake decorating shop.

PATRICIA GARZA
WESTERN COOKBOOK

CANDY CANES AND CHRISTMAS WREATHS

1¼ cup (2½ sticks) butter
1 cup confectioner's sugar
1 egg
1 teaspoon vanilla
½ teaspoon almond extract
3½ cups sifted flour
1 teaspoon salt
Red and green decorating sugar
Cinnamon candies

Cream butter. Add sugar and mix well. Add egg and flavorings, then flour and salt which have been sifted together. Set aside half of the dough. Divide the other half in two parts. Tint one part light green and the other light red with food coloring. For candy canes, roll 1 teaspoon full of white dough and one of the red into strips of about 4 inches long. Place strips side by side and twist together lightly. Carefully put on ungreased baking sheet and curve the top down to form handle. Brush with egg white and sprinkle with red sugar. Bake in a preheated oven 350 degrees, for 10 to 12 minutes. For wreaths, use 1 teaspoon of white dough and 1 of green. After twisting them together, form into a circle on the cooky sheet. Brush with egg white and sprinkle with green sugar. Use cinnamon candies for garnish and bake same way.

JIM DOCKERY/PEGGY DOCKERY
JUNIOR STEER RIDING
CHAIRMAN

MEXICAN PECAN CANDY

2⅓ cup sugar
Pinch of baking sugar
¼ cup white Karo syrup

Just enough sweet milk to moisten sugar. Cook over low heat until a small amount balls up in a cup of cold water. Remove from fire and add:

2 teaspoons vanilla
1½ cups of pecans

Stir until creamy, dip out with tablespoons onto waxed paper. Remove when cool to dish or wrap each piece separately.

BETTY LUCE

EASY PRALINES

1 package vanilla pudding
    and pie filling mix
1 cup powdered sugar
½ cup brown sugar
½ cup evaporated milk
1 tablespoon margarine
1 tablespoon vanilla
1½ cups pecans

Combine first four ingredients in a large pan and cook over medium heat until mixture becomes thick and changes color, or until a ball forms in water. Remove from heat, add margarine, vanilla and pecans. Return to heat and stir until thick.

Drop candy by teaspoonfuls onto waxed paper.

ROBYN MERCHANT
AUCTION SALE

LECHE QUEMADA

1 cup broken pecans and walnuts
1 cup sweetened condensed milk
⅔ cup brown sugar
¾ cup butter
2 teaspoons vanilla

Brown nut meats in slow oven. Combine sweetened condensed milk, brown sugar and butter in saucepan. Heat until boiling, stirring constantly until it begins to harden (I prefer a softer, more creamy candy, I therefore take candy off heat just a few minutes after boiling). Remove from heat. (Don't cook too long) Let cool a few minutes. Stir in vanilla and nut meats. Spread on a greased mold and refrigerate. When cold, cut into squares. Candy should resemble fudge but with a finer texture.

GEORGE B. WOODS
AUCTION SALES

FUDGE

2 9x13 buttered pans
4½ cups sugar
1 teaspoon salt
½ cup butter
1 13-ounce can evaporated milk
1 12-ounce package chocolate chips
4 bars german chocolate (break into squares)
1 8-ounce chocolate bar, plain
1½ jars marshmallow creme
2 teaspoons vanilla
4 cups toasted pecans

Combine sugar, salt, milk, and butter; bring to a simmer on medium heat. When first *bubble* is seen, boil exactly eight minutes. Remove immediately from heat. Stir in other ingredients. Blend thoroughly. Pour into pans, cover with foil until firm.

MONICA GOSE
LIFE MEMBER

DIVINITY CANDY

3 cups sugar
1 cup white Karo syrup
1 cup water
1 tablespoon vinegar

Boil the above ingredients until a little will form a soft ball in cold water.

1 cup sugar
½ cup water

Boil the above two ingredients until it will thread. Combine the two, beating constantly until thick then add 2 cups of nuts.

KATY "DID"

DATE CANDY ROLL

3 cups sugar
¾ cup milk
¼ cup canned milk
½ stick oleo
1 tablespoon white Karo syrup
1 large package dates, chopped
2 cups pecans, chopped

Cook sugar, milk, oleo, and Karo syrup over medium heat, until it forms a soft ball when dropped in cold water. Add dates and cook until it forms a firm ball. Remove from fire, add pecans and beat until stiff. Pour onto a clean damp cloth and roll up. Let it get cold before removing and slicing.

ROSALINE CARTER
LIFE MEMBER

CHOCOLATE MOUNDS
(Candy)

2 boxes powdered sugar, sifted
2 sticks margarine
1 7-ounce can coconut
Add:
2 cups pecans, almonds or walnuts
1 can condensed sweetened milk
1 teaspoon vanilla

Refrigerate for one hour. Roll into bite size balls. Melt 1 parafin wax (a block) and add one 12 ounce package chocolate chips. Mix well and dip above using toothpick and place on wax paper.

MICKEY HUBER
CALF SCRAMBLE

CHOCOLATE FUDGE SQUARES

1½ sticks of margarine
4 eggs
2 cups sugar
1 cup flour
¼ teaspoon salt
2 squares bitter chocolate
(NOT semi-sweet)
1 teaspoon vanilla
1 cup chopped nuts

Beat soft margarine, add eggs one at a time. Blend in sugar and flour, about ½ cup at a time, then add melted chocolate (which has been cooled), vanilla and nuts.

Pour batter into well greased 9x13-inch pan and bake at 350 degrees for 35 to 40 minutes. Check during baking so as not to allow mixture to dry out. Cut into 3x3 inch squares. Serve topped with whipped cream, ice cream, or frost, as desired.

ROBYN MERCHANT
SOUVENIR PROGRAM

CANDY POPCORN

⅔ **cups Karo syrup**
⅔ **cups sugar**
½ **teaspoon salt**
2 quarts popped corn

Mix Karo syrup, sugar and salt in heavy saucepan; cook over moderate heat for 2 minutes or until sugar is dissolved, stirring constantly. Pour over popped corn in deep kettle and stir over medium heat 3 to 5 minutes, or until corn is evenly and completely coated with mixture. Remove from heat and form balls.

MARY ELLEN PENWELL
SOUVENIR PROGRAM

MICROWAVE QUICKIE SUGAR FUDGE

1 pound box powdered sugar
½ **cup cocoa**
¼ **cup milk**
Pinch salt
¼ **pound butter**
1 teaspoon vanilla
½ **cup chopped pecans**

In 1 quart casserole, add powdered sugar, cocoa, milk, salt and butter. Cook two minutes. Remove and stir to blend ingredients. Add vanilla and nuts and blend well. Pour fudge into pie plate lined with wax paper and chill until firm.

SHARON & TERRY BISHOP
ENTERTAINMENT

Western Parade

The first parade in February 1950 was a project of the San Antonio Junior Chamber of Commerce. The following year Alton Rieden was named chairman and remained in that position until 1972. Jack Sellars has headed up the Horse Committee since the beginning in 1950. The first year was somewhat of a struggle to get as many horses and horse groups as possible. Today, that group is the largest with 11 trail rides and many other horse groups such as Charros and Mounted Posses.

The in-town float committee headed by Armin Puck challenges Fritz Toepperwein and his out of town float committee each year on the number of entries. They both gang-up on Jack Sellars when it comes to horse drawn units.

Parade day is all important and the smoothness of the operation can be attributed to the marshaling by the Texas National Guard and the control by the San Antonio Police Department.

BILL ROTH
CHAIRMAN

1882 IN THE CHEROKEE STRIP
(TEXAS, OKLAHOMA, NEW MEXICO)

Cowboys wore the best clothes that they could buy and took a great pride in their personal appearance.

Texas cowhands went to work in 1872 for $20.00 per month by the year, work or play. Wages increased a little by the 1880's on most ranches from Texas northward. The records of a Panhandle Ranch in 1885 paid wages averaging $38.72 but that dropped to $32.24 in 1890.

Cowhand $35.00 per month
Top Hand $40.00 to $45.00
Trail Bosses $50.00 to $65.00
Range Foreman or Wagon Boss $125.00
Cook $40.00 to $45.00 same as a tophand
Ranch Headquarters Cook $50.00

In the 1880's most men quit cowpunching after 10 or 15 years. The work was rough and sleeping in the open and not taking care of health or injuries would often create a "stoved-up" cowboy — one who spent the rest of his life nursing poor health.

Why cowboys moved on is anyone's guess. Some may have been running from the law, others searching for something or hoping their luck would get better elsewhere. Perhaps the vast open spaces acted like a magnet and drew the restless cowboy beyond the horizon. The plains undoubtedly had an effect on the mind of the cowboy, as suggested in a little-known song, "The Wandering Cowboy."

I am a wandering cowboy,
From ranch to ranch I roam;
At every ranch when welcome,
I make myself at home.

The saving of a few dollars was often reason enough for a cowboy to quit and move on.

DUTIES OF HORSE WRANGLER

On camping
  Unhook the team
  Set the wagon tongue up on the neck yoke
  String the harness on the pole,
  Set the cook stove on the ground six feet back, and
    slightly to the right of the grub box door when let down
    on one center leg.
  Put in poles and stand the 12x14 foot tent in back of the
    wagon over the stove and guy it good
  Next, set up the corral, consisting of one-inch rope,
    forked poles and guy ropes, about 200 feet from the
    chuckwagon.
  Keep track of the horses day and night.

FROM A RANCH IN THE CHEROKEE STRIP

The quality of food served up by a ranch cook was often a determining factor in keeping good cowboys.

The supplies aboard a ranch wagon tell us much about the needs and eating habits of cowboys at spring round-up.

  Forty pounds Climax Plug
  Twenty pounds Bull Durham
  Several candies and packs of smoking tobacco
  A dozen .45 Colt single-action pistols
  Twenty Boxes of Cartridges
  A roll of half-inch rope
  Ten gallons of kerosene
  A caddy of matches
  One hundred pounds sugar
  One 160 pound sack of green coffee
  Five hundred pounds of salt pork
  Twenty sacks flour
  Two hundred pounds beans
  Fifty pounds country dried apples
  A box of soda
  A sack of salt

RANCH HOUSE SOAP RECIPE

1 can lye
1 quart water
2½ quarts grease (6 pounds — any waste fat)
1 cup powdered ammonia
4 heaping tablespoon powdered borax
1 teaspoon lysol or
citronella as desired for fragrance or disinfectant

Dissolve lye in water, stir until lukewarm. Add grease and stir constantly. Add ammonia and borax powder together with lysol or citronella. Stir until too thick to be handled. Pour into cloth lined pan or box. Let cool. Then cut into bars and let set 1 week or more is better to let set 3 or 4 weeks if possible as soap is yellow when made — but will turn "snow white" as it sets. This soap will last and will not hurt your hands.

CAUTION: be sure you use a wooden spoon to stir soap with.

BETTIE RUTLEDGE
AUCTION COMMITTEE

REMEDIES

For a **cowboy cough and sore throat remedy** slice a large onion about ⅛ inch thick. Place a layer in cereal bowl. Sprinkle sugar freely over layer. Repeat until all onion is used. Let stand to draw off juice. As needed, dip spoon into mixture, pressing down on onion to extract juice.

****

To kill a **boil** when it first appears, apply turpentine.

****

For a **wasp sting,** rubbing with a slice of onion is a sure cure.

****

For **coughs,** use ⅓ honey ⅓ lemon ⅓ whiskey.

****

For **arthritis,** 1 quart bathtub gin, 1 cup raisins. Let stand three days and take one ounce every morning.

For **snake bites,** take one ounce bootleg whiskey and clean the snake bite wound. Then drink the rest and visit your doctor.

****

Sniffing lemon juice into the nostrils will cure a **nose bleed.**

****

To prevent **scars** from scalding and burns, rub good sweet oil into the new skin daily. Keep this up until the new skin is soft and flexible.

****

To draw a **splinter** out from under a finger nail, apply common yellow soap mixed with brown sugar. Another way is to bind a cold water bandage kept wet around the top of the finger.

****

To improve **complexion,** drink buttermilk or use on skin.

****

Corns will disappear when nitrate of silver is used.

****

Nausea may be stopped by sucking small pieces of ice.

****

To stop a **sneezing attack,** slowly swallow three or four tablespoons of milk.

****

For relief of **headaches,** add the juice of a lemon to a cup of hot black unsweetened coffee.

****

To prevent **odor on the breath,** after eating onions, eat a half dozen sprigs of parsley which have been dipped in salt or vinegar.

****

To make medicine tasteless, eat a small amount of cayenne pepper or chew a piece of orange peel before taking the medicine.

****

For **rheumatism,** 1 tablespoon vinegar, 1 tablespoon bootleg whiskey. Of course, take at your own risk!

****

Make **linament** by mixing equal portions of vinegar and turpentine and the whites of two eggs. Shake well.

****

To soothe **itching** use a paste of bicarbonate of soda.

GENERAL
REMEDIES

1 Feed plants the water from boiling eggs as it has many minerals.

2 Boil potato peelings in your teakettle to take out lime. Empty and wipe dry.

3 Frying meat will not splash if you sprinkle a little salt in the frying pan before putting the meat in.

4 To keep weevils out of flour or corn meal, put several bay leaves in container. It will not change the taste.

5 A cloth moistened with vinegar will whiten piano keys.

6 The water mark left in a bowl of flowers may be removed by soaking the bowl in sour milk overnight.

7 To remove the printing on flour and sugar sacks, pour kerosene on them and salt. Roll them tightly and allow to soak at least ½ day. Wash with soap and water.

8 Always scald a mouse trap after a mouse has been caught in it, otherwise, mice will not go near it.

9 Keep tobacco fresh by placing a few freshly cut pieces of apple in the box with the tobacco.

10 Smile, it takes 72 muscles to frown and only 14 to smile.

11 "Life is like an onion, you peel it off one layer at a time, and sometimes you weep"

12 SILVER SOAP:

For cleaning silver and britannia. You may use the following:

1 bar of turpentine soap
3 tablespoons of spirits of turpentine
½ tumbler of water

Let it boil ten minutes. Add 6 tablespoons of spirits of hartshorn. Make a suds of this, and wash silver with it.

13 TO CLEAN BRASS:

If stained, rub over with oxalic acid or strong vinegar; polish with rottenstone pulverized with whiskey or sweet oil, or turpentine; then rub with soft leather or buckskin. In the beginning of warm weather, when there is no further use of andirons, wrap them carefully so tastily with the former as to make a handsome parlor ornament.

14 FLOWER WATER:

1 pint lemon-lime carbonated beverage
1 pint water
½ teaspoon clorox

Mix together. Pour over flowers in vase. Will keep much longer in this water.

FAVORITE SON-In-LAW'S (JOE KAUFMAN) HINT for RIDDING FLOUR OF WEEVILS

15 Open bag of flour, pour in a dab of salt, stir into flour. The weevils will eat the salt, become thirsty and crawl out of the bag looking for water. When this occurs, quickly dump flour into air tight container. May be repeated if necessary.

MRS. E. R. LITTLETON
(FAVORITE MOTHER-IN-LAW OF JOE KAUFMAN)
DEVINE, TX

"DRAWING MEDICINE"

When doctors were not available, it was necessary that the pioneers use their knowledge of "home remedies" to treat their families. The term "drawing" applies to drawing out the infection as the core from a boil or a splinter from a foot. The following is a recipe for drawing medicine.

     2 pounds hog lard
     1 pound rosin
     1 pound wax (beeswax)

Melt in a cooker. Cool the above ingredients add 2 ounces of oil of spice. Stir and pour into small containers for future use.

COFFEE CLUES

Always start with a coffee maker that is empty

Never brew coffee at less than ¾ of the coffee maker's capacity — If a smaller quantity is all that's needed, invite a critter or two to share coffee

Freshness is vital to a good cup of coffee. Use fresh coffee and fresh creek water

Serve hot steaming coffee as soon as possible after brewing. Hold at serving temperature over camp fire.

HOW TO KEEP THIS COOKBOOK CLEAN IN YOUR KITCHEN

Simply open the page to the recipe you will be using and slip the opened book into clear plastic bag. The bag will be your bookmark, and will protect the book.

TIDBITS

For many, the start of the new year also means the start of a new diet. Those wanting to shed excess pounds should know that the best diet is made up of a variety of foods that are high in nutrients and relatively low in calories. Lean cuts of beef as well as lamb and veal, are excellent "diet foods" and should be included often in a well-balanced weight reduction diet.

Where's It Located?

The location of beef muscles on the carcass is a clue to tenderness. In general, the more tender muscles are suspension muscles that are not used in movement and have little connective tissue. These include muscles from the rib, short loin and sirloin section. Less tender muscles are used in locomotion and have more connective tissue. These muscles are found in the chuck, brisket, foreshank and round sections.

In A Hurry?

Some of the easiest to prepare "convenience" foods can be found in the meat case. Ground beef patties, beef and pork cubed steaks, ham slices and naturally tender beef steaks can be ready for the table in minutes when broiled, pan-broiled or panfried.

Eye-Opening Breakfasts

If breakfast skipping is the trend at your house, stop them in their tracks with some non-traditional breakfast foods. The day is sure to run a little smoother when you lead in with favorite foods as hamburgers, meaty tacos or sausage piz-za. Other eye-opening possibilities include corned beef hash, meat balls, ham or meat cubes in a sauce served over biscuits, pancakes or cornbread.

Freeze It Fast

To maintain optimum quality, meat should be frozen quickly at 0°F. or lower. To speed freezing, allow space for air bet-ween packages during the initial freezing period. Also avoid freezing a large quantity of meat at one time since this cause the freezer to overload, resulting in higher temperatures.

GULF COAST CATTLEMAN

EQUAL PORTIONS

Pinch or dash	Less than ⅛ teaspoon or a portion between the finger tip and thumb.
3 teaspoons	1 tablespoon
2 tablespoons	⅛ cup or 1 ounce
4 tablespoons	¼ cup
5 tablespoons + 1 teaspoon	⅓ cup
8 tablespoons	½ cup
10 tablespoons + 2 teaspoons	⅔ cup
12 tablespoons	¾ cup
16 tablespoons	1 cup
8 ounces	1 cup
½ pint	1 cup
1 pint	2 cups
1 quart	4 cups
1 gallon	4 quarts
1 peck	8 quarts
1 bushel	4 pecks
12-14 egg yolks	1 cup
8-10 egg whites	1 cup

TO INCREASE RECIPES

To double a recipe, use exactly twice the amount of each ingredient. Add extra minute of beating for cakes.

If the increased recipe calls for uneven amount of ingredients, it is a help to remember that

⅔ cup = ½ cup plus 1⅔ tablespoons
⅝ cup = ½ cup plus 2 tablespoons
⅞ cup = ¾ cup plus 2 tablespoons

Be sure to use twice as many pans of the same size indicated for the original recipe or a pan double in area . . . so that the batter will be the same depth in the pan and same baking time and temperature may be maintained.

SWAPPING INGREDIENTS

If recipe calls for	You may swap the following
1 tablespoon cornstarch (to make it thicker)	2 tablespoons flour
1 cup cake flour	1 cup sifted all-purpose flour minus 2 tablespoons
1 cup sweet milk	½ cup evaporated milk plus ½ cup water
1 cup sour milk or buttermilk	1 tablespoon lemon juice or vinegar plus enough fresh milk to make 1 cup
1 cup honey	¾ cup sugar plus ¼ cup liquid
1 cup canned tomatoes	about 1⅓ cup — cut up fresh tomatoes, simmered 10 minutes
1 square unsweetened chocolate (1 ounce)	3 tablespoon cocoa plus ½ teaspoon shortening or 3 tablespoon cocoa plus 1 tablespoon butter

TO REDUCE RECIPES

To half a recipe, use exactly one-half the amount of each ingredient.

If the divided recipe calls for less than 1 egg, beat up a whole egg. Measure with a tablespoon and DIVIDE.

Baking pans used for half recipes of cakes, pies, etc. should measure about half the area of those for the whole recipe. Approximate baking time and oven temperature the same.

COWBOY RECIPES

BULLET'S POT LUCK

1 large soup bone (with three months well protected
   burying time on it.)
2 cups savory beef stock
2 cups dog food, dry
2 bites Busby's left over sandwich.

Mix well let stand for two or three minutes, sniff testing, while continually checking that no other dogs are around. Upon complete satisfaction no intruder is in snitching distance devour in one or two large bites.

BEATEN BISCUIT

Of course I'll gladly give de rule
I meks beat-biscuit by,
Dough I ain't sure dat you will mek
Dat bread da same as I.

'Case cooking's like religion is —
Some's 'lected, an some ain't,
An rules don't no more mek a cook,
Den sermons mek a Saint.

Well, 'bout de grediances required,
I needn't mention dem,
Of Course you knows of flour an things,
How much to put, an when;

But soon as you is got dat dough
Mixed up all smoove an' neat,
Den's when your genius gwine to show,
To get them biscuit beat!

Two hundred licks is what I gives
For home-folks, never fewer,
An' if I'm spectin' company in,
I gives five hundred sure!

Author Unknown

Our "Thanks" to Janet Rogers for our division pages. Copies of these pictures may be purchased by contacting Janet at the address indicated below:

Janet Rogers
Janet the Photographer
2829 Nacogdoches
San Antonio, Texas 78217

APPETIZERS

Chafing Dish

Appetizer Meat Balls	36
Mushroom Balls	28
Mushroom Royale	30
Salmon Puffs	35

Cowboy Finger Foods

Cheese Crackers	29
Cucumber Finger Sandwich	26
Jalapeno Cheese Sticks	38
Marinated Carrots	25
Marinated Mushrooms	31
Pecans, Roasted	39
Pecans, Sugar	39
Pecans, Sugared	38
Pecans, Spiced	37
Sausage Nibbles	28

Dips

Broccoli Dip	18
Broccoli Dip	18
Chili con Queso de Wolfe	21
Chili Bean	20
Hot Beef Stroganoff	20
Hot Crab	24
Hungry Man	21
Joe Boy's Hot Sausage	15
Mexican	22
New Year's Black-Eyed Pea	33
Picadillo Dip	23
Pizza Cocktail Dip or Spread	36
Popeye	16
Six -Layer Dip	19
South of the Border	19
Spinach	17
Spinach	17
Texas Caviar	33
The Dip	16

Hot Hors d' Oeuvres

Fried Cheese (Saganaki)	27
Fried Cheese	27
Mushroom with Meat Stuffing	32
Nachos de Camaron	34
Pizza Snacks	37

Spreads

Bacon-Onion	26
Cheese Ball	26
Cheese Ball	14
Chicken Liver Pate	23
Crab Pate	25
Curry Pate	24
Desert Cheese Centerpiece	15
Paresa	37
Pineapple-Cheese Ball	29
Pizza Cocktail Dip or Spread	36
Salmon Ball	14
Salmon Party Ball	35
Spinach Balls	22

BATTER

Batter for Onion Rings	126
Onion Ring Batter	126
Possum Fritters	127

BEVERAGES

Aggravation	50
Almond Liqueur	54
Artillery Punch	47
Bloody Mary Drink	52
Border Buttermilk	44
Christmas Hooch	55
Citrus Punch	45
Cowboy Margarita	46
Cranberry Punch	54
Daiquiri Punch	50
Frozen Strawberry or Peach Daiquiri	53
Hot Buttered Rum	48
Kahlua	49
Kahlua	50
Lemonberry Pitcher Punch	57
Margarita	43
Margarita	46

Western Cookbook Committee
San Antonio Livestock Exposition, Inc.
Post Office Box 20228
San Antonio, Texas 78220

Please send _____ copies of COWBOY COUNTRY at............................$10.00 each

Plus postage and handling.. 1.50 each

State Tax for Texas residents...55 each

Enclosed is my check or money order in the amount of: _____

NAME _____

ADDRESS _____

CITY _____ STATE _____ ZIP _____

No COD's Please

Western Cookbook Committee
San Antonio Livestock Exposition, Inc.
Post Office Box 20228
San Antonio, Texas 78220

Please send _____ copies of COWBOY COUNTRY at............................$10.00 each

Plus postage and handling.. 1.50 each

State Tax for Texas residents...55 each

Enclosed is my check or money order in the amount of: _____

NAME _____

ADDRESS _____

CITY _____ STATE _____ ZIP _____

No COD's Please

Western Cookbook Committee
San Antonio Livestock Exposition, Inc.
Post Office Box 20228
San Antonio, Texas 78220

Please send _____ copies of COWBOY COUNTRY at............................$10.00 each

Plus postage and handling.. 1.50 each

State Tax for Texas residents...55 each

Enclosed is my check or money order in the amount of: _____

NAME _____

ADDRESS _____

CITY _____ STATE _____ ZIP _____

No COD's Please

Western Cookbook Committee
San Antonio Livestock Exposition, Inc.
Post Office Box 20228
San Antonio, Texas 78220

Please send _____ copies of COWBOY COUNTRY at............................$10.00 each

Plus postage and handling...1.50 each

State Tax for Texas residents ....55 each

Enclosed is my check or money order in the amount of: _____

NAME _____

ADDRESS _____

CITY _____ STATE _____ ZIP_____

No COD's Please

Western Cookbook Committee
San Antonio Livestock Exposition, Inc.
Post Office Box 20228
San Antonio, Texas 78220

Please send _____ copies of COWBOY COUNTRY at............................$10.00 each

Plus postage and handling...1.50 each

State Tax for Texas residents ....55 each

Enclosed is my check or money order in the amount of: _____

NAME _____

ADDRESS _____

CITY _____ STATE _____ ZIP_____

No COD's Please

Western Cookbook Committee
San Antonio Livestock Exposition, Inc.
Post Office Box 20228
San Antonio, Texas 78220

Please send _____ copies of COWBOY COUNTRY at............................$10.00 each

Plus postage and handling...1.50 each

State Tax for Texas residents ....55 each

Enclosed is my check or money order in the amount of: _____

NAME _____

ADDRESS _____

CITY _____ STATE _____ ZIP_____

No COD's Please